retired, he had sponsored or cosponsored more legislation than any senator at the time....

Senator Hatch was also a man of deep faith; a gentle soul who wrote songs and poems and shared them with friends, colleagues, and the world. This was the Orrin who looked out for the people who often didn't have a voice in our laws and our country. I saw this in his efforts to pass the Americans with Disabilities Act and the Children's Health Insurance Program....He was, quite simply, an American original.[6]

—President Joe Biden

He loved God, and he loved his neighbors. And that enabled him to see others who had differences of opinion with him in very noble terms. I think that's at the center of who Orrin Hatch was. That breaks down a lot of political walls that otherwise separate Americans. He saw his opponents as equal to himself, believing that we are all the offspring of heavenly parentage. When you see others as a brother or a sister, regardless of race or ethnicity or national origin or sexual orientation, that enables you then to treat them with respect and give them the dignity that should be accorded to all of divine heritage.[7]

—Former US senator Gordon Smith

6. Statement by President Joe Biden on the passing of former senator Orrin Hatch, April 24, 2022, https://www.whitehouse.gov/briefing-room/statements-releases/2022/04/24/statement-by-president-joe-biden-on-the-passing-of-former-senator-orrin-hatch/.
7. Author interview.

From 1973, the year our data begins, to his retirement in early 2019, Senator Orrin Hatch was the top senator of any party in our center's Cumulative Legislative Effectiveness score, that adds up legislative effectiveness across a member's entire time in Congress. Senator Ted Kennedy came in second among senators by that measure.

Hatch also was ranked as the #1 senator of any party in frequency of appearances in the center's Exceeds Expectations category for that period.

Finally, using a third measurement of effectiveness, the center ranked Hatch as the #1 Republican senator for that period in the number of 'substantive and significant' bills the member sponsored that became law.[1]

—Professor Craig Volden and Professor Alan Wiseman,
Center for Legislative Effectiveness, research institution
hosted jointly by the University of Virginia and
Vanderbilt University

Because of Senator Hatch's heightened sensitivity to the promise of life, and because of his deep-seated faith and belief in the goodness of humankind, he always reached out to those in need.[2]

—A. Scott Anderson, Utah business leader and friend

The Ryan White Comprehensive AIDS Resources Emergency (CARE) Act would never have happened without him, there's no doubt about that. As someone who has worked on AIDS for over thirty years, there is no doubt in my mind that the US response to AIDS would have been significantly more delayed if it wouldn't have been for Hatch. Especially in the early days when the response to AIDS was so stuck in fear, that without Orrin Hatch, the US response to AIDS would have waited a lot longer had it not been

---

1. Author interview.
2. Remarks at the funeral service for Orrin G. Hatch, May 6, 2022.

for someone like him who was willing to put partisanship aside and do something big and important for the country.

We will be forever indebted to him for that—forever.[3]

—Michael Iskowitz, former chief counsel for poverty, disability, and family policy, United States Senate Committee on Labor and Human Resources

If it wasn't for Senator Hatch, we would still be fighting (over) the Americans with Disabilities Act, and there probably wouldn't be final passage of the ADA.[4]

—Patrisha Wright, former director of government affairs, Disability Rights Education and Defense Fund

For the last forty-two years, Senator Hatch has proudly represented the people of Utah, sponsoring more bills that have become law than any living legislator. From rewriting our tax code to helping just hardworking Americans get through life to reshaping our courts to uphold the vision of our founders to protecting the religious freedom of all Americans, his achievements are too numerous to count.

Senator Hatch is a true American statesman.[5]

—President Donald J. Trump

He was the fighter who carried with him the memory of his humble upbringing near Pittsburgh, who never humored a bully or shied from a challenge. The young man who, upon receiving his degree from Brigham Young University, was the first in his family to graduate college; the young lawyer who built a successful law practice; and the senator who sprinted from meeting to meeting because there was so much to do—indeed, when Senator Hatch

---

3. Author interview.
4. Author interview.
5. Remarks at White House Medal of Freedom Ceremony, November 16, 2018.

TITAN

OF THE SENATE

TITAN
OF THE SENATE

ORRIN HATCH

AND THE ONCE AND FUTURE
GOLDEN AGE OF BIPARTISANSHIP

WILLIAM DOYLE

CENTER
STREET

NEW YORK • NASHVILLE

Center Street
Hachette Book Group
1290 Avenue of the Americas, New York, NY 10104
centerstreet.com
twitter.com/centerstreet

Originally published in hardcover and ebook by Center Street in September 2022
First trade paperback edition: September 2023

Center Street is a division of Hachette Book Group, Inc. The Center Street name and logo are trademarks of Hachette Book Group, Inc.

The publisher is not responsible for websites (or their content) that are not owned by the publisher.

The Hachette Speakers Bureau provides a wide range of authors for speaking events. To find out more, go to hachettespeakersbureau.com or email HachetteSpeakers@hbgusa.com.

Center Street books may be purchased in bulk for business, educational, or promotional use. For information, please contact your local bookseller or the Hachette Book Group Special Markets Department at special.markets@hbgusa.com.

Library of Congress Cataloging-in-Publication Data

Names: Doyle, William, author.
Title: Titan of the Senate : Orrin Hatch and the once and future golden age of bipartisanship / William Doyle.
Description: First edition. | New York : Center Street, 2022. | Includes bibliographical references.
Identifiers: LCCN 2022019465 | ISBN 9781546001454 (hardcover) | ISBN 9781546001478 (ebook)
Subjects: LCSH: Hatch, Orrin, 1934-2022. | Legislators—United States—Biography. | Legislators—Utah—Biography. | United States. Congress. Senate—Biography. | United States—Politics and government—1977–1981. | United States—Politics and government—1981–1989. | United States—Politics and government—1989–
Classification: LCC E840.8.H29 D68 2022 | DDC 328.73/092—dc23/eng/20220607
LC record available at https://lccn.loc.gov/2022019465

ISBNs: 9781546001461 (trade paperback), 9781538709634 (ebook)

Printed in the United States of America

LSC-C

Printing 1, 2023

To Naomi and Brendan

ORRIN HATCH
In His Own Words

I fought for what I believed in, and I won an awful lot of battles.[1]

The Founders, in all their prescient wisdom, understood that diversity is the boon—not the bane—of our democracy.[2]

I've authored more bills that have become law than any member of Congress alive today. I played a central role in the creation of the modern generic drug industry, the passage of the landmark Americans with Disabilities Act, and the confirmation of every current member of the United States Supreme Court.

I helped lead the effort to pass historic, comprehensive tax reform. One of my proudest legislative achievements is the Religious Freedom Restoration Act, which guarantees vigorous religious liberty protections for all Americans.[3]

I can be the son of working-class parents and also a pro-business Republican.

I can be a bipartisan dealmaker and also a consistent conservative.

I can be an ally to the transgender community and also a committed Christian.

As much as my critics would like to pigeonhole me—dismissing more than eight decades of accrued wisdom and life experience based solely on the 'R' that follows my name—I can't be reduced to a party platform.[4]

CONTENTS

Introduction

I F GREATNESS IS MEASURED by achievement, Orrin Hatch was the greatest United States senator of the past half century.

This is not a partisan or an ideological opinion; it is a judgment based on empirical fact.

According to scholars at the nonpartisan Center for Effective Lawmaking, a research institution hosted jointly by the University of Virginia and Vanderbilt University, Orrin Hatch is the number one "most effective" senator of all Republicans and Democrats from 1973 (the year the Center's data begins) to 2019, when measured by the Center's "Cumulative Legislative Effectiveness" score that adds up legislative effectiveness across a member's entire time in Congress. The number two spot in the ranking is held by Senator Edward "Ted" Kennedy, Democrat from Massachusetts, Hatch's periodic nemesis, friend, negotiating partner, and brother figure. Hatch also was ranked as the number one senator of any party in the Center's "Exceeds Expectations" category for that period. Finally, using a third measurement of effectiveness, the Center ranked Hatch as the number one Republican senator for that period in the number of "substantive and significant" bills the member sponsored that became law. Hatch also sponsored or cosponsored 791 bills that became law, more than any other senator of the post-Watergate era.[5]

The "most effective senator" designation is the product of Orrin Hatch's longevity, tenacity, and accumulated power in the Senate committee system, but it is also a measure of personal skill, political brilliance, staff quality, and the ability to work as a bipartisan leader on great issues.

In late 2019, I came across Hatch's number one position in the scholars' ranking of senators and was intrigued. As I researched his career, I began to fully appreciate a striking paradox: over the course of his forty-two years in the Senate, Orrin Hatch was one of America's most powerful and passionate conservative Republicans, but he was also a man who worked with members of both parties to sponsor or cosponsor and pass nearly eight hundred federal laws on a host of issues that impact the lives of Americans, more than any other senator—and a great many of these laws were bipartisan achievements.

Laws help define a society and a government, and Orrin Hatch is a chief legislative architect of the modern American nation. Put simply, Orrin Hatch "got more done" than any other US senator in the post-Vietnam, post-Watergate era. He was, in terms of accomplishments, a "titan of the Senate."

Greatness is in the eye of the beholder, and your opinion of Orrin Hatch may well depend on what your politics are. But no matter what your political persuasion is, and whether or not you agree with Hatch's actions and positions over his decades in power, the Center for Effective Lawmaking analysis demonstrates that he was arguably the most significant and consequential American senator of his time, a titan of Congress whose stature and impact were comparable to, and in important ways exceeded, many of the US senators in American history who are considered to be "great."

Hatch began his political career as a little-known trial attorney with no political experience, and ended it as president pro tempore of the US Senate, third in the constitutional line of succession to the presidency. I speculated that by exploring highlights in the career of Orrin Hatch, and by examining several of his most dramatic moments in depth, one could gain critical insights into what makes an effective lawmaker, as well as gain fascinating perspectives on the epic personalities and issues of modern American history and politics over the last two generations, from a view deep inside the corridors of power.

There are at least two sides to Orrin Hatch, who is, like many people, complex, contradictory, and perfectly capable of making mistakes over the course of a long career. The most familiar image of Hatch is that of a strong conservative crusader, fighting for conservative Supreme Court justices and originalist interpretations of the US Constitution, opposing judicial activism, backing the conservative domestic and foreign policies of Republican presidents, promoting limited government and individual liberties, fighting against abortion, supporting pro-growth and fiscally conservative policies, and working to ensure the long-term fiscal sustainability of federal social programs.

But there is another lesser-known and equally consequential side to Hatch, and it is the main focus of this book—that of the most effective US senator of our times, the man who engineered not only the most legislation of any senator in the post-Vietnam, post-Watergate era, but some of the greatest congressional bipartisan accomplishments of that period.

If you live in the United States today, you live in a nation that was legislatively engineered in part by Orrin Hatch. When you cross a street, board a bus or a train, enter a building, or use a communications device, you are moving in an environment that has been shaped by the Americans with Disabilities Act, the landmark piece of legislation championed by Hatch over three decades ago that reshaped the nation and guarantees fair treatment and access to all our fellow citizens.

If you experience high blood pressure, diabetes, a heart condition, or any one of a host of other medical conditions that require prescription drugs, and if you rely on generic medications, you are paying a small fraction of the cost of a brand-name drug, thanks to the Hatch-Waxman Act of 1984, a piece of legislation that effectively created the modern generic drug market.

If you or someone in your family or community faces the challenges of HIV/AIDS, addiction, cancer, an organ transplant, a traumatic brain injury, autism, ALS, the need for an orphan drug, the need for medical insurance for a child in a low-income family, or any one of a host of other medical and social issues, there is a good chance that your life has been touched by legislation written, shaped, and championed by Orrin Hatch. If your life has been affected by a US Supreme Court decision, then your life has probably been touched by the work of Orrin Hatch, who successfully supported the confirmation of seven out of the nine justices sitting on the court today, including the chief justice.

If you or your religious community is threatened with discrimination or limitations on the First Amendment guarantee of freedom of religious worship, the Religious Freedom Restoration Act backed by Hatch and the related measures that were inspired by it can act as your shield.

I came to realize that some of Hatch's greatest achievements forged a link not only to a distant past of periodic bipartisan cooperation that I call a "Golden Age of Bipartisanship," but also to a potential future such age, when Republicans and Democrats could pause their vicious, personal, and unrelenting ideological combat at least for a while, reach across the aisle, and do great things for the nation on a wide range of critical issues.

The Golden Age of Bipartisanship was not an age of continuous time, but a series of moments in our nation's history when Orrin Hatch joined with and often inspired other Republicans to work across the aisle with Democrats and create major legislative achievements that affected a broad spectrum of American life, including generic drugs, AIDS research and treatment, the rights of Americans with disabilities, stem cell research, religious tolerance and freedom, orphan drugs, education of the handicapped, children's health insurance, strengthening Medicare, and school safety. In many of these cases, Hatch played a leading and often critical role.

In February 2020, when I first met Orrin Hatch in Utah, he was busy establishing his new foundation after retiring from the Senate the year before. I was impressed by his humility, his approachability, his strong religious faith, his willingness to admit mistakes, and his powerfully optimistic and hopeful vision of America. "There's no use kidding about it," Hatch told me as we gazed at the mountains of his beloved Utah from a Salt Lake City conference room. "I had a storybook career in the United States Senate."

This book was written with the cooperation of Orrin Hatch. He and many of his current and former aides and Senate colleagues helped me with invaluable advice, research, interviews, and fact-checking. Hatch generously allowed me to have free access to his papers and gave me a series of wide-ranging interviews in 2020 and 2021. Additionally, I explored many thousands of pages from the files of the Senate Historical Office and from the Center for Legislative Archives of the National Archives and Records Administration.

Rather than offer a "microhistory" of all of Hatch's career, or his religious faith and family life, or his many interests outside politics such as physical fitness and music—he was a prolific and Grammy-nominated songwriter—this book instead focuses on several critical events that most vividly illustrate his experiences in action as the "most effective senator." Over the years, Hatch served as chairman of three powerful Senate panels, all of which are by definition ideologically contentious: the Education and Labor Committee (which since 1999 has been known as the Health, Education, Labor and Pensions Committee); the Judiciary Committee; and the Senate Finance Committee. Additionally, he served for many years on the Senate Intelligence Committee, where he played a key role in providing congressional support and oversight to the intelligence agencies of the federal government. I have chosen to focus mainly on domestic affairs since American intelligence and foreign policy are primarily led by the executive branch.

This is not technically an authorized biography, since the editorial control is mine alone. The only promise I made to Orrin Hatch was that I would try my best to create an intellectually honest and nonpartisan historical account of key moments in his Senate career.

Orrin Hatch died on Saturday, April 23, 2022, in Salt Lake City, Utah, surrounded by family. He was eighty-eight years old. He was laid to rest in Newton, Utah, the small town where his wife, Elaine, grew up.

The story begins near the end, during a moment when Orrin Hatch secretly prepared to take command of ten thousand nuclear warheads—and join a series of events that would bring much of the world to an end.

CHAPTER 1

The Vanishing

O N THE MORNING of January 20, 2017, inside a secret military installation outside Washington, DC, an eighty-two-year-old man saw the face of the Apocalypse.[6]

The man was Orrin Grant Hatch of Utah, the senior Republican in the United States Senate, the president pro tempore of the Senate, and the longest-serving Republican senator in US history.

The face belonged to an American military officer stationed a few yards away who carried a bulging, forty-five-pound aluminum-framed, leather-encased briefcase known as the "president's emergency satchel" and nicknamed the "nuclear football."

The football contained the codes and communications equipment that would, when activated, enable Orrin Hatch to authorize the launch of thousands of nuclear weapons and bring much of the world to an end. A similar object carried by a military aide has closely followed every president since the climax of John F. Kennedy's Cuban missile crisis in 1962. It is not clear where the name "football" came from. Some sources report that it was inspired by a Cold War plan called Operation Drop Kick, but that referred to an insect warfare test, not a nuclear one. There was a fictional nuclear warfare rehearsal plan of the same name in Stanley Kubrick's end-of-the-world black comedy *Dr. Strangelove*, which may have inspired the nickname.

Senator Orrin Hatch was one of the most prominent legislative architects of the post-Vietnam American nation, but now he was on the verge of gaining the power to join a series of events that would result in its utter destruction.

Hours earlier, Hatch had vanished from sight. He was third in the line of succession to the presidency after the vice president, and perhaps the most familiar face on Capitol Hill, having served there for forty years. He was the top Republican in the Senate, celebrating the election triumph of the first candidate of his party to assume the presidency in eight years. He was expected to be at the head of a procession of congressional leaders escorting Donald Trump through the halls of Congress to the West Front of the Capitol for his inauguration as the forty-fifth president of the United States. At Hatch's invitation, the famed Mormon Tabernacle Choir from his home state of Utah was preparing to sing "America the Beautiful" on the steps of the Capitol Building.

On this cold, gray day, more than three hundred thousand people were gathering in the nation's capital for the historic transfer of power, along with twenty-eight thousand security officers from the Secret Service, Transportation Security Administration, Coast Guard, National Guard, FBI, US Park Police, and US Capitol Police. They were joined by outgoing president Barack Obama; outgoing vice president Joe Biden; former presidents Jimmy Carter, Bill Clinton, and George W. Bush; former vice presidents Dan Quayle and Dick Cheney; members of the Supreme Court; and Trump's vanquished opponent in the bitter 2016 election, Hillary Clinton. Orrin Hatch was nowhere to be seen.

Sixty-seven Democratic members of the US House of Representatives were boycotting the event, for what they called Trump's divisive policies, his criticism of civil rights icon Congressman John

Lewis, and what they cited as foreign interference in the election. Scattered protests and sporadic violence erupted on this day as demonstrators attempted to blockade the inaugural parade route, broke store windows, started fires in the street, and ignited a limousine, prompting police in riot helmets to fire tear gas, concussion grenades, and chemical spray.

On the Capitol steps, First Lady Michelle Obama's face registered complete dejection at the prospect of Trump's swearing-in. In the background, a military officer carrying a nuclear "football" discreetly prepared to shift his allegiance at the stroke of noon from Obama to Donald J. Trump, a man who, once he became the Republican Party nominee, had been strongly supported in his campaign for president by party giant Orrin Hatch. But where was Hatch? Friends and colleagues strained their necks to spot him in the procession down the Capitol steps, but he had vanished.

At that moment, in fact, the senator was serving as a nuclear-armed, backup president of the United States and sitting at a desk inside a top secret command-and-control location outside Washington, DC. He was accompanied by his wife, a few aides, and a security detail. Within close reach, a military officer was carrying a nuclear football identical to the one on the US Capitol steps. A small phalanx of government officials was standing by with briefing books, prepared to help Orrin Hatch take over the United States government.

For this Inauguration Day in 2017, as Obama and Trump administration officials gathered at the Capitol, Hatch was, at President-elect Trump's request, secretly serving as the "designated survivor" or "designated successor" in case a disaster, nuclear or otherwise, wiped out the top officials at the ceremony, including the president, the vice president, and the Speaker of the House. According to the Presidential Succession Act of 1947, Hatch, as president pro tempore and senior officer of the Senate, was next in the line of succession and would become president.

Hatch was arguably the ideal choice to be a "designated

survivor"—no elected official in the country at that time had more experience in the highest levels of federal government than he did. He had done this once before, in 2016, serving as "designated survivor" during President Obama's final State of the Union address. Hatch knew the finest working details of the vast federal government, having served as chair of the Senate Finance Committee and the Judiciary Committee, and also serving on the Senate Intelligence Committee. At eighty-two years of age, he would be the oldest president in the nation's history, four years older than Ronald Reagan was on his last day in office. He would also be the first member of The Church of Jesus Christ of Latter-day Saints,[7] often colloquially referred to as the Mormon Church, to assume the office.

And now, on Inauguration Day in 2017, Hatch was preparing to become president of all Americans in the event of a catastrophe in the nation's capital.

*   *   *

The specific history and details of the designated survivor process are largely shrouded in secrecy, but the tradition traced back to the Truman-Eisenhower-Kennedy-era Cold War planning for "continuity of government" in the event of a national emergency, and to the 1981 inauguration, when, by mutual agreement, outgoing Carter administration defense secretary Harold Brown stayed on for several hours into Ronald Reagan's first term until the new administration's team was fully in place.

During the 1986 State of the Union address, Reagan's agriculture secretary, John Block, was selected as designated survivor and dispatched by commercial plane to spend the night with his wife at a friend's house in Montego Bay, Jamaica. He traveled with no aides, no nuclear football, and no briefings on what to do if he became president.[8]

By the 1990s, the process had advanced in sophistication, but not by much. During the 1997 State of the Union address, designated survivor Dan Glickman, President Bill Clinton's agriculture secretary, was escorted by aircraft and motorcade to his daughter's apartment in New York City, where he watched the speech on TV. Surprisingly, recalled Glickman, "I was not given a briefing on what to do if something happened,"[9] even though a military officer nearby was carrying a briefcase he assumed was the nuclear football. When the speech was over, his Secret Service detail vanished and Glickman was reduced to trying to catch a cab in the pouring Manhattan rain.

In the wake of the attacks on September 11, 2001, both the continuity of government and designated survivor programs were sharply upgraded and expanded to a scale that could weigh heavily on those chosen to play the role of "backup president."

In 2006, Secretary of Veterans Affairs Jim Nicholson was selected as designated survivor for President George W. Bush's State of the Union address to a joint session of Congress. In 2020 he recalled of the experience, "It really focuses your mind on the enormity of the job of president. They take you to an undisclosed location in a helicopter, you start getting briefings, and they even call you Mister President. It's kind of surreal but you take it seriously. It's being done that way because of the possibility, one hopes remote, that it could happen that you end up becoming the commander in chief. That really kind of gets your attention and makes you think of the unrelenting challenges and issues and demands on the president, constantly making decisions, usually without all the facts. It's all in anticipation of what would be a cataclysmic occurrence, if you did wind up being the last man standing. Given the technology of today and the intensity of our enemies, it's not just science fiction. It could really happen in an instant."

After what he described as a "fantastic" steak dinner catered by White House chefs who were flown to the secret location with him, Nicholson watched Bush's speech on TV and braced himself for the worst. Over and over, he mumbled a prayer that no catastrophe would happen. He mused about how devastated and chaotic the nation would be if a "decapitation" attack succeeded and he had to assume the presidency. Nicholson recalled, "I had no desire to become president, especially under those circumstances." When Bush's speech was over and the call came, "POTUS has closed back into the White House; you can go home," Nicholson flew off, tremendously relieved.[10]

For the State of the Union address the following year, designated survivor Alberto Gonzales was offered a choice between two undisclosed locations, one on the ground and one in the air. Choosing the airborne option, Gonzales was taken to Andrews Air Force Base outside the capital and sent aloft, possibly in a US Air Force Boeing E-4B Advanced Airborne Command Post Nightwatch aircraft, which is a modified Boeing 747 "doomsday plane" capable of providing the president with emergency nuclear command and control. "Although the aircraft did not have all of the comforts and technology of Air Force One, it was equipped to serve as a flying command center," Gonzales recalled. "A senior member of every major federal department accompanied me, each carrying thick binders laying out protocols and classified procedures to advise me in the event I assumed the presidency following a disaster in Washington. As we departed for places unknown to me, I received a series of classified operational briefings and then I settled in to watch the State of the Union address on a large monitor aboard the plane."[11]

It is not known exactly where Orrin Hatch was taken to serve as designated survivor on January 20, 2017, but it is probable that his destination was one of two mammoth, nuclear-blast-hardened government "doomsday" facilities within a short flight from Washington, DC. One of them, the Mount Weather Emergency Operations Center in Virginia, located approximately sixty miles west of Washington, DC, is run by the Federal Emergency Management Agency and is designed to host civilian government leaders like the president, cabinet officers, Supreme Court officials, and congressional leaders in the event of a disaster.

Another likely destination for Hatch was the "backup Pentagon" known as Raven Rock, or Site R, a small-city-size complex carved deep inside a mountain near Blue Ridge Summit on the Pennsylvania-Maryland state line and about seven miles north of the presidential retreat at Camp David.

Raven Rock serves as a fully equipped alternative to the Pentagon "war room," or National Military Command Center, and it was believed to have been used by Vice President Cheney and other officials after the attacks on September 11, 2001. Author James Bamford described Raven Rock as "a secret world of five buildings, each three stories tall, computer-filled caverns, and a subterranean water reservoir,"[12] all underground and accessible by a helipad and a giant tunnel. According to author Garrett Graff, the site has "power stations, underground water reservoirs, a small chapel, clusters of three-story buildings set within vast caverns, and enough beds to accommodate two thousand high-ranking officials from the Pentagon, the State Department, and the National Security Council." Graff added, "You can add to that list police and fire departments, a cafeteria, and everything else you would find in a normal small city."[13]

As designated survivor on Inauguration Day in 2017, Senator Hatch was shadowed through the day by a military officer carrying the "nuclear football," one of the most powerful instruments of mass murder that humankind had ever created. It was a bulky black briefcase, an ordinary-looking leather satchel that was specially modified with zippers and pouches for documents and secure communications equipment.

If the president, vice president, and Speaker of the House were killed or incapacitated at the inaugural site, Orrin Hatch would automatically become president, his military aide's football would be activated, and the aide would quickly move to Hatch's side. Then a grim, high-speed choreography would unfold, a process coordinated by well-rehearsed sections of the Defense Department, the Federal Emergency Management Administration, the White House Military Office, and the White House Communications Agency.

Through the football and other available communications tools, Hatch would be linked by voice and video to the Department of Defense's National Military Command Center at the Pentagon, known as the Pentagon's "war room," and to Strategic Command headquarters, or STRATCOM, at Offutt Air Force Base south of Omaha, Nebraska, which commands the nation's arsenal of strategic nuclear weapons on missiles, submarines, and bombers. If the secretary of defense, national security adviser, and chairman of the Joint Chiefs of Staff survived the attack and could be reached, they and other high military officials would be patched into the call, but the decision to launch nuclear weapons would be President Hatch's alone, presumably with the concurrence of one or more of the top Pentagon leaders.

Even if the Pentagon was also destroyed in a series of Inauguration Day attacks, nuclear command would easily switch to the "backup" Pentagon at Raven Rock. "If Hatch is right there, he's good to go," reported Bruce Blair, a former Minuteman missile launch control officer and nuclear weapons historian at Princeton University. "You can even issue a launch order directly from Raven Rock to all the nuclear forces."[14]

Blair explained, "Hatch would be rushed by the military aide into the Raven Rock command center room. Screens would light up and Hatch would hold an emergency teleconference with the deputy director for operations at the war room of the Pentagon or his surrogate, a one-star general or a colonel, depending on who's there at the moment. The main talker would be the four-star head of US strategic forces, who explains the available options, such as a nuclear strike plan against North Korea hitting eighty targets, largely nuclear weapons facilities, forces, and associated facilities. The new president, Hatch, may or may not ask others for their advice before picking one. If the conference was prompted by indications of an incoming nuclear attack, then the briefing may not last longer than half a minute, and he may have no more than six minutes to deliberate."

If President Hatch did decide to launch a nuclear response, he and the military aide would quickly review the options listed in a briefing book inside the football. The American version of the football is not believed to contain a "red button" or to consist primarily of elaborate computer-style gear—unlike Russian president Vladimir Putin's nuclear football, the *Cheget*, which is believed to consist mainly of a high-tech laptop device—but communications equipment and simplified charts illustrating the various options and targets to select from the latest US nuclear war plan, known as OPLAN 8010-12. Hatch's launch response could range from a single nuclear-tipped cruise missile to hundreds of intercontinental ballistic missiles.

To issue Hatch's launch order to the Pentagon war room or an alternate command post, his military aide would reach into the football and produce a small object resembling a credit card, nicknamed the "Biscuit," upon which is written the "Gold Code," a sequence of alphanumeric symbols that Hatch would read aloud to authenticate his identity as commander in chief. If Hatch were already positioned inside Raven Rock, this step wouldn't be necessary, as the military staff there would have already verified his identity.

The reading out loud of the Gold Codes on the Biscuit would be the final step for Hatch to launch nuclear weapons, making the Biscuit the most dangerous object on the planet. But at least two American presidents have managed to lose track of theirs. In the 1970s and 1980s, when the Gold Codes were kept on a Biscuit card that the chief executive usually carried on his own person rather than inside the football, Jimmy Carter is believed to have misplaced his Biscuit when his suit was sent to the dry cleaners. In 1981, Ronald Reagan's copy was sealed away for five days by the FBI after George Washington University Hospital emergency room staff cut off Reagan's thousand-dollar business suit and put the card in a medical bag in the wake of his attempted assassination.

President Bill Clinton kept his Biscuit and his credit cards wrapped up with a rubber band, but, incredibly, he managed to lose it for a substantial length of time, according to a top military official. "The codes were actually missing for months," wrote General Hugh Shelton, Clinton's chairman of the Joint Chiefs of Staff from 1997 to 2001. "That's a big deal—a gargantuan deal."[15]

On Inauguration Day in 2017, in the case of a catastrophic emergency like a mass launch of Russian or Chinese nuclear weapons aimed at the United States, or a single nuclear warhead launched at the Capitol Building from an offshore submarine, the military aide assigned to Senator Hatch would have taken the Biscuit out of the football and passed it to Hatch, who would read the authentication code over the communications link to military officials. According to nuclear weapons historian Bruce Blair, "Then the order goes out almost immediately to all the alert nuclear forces, which in 2017 would have amounted to four hundred land-based, single-warhead rockets or ICBMs [intercontinental ballistic missiles] deployed in silos in five states in the Great Plains and Midwest, and about four hundred more warheads in SLBMs [submarine-launched ballistic missiles] on ready alert in the Atlantic and Pacific Oceans that would have been ready to receive a launch order. Hatch would have had a total of eight hundred warheads immediately available to fire."

Within three or four minutes of Hatch's order, missiles would shoot out of their silos in the Midwest, then about ten minutes later the submarines would start firing missiles out of their tubes, one at a time, every fifteen seconds. The ICBMs would fly high above the earth's atmosphere and travel at speeds of 14,000 mph, descending to targets in, for example, Russia, China, or North Korea, in twenty-five minutes. The submarine-launched missiles, fired from waters closer to their aim points, could have flight times of as little as twelve minutes. None of the missiles could be recalled.

If Hatch ordered even a portion of the US strategic missiles on alert to be fired, it would easily mean all-out war, and within a few hours, large parts of the earth would be plunged into a rough approximation of Armageddon. Untold millions of people would be smashed, blasted, crushed, vaporized, and burned to death. The initial blasts would create radiation-filled shock waves of outward pressure millions of times greater than the atmosphere, toppling skyscrapers, shredding people with flying glass and debris, and hurling them across cities. Electromagnetic pulses from the air-bursts would decapitate the nervous systems of the world's economy by blowing out fiber-optic lines, power grids, cell phones and electrical circuits, banking systems, and air-traffic-control networks.

Seconds after the initial explosions, fireballs and thermal pulses from groundbursts would incinerate exposed people and flatten buildings in a ten-mile radius. The fireballs would transform into mushroom clouds of condensed water and debris that would rise high into the stratosphere, expand to fifty-mile diameters, and shower the earth with radioactive fallout for decades to come. By the end of the first day, hospitals would be overwhelmed, mass fires would rage, and cities and suburbs would be consumed with riots, chaos, and attempted mass migrations. Nations would be in full-scale collapse, and hundreds of millions of people would be dead inside of a week. As President Dwight Eisenhower once said, if nuclear war happened, "there just aren't enough bulldozers to scrape the bodies off the street."[16]

In the face of this awesome responsibility, Orrin Hatch was apprehensive, but calm, almost serene. "He projected a sense of inner strength and inner peace, no matter how stressful the situation was," said a government official who was with Hatch on this day. "He had seen it all, and he was fully prepared to be president. Here was a person who was a senior legislator for forty years, a senior member of the Senate Intelligence Committee, a man who had a profound interest in our nation's military. He was ready to go."[17] When TV images appeared of the Mormon Tabernacle Choir singing "America the Beautiful" on the Capitol steps, the official saw Hatch become teary-eyed.

"I hated to miss all the goings-on at the inauguration, but it was one of the most interesting experiences of my life, a great honor," Hatch later explained. "We were very much taken care of by the Secret Service and others. I was prepared to do it. I had been quite cognizant of the responsibilities of the presidency. That's one reason I was chosen. I didn't expect anything to happen; I expected to come back safe and sound. But it was interesting, no question about it. If anything happened to the president at that time, I would have been president. It was a little bit scary. I was worried that maybe something could happen."[18]

On this Inauguration Day, a series of bizarre, hair-raising possibilities was unfolding behind the scenes. Very few people inside or outside the US government knew it, but under certain circumstances—such as a mass-casualty attack during a gathering of most of the senior government officials like a State of the Union address or on Inauguration Day, especially one involving a handover from one party to another—the chain of succession to the presidency was so fragile and complex that it was a recipe for total confusion and raised the possibility of multiple claimants to the presidency and even a de facto political coup d'état. "The inauguration is a much freakier period than most people realize," noted John Fortier, the director of governmental studies at the Bipartisan Policy Center and a leading scholar on the subject.

Compounding the potential confusion on this day was the fact that in addition to Orrin Hatch, there was in fact a *second* nuclear-capable designated successor who was standing by to assume the presidency at a moment's notice. He was stationed at a different undisclosed secure location—and he had no idea that Hatch not only was also serving as a designated survivor, but that Hatch outranked him.

Technically, the terms of the president and vice president cease at noon on January 20, but due to a constitutional ambiguity, their cabinet officers stay in office until either their resignation is effective or their successors in the new administration are confirmed by the Senate—but this doesn't happen for a few hours or possibly days after an inauguration. To avoid serving even for a few days or hours into a new administration's reign, especially one of an opposing political party, cabinet officers usually submit their resignation weeks or months before the handover and postdate it to be effective at noon on Inauguration Day, or the night before. For those intervening few hours or days, the new president does not formally have a new cabinet until the Senate confirms his or her nominees.

In other words, the presidential line of succession—which constitutionally runs in the order of vice president; Speaker of the House; president pro tempore of the Senate; the Big Four cabinet members of secretary of state, secretary of the Treasury, secretary of defense, and attorney general; then the rest of the cabinet members in the order of the dates their departments were created—is ruptured, for the few hours or days it takes to confirm new cabinet secretaries.

This presents a strange, Rube Goldbergian calculus that could unfold if enough of the top officials gathered at the Capitol were killed or incapacitated on an Inauguration Day. Such catastrophic conditions were not impossibly far-fetched in an era when, on March 30, 1981, President Ronald Reagan had a bullet fired to within an inch of his heart; and on September 11, 2001, when large commercial jets were hijacked to explode upon the Pentagon, the World Trade Center, and, apparently, the Capitol Building, ultimately killing a total of 2,977 people.

With a mass-casualty attack on the inaugural ceremony, the presidency could instantly pass to a lower-ranking Senate-confirmed official of the outgoing administration like the under secretary of state, who would become acting secretary of state upon his or her boss's resignation, and would then become president upon the death or incapacitation of those senior to him or her in the line of succession. However, according to the Presidential Succession Act, this person could be "bumped" out of the job a few days or weeks later by a new Speaker of the House or new president pro tempore from either party, who was chosen by surviving members of a "reconstituted" Congress, the legitimacy of which could itself be disputed.

This extraordinary "bumping procedure" enabling congressional leaders selected for leadership roles after an attack to displace a cabinet member who has already assumed the presidency could potentially lead to multiple presidents in a short span of time. The daisy chain would become even more bewildering if officials who were thought to be dead were instead discovered alive in the rubble somewhere, or if, for example, someone who was vice president at the time of the attack, and was grievously wounded and believed to be permanently incapacitated in a coma, was to recover, was declared fit for office by his or her medical team, and then claimed the presidency. The law is ambiguous in such scenarios, and each claim to the presidency could be disputed by the leadership of the opposing political party. The military aides carrying the nuclear footballs might not know which way to turn.

But the fact that Hatch, as president pro tempore and number three in the line of succession, was serving as designated survivor in a highly secure location away from the Capitol Building actually sharply reduced the risk of confusion in the event of a disaster, as did the fact that there was also a "backup" *second* designated survivor assigned to duty on this day. There was precedent for this extra precaution: at least one previous president pro tempore, Republican senator Ted Stevens of Alaska, had served as designated survivor during George W. Bush's 2005 State of the Union address at the same time that Bush's commerce secretary, Don Evans, also served as designated survivor. Stevens also served as designated survivor during Bush's 2006 State of the Union address, when Attorney General Alberto Gonzales also stepped into the role.

On January 20, 2017, there was a different designated survivor standing by at another secure location who was, incredibly, totally unaware of Orrin Hatch's role. He was outgoing president Barack Obama's secretary of Homeland Security, a Democratic attorney named Jeh Johnson, who thought he was the only designated survivor, and who had his own entourage of Secret Service officers and his own military aide with a nuclear football. As secretary of Homeland Security, the Secret Service reported to Johnson, along with federal immigration, customs, transportation safety, and emergency management agencies. The previous year, both Johnson and Hatch served as designated survivors for the 2016 State of the Union address, but this time, Johnson was unaware that Hatch was repeating the role.

In the days before the 2017 inauguration, President Obama asked Johnson to serve as the designated survivor. According to Johnson, "I had to withdraw the resignation letter that I'd written months before that originally said I'm resigning effective noon on January 20, 2017. I amended it to say that I would resign when my successor was approved by the Senate, presumably on the evening of January 20. I wanted to be sure that the president-elect knew I was staying on, so I went to Tom Bossert [Trump's incoming deputy secretary of Homeland Security] and said, 'Tom I just want to be sure the president-elect understands I am not resigning, I am staying into his administration to be designated survivor.'"[19] According to Johnson, the Trump team agreed, but unknown to him, they would also line up their own designated survivor—Orrin Hatch.

Among the very few people who had a complete picture of the potential game of "nuclear musical chairs" would have been those in the White House Military Office, which controlled the choreography of the nuclear footballs, and presumably a small handful of top officials in the Obama and Trump chiefs of staff offices, who would have privately agreed to appoint two designated survivors.[20]

And so it came to pass that Jeh Johnson, the secretary of Homeland Security, to whom the Secret Service reported, and who on a normal day ranked number fourteen in the line of succession that ran through the cabinet, didn't have the slightest idea that instead of being the only designated survivor on that day, he was merely a "backup" to the more senior government official Orrin Hatch, who had his own Secret Service detail and nuclear football.

If the time came, and both men survived an Inauguration Day catastrophe, Hatch, as president pro tempore of the Senate and number three in the line of succession, would have automatically "bumped out" Johnson. To the total surprise of everyone including Johnson, Hatch would have become president of the United States and grasped the reins of power by giving a pre-scripted emergency address to the nation delivered through the Pentagon's Milstar nuclear-blast-and-jamming-resistant satellite communications network, declaring the continuity of the American government and appealing for calm.

As it happened, Inauguration Day in 2017 went off without an enemy attack or a constitutional hitch.

At the end of the day, Orrin Hatch returned to the capital with his wife and resumed his normal life. Jeh Johnson did the same—and was soon thoroughly perplexed to read news reports that he was not the only nuclear designated survivor that day.

But if Orrin Hatch had become president that day, the United States would have gained one of the most governmentally experienced chief executives the nation had ever seen.

His journey through the corridors of power began on a winter day forty-one years earlier, inside a building that houses a legislative body that *New York Times* chief congressional correspondent William White referred to as "the one touch of authentic genius in the American political system,"[21] and British statesman William Gladstone called "the most remarkable of all the inventions of modern politics"[22]—the United States Senate.

CHAPTER 2

Into the Labyrinth

O N JANUARY 4, 1977, a tall man from the American West appeared in the US Capitol Building and strode toward the Senate chamber, accompanied by his wife and parents. He was forty-two years old, and this was one of the greatest days of his life—the day he would raise his hand and take an oath administered by the vice president of the United States on the floor of the Senate chamber to become the junior United States senator from Utah.

His name was Orrin Grant Hatch.

He cut a striking figure in the baroque, labyrinthine Senate hallways with a lanky, rail-thin frame and a face that seemed designed to be chiseled in marble. The *New York Times* would later write of him, "He is widely regarded as one of the most gracious and mannerly members of Congress, with little of the evident self-importance that abounds there. He is tall and neat, and he has an almost translucent complexion that in a certain light, gives him the appearance of being crafted out of porcelain."[23] The political magazine *National Journal* once described Hatch as always looking like he "just stepped out of an advertisement for fine men's clothing,"[24] and *Washingtonian* magazine would dub him one of the Capitol's best-dressed Republicans, citing his "nice shoes, great shirts and handsome suits."[25]

Before the swearing-in ceremony on the Senate floor, Hatch and his family were escorted into the cavernous, ornate Capitol office of the vice president, a few paces off the Senate floor. Vice President Nelson Rockefeller wanted to have a look at him.

For a fleeting moment, as Rockefeller and Hatch shook hands, the past and the future of the Republican Party came face-to-face. Rockefeller peered at Hatch through thick spectacles perched on his beer-barrel-shaped head and said, "Well, you are to be congratulated on your stunning victory."[26]

The sixty-eight-year-old Rockefeller, a normally effervescent man who spent much of his life joyfully slapping backs, squeezing arms, and exclaiming his trademark greeting, "Hiya, fella!" to total strangers while savoring life as one of America's wealthiest men, on this day "seemed dejected and very lonely,"[27] in Hatch's words.

The former New York State governor was the last great political dinosaur of a species that would soon be extinct: a liberal Republican, who fully embraced the traditions of New Deal–style big government and social intervention. Orrin Hatch, in sharp contrast, was a staunch small-government conservative.

In Hatch, Nelson Rockefeller might have sensed he was looking at the party's future, a future that had little use for him, and there were many reasons for him to feel dejected on this day. In two weeks he would be out of a job, cast aside by his party after having glumly endured a miserable two years as vice president to the moderate Republican Gerald Ford. He had already been effectively fired-in-advance five months earlier by Ford, who was facing a strong threat from former Hollywood actor and former California governor Ronald Reagan for the Republican presidential nomination. In an act that Ford confessed was the most "cowardly" thing he'd ever done,[28] he tossed Rockefeller overboard from the 1976 Republican ticket for being too liberal and chose Kansas senator Bob Dole as his vice presidential running mate. Ford lost anyway, to Democratic former Georgia governor Jimmy Carter.

In 1974, Ford had promised the hyperactive Rockefeller that he would be a "partner" in governing, but early in his tenure as Ford's appointed, nonelected vice president, Ford's White House officials eviscerated Rockefeller's influence and cut him out of decision-making. Once a week, the two men had a courtesy meeting, and Ford recalled that Rockefeller "would sit down, stir his coffee with the stem of his horn-rimmed glasses and fidget in his chair as he leaped from one subject to another."[29] When someone once asked him what he did as vice president, Rockefeller answered, "I go to funerals. I go to earthquakes."[30] A connoisseur of art, Rockefeller hated the design of the vice presidential seal, so he micromanaged its redesign. One day, when an aide walked into Rockefeller's office during a long streak of bad news, the vice president pointed at his new design and sighed before exclaiming, "See that goddamn seal? That's the most important thing I've done all year."[31] Rockefeller once said, "I've known all the Vice Presidents since Henry Wallace. They were all frustrated, and some were pretty bitter."[32] He was describing himself. In two weeks, Rockefeller would be gone from politics, and in two years he would be dead of a heart attack in his New York brownstone, reportedly in the presence of his mistress and boxes of take-out Chinese food.

Orrin Hatch, on the other hand, was the polar opposite of Rockefeller in nearly every way, and he was bursting with enthusiasm on this day. Born into poverty, Hatch was a lifelong devout member of The Church of Jesus Christ of Latter-day Saints and a devoted family man, and he'd never had a smoke or a drop of hard liquor (he sipped a beer once and didn't like it) and avoided coffee and tea. He was a conservative Republican who had never held public office before, and he'd been politically active for little more than a year. Until recently, he had never even seen the inside of the Senate. Until 1976 he was an unknown trial attorney from Salt Lake City who handled legal affairs for small businesses and regular folks. He was a quarter century younger than Rockefeller, was a former union laborer, and was an early vanguard of the "New Right" and "Reagan Republican" politicians who would soon sweep into the corridors of power and turn American history in an entirely new direction. There was little room for liberal Republicans like Rockefeller in their worldview.

In 1976, as a novice political candidate, Hatch was anointed as a political star in the making by no less than Ronald Reagan, the fast-emerging "Sun King" and father figure of modern conservatism. Reagan's endorsement helped Hatch launch a one-man conservative uprising in Utah that overthrew a powerful three-term incumbent Democrat to capture Hatch's very first and only public office, a seat in the US Senate. Hatch would be one of thirty-eight Republican senators in a Congress dominated by Democrats, who had just retaken control of the presidency.

At the dawn of 1977, Orrin Hatch had a brilliant political future ahead of him. He was young, aggressive, was a "clean slate" unburdened by obligations to special interest groups and networks of political benefactors, and he was free to chart his own course. He had no voting record as an elected official and no detailed policy positions other than those outlined in his campaign speeches and materials. Hatch would go on to serve in the Senate for a remarkable length of time—a full forty-two years, or seven terms, more than any other Republican senator in history.

Hatch would serve as senator from the dawn of Jimmy Carter's presidency through Donald Trump's first years in office. It was an era that spanned the ashes of the Indochina Wars and the Watergate scandals, economic recessions, stock market plunges and booming economies, several wars in the Middle East, the fall of the Berlin Wall, and the collapse of the Soviet Union. It would span a presidential impeachment, the rise of the internet, epic battles between Democrats and Republicans over health care and a host of other issues, the rise of global terrorism, tax reform, tumultuous Supreme Court nominations, the attacks of September 11, 2001, the election and reelection of a Black man as president, the Tea Party, the coming of Donald Trump, and great tensions with China and Russia. Hatch would conclude his career as the senior officer of the Senate, its president pro tempore, the third person in the constitutional line of succession to the presidency.

Hatch would experience victory and defeat, blessings and disappointments, triumphs and mistakes, and he would confer with schoolchildren, farmers, businesspeople, Native American tribal leaders, revolutionaries, elderly constituents, women's groups, Mother Teresa, Ronald Reagan, Bill Clinton, both Presidents Bush, Barack Obama, Donald Trump, Margaret Thatcher, Pope John Paul II, the Queen of England, and the supreme leader of the People's Republic of China. He would become one of Israel's strongest supporters in Congress, and he would back US interventions in Iraq and Afghanistan.

Hatch was a red-blooded, hard-line American conservative, and over the decades he would champion a wide range of conservative causes. He opposed the Panama Canal Treaties, blocked what he saw as an unfair power grab by union bosses, opposed abortion as immoral, opposed the Equal Rights Amendment as unnecessary, supported voluntary affirmative action while condemning racial quotas, supported Second Amendment gun rights, proposed a balanced budget amendment to the Constitution, backed conservative policies of the Reagan and two Bush administrations, denounced Obamacare, fought for both conservative and liberal Supreme Court justices, and pushed through a major reform of the tax code—the Trump-backed Tax Cuts and Jobs Act of 2017. He fought a bruising televised battle for Supreme Court nominee Clarence Thomas against Anita Hill's sexual harassment charges in Senate confirmation hearings in 1991, earning the enmity of many critics in the process. He was involved in the confirmation processes of eighteen hundred members of the federal judiciary and fought for a multitude of conservative candidates. "Few senators can claim a fraction of the influence of Orrin Hatch on the direction and makeup of the United States Supreme Court,"[33] noted George Washington University law professor Jonathan Turley.

Among Hatch's most historic achievements, however, were some of the greatest bipartisan moments of the last half century, when Republicans and Democrats reached across the aisle to shape history for the benefit of all Americans. In fact, Hatch's willingness to work with Democrats and liberals periodically earned him approbation and condemnation from some of his fellow Republicans and conservatives. Hatch would become one of the most consequential and complex political leaders in congressional history—a passionate, conservative champion who simultaneously engineered some of the greatest bipartisan achievements of the US Congress in the modern era, and the most effective lawmaker of his time.

Hatch would fight for landmark bipartisan legislation that included one of the strongest pieces of pro-consumer legislation ever enacted, the Hatch-Waxman Act of 1984, which created the generic drug industry and saved consumers over a trillion dollars; and the greatest civil rights bill since the 1960s, the Americans with Disabilities Act of 1990, which literally reshaped the architecture of the nation to honor the full citizenship of people with disabilities. It included the Ryan White CARE Act of 1990, which capped a series of Hatch-backed measures that dramatically expanded federal funding for AIDS research, education, and treatment; the Religious Freedom Restoration Act of 1993, which guaranteed strong religious liberty protections for all Americans; and the State Children's Health Insurance Program, or SCHIP, of 1997 and its reauthorizations, which extended health insurance to millions of American children of the working poor.

In 2017 and 2018, Hatch would end his Senate career as the president pro tempore by helping to pass a flurry of bipartisan legislation to strengthen Medicare, foster care, children's health insurance, and school safety.

How did Hatch leave such a deep mark in American legislative history? "He's got to be one of the most effective U.S. senators because he works his butt off," speculated the late Dee Benson, Hatch's former chief of staff, who later became chief judge of the US District Court of Utah. "He's in the middle of a lot of stuff. He loses some, but it's not for lack of trying. If you had to pick one Republican to blast something through, he's the only guy you want to sponsor it and get it done."[34] Over the years, Hatch would work extremely hard, sleep little, and love his job. "I'm complex," Hatch once declared. "I'm always keyed up," he explained. "My mind is racing all the time. I get so caught up in what's going on."[35] In 2003, Hatch told a reporter, "Every day I pray that I can do better. I wish I had more hours in the day. I wish I had more ability to read more. I wish I had more ability to understand. I wish I could meet more with people than I do. I just wish I had more capacity."[36]

Over the years, journalists would work themselves into contortions while trying to explain Hatch. Bob Bernick, an editor at Hatch's hometown daily newspaper *Deseret News*, wrote in 1999: "Wearing starched collars, standing straight-backed in finely tailored suits, Hatch is seen by some as a caricature of a stiff moralistic leader. But others praise the compassionate Hatch, a deeply religious man who counsels, forgives, encourages."[37] Four years later, Bernick's colleague Doug Robinson wrote of Hatch, "After talking to acquaintances, this is what you learn: He's talented, intelligent and passionate. He's perceived as egotistical, but most of it still springs from the insecurity of his youth, the poor lather's son trying to win acceptance and prove himself. He can be shrill, overwrought, and a bit stiff and uptight, but at other times remarkably eloquent, witty and personable. He's deep; he's shallow. He's sensible and sharp; he's embarrassing."[38] But the real embarrassment could properly be assigned to those people over the years who would dismiss Hatch merely as a conservative ideologue, or would underestimate Hatch's political skills and the impact he would have, often behind-the-scenes, on American history.

Matt Sandgren, a former chief of staff for Hatch, recalled in 2021 that "Orrin is a multifaceted person. He's the loving and doting husband, the proud father, the encouraging grandfather, and the master legislator. He represented a generation of lawmakers brought up on the virtues of bipartisanship and compromise. Orrin was genuinely beloved by colleagues on both sides of the aisle, making him a true anomaly in tribalistic times—but don't mistake his kindness for weakness. Always to be remembered is Orrin's legal prowess. He was a prosecutor to the core who could lap any of his colleagues along the dais."[39]

As a politician, Hatch could debate the issues with passion, effectiveness, and sometimes righteous anger. "Once you determine that he will be your opponent, you'd better damn well be ready for a bloody battle," asserted Laura Murphy Lee, director of the American Civil Liberties Union office in Washington, DC. "He's dedicated, and he's focused, and he's thorough."[40] But as a personality, Hatch was so genial and approachable that at least one of his top aides would get frustrated by the streams of strangers who routinely approached him and slowed him down in the halls of Congress, in airports, and pretty much everywhere, often to be rewarded with a welcome and a chat from the senator. It was impossible for Hatch to remember the names of most of the people he'd met over forty years of public service, so he developed a standard, disarming greeting, "There you are!"[41] He considered most everyone a friend, and the feeling was often mutual.

Hatch engendered fierce loyalty from many of the people who worked for him over the decades, such as his longtime staffer Melanie Bowen, who joined his staff at the beginning of his Senate career and now helps lead his post-Senate policy foundation. In 2022, Bowen recalled, "He stood tall among his peers—he portrayed an inner confidence crafted and cultivated at a young age through hard work and faithful living. His thirst for knowledge, unabashed determination, and relentless commitment to finding solutions were his signature traits. As a compassionate conservative, he loved and served his constituents—regardless of their social or economic status. His casework accomplishments for constituents will likely never be repeated again; he helped lift the burdens of countless individuals and families. While many would read about some of the more public successes, most of Orrin's casework was done quietly behind the scenes. Many things can be attributed to this great man but to me, Orrin Hatch is a man who truly loved his nation, family, and God."[42]

Hatch was a longtime member of the clergy of The Church of Jesus Christ of Latter-day Saints, he prayed and studied the Scriptures every day, and through his life he was steered by strong currents of compassion, self-reliance, pragmatism, confidence, and perseverance that flowed from this faith.

On January 3, 1977, Orrin Hatch's career as a US senator lay before him. In one of his last official acts as vice president, Nelson Rockefeller led Hatch to his destiny, guiding him and a group of other senators-elect and senators onto the Senate floor, where he swore them into office in groups of four.

When Hatch finished his oath of office, his wife, Elaine, and parents, Jesse and Helen, stood up and applauded from the elevated visitors' gallery.

Hatch had now joined one of the most elite and powerful political fraternities on earth, the community of one hundred men and women who were members of the US Senate.

* * *

"I rose like a rocket,"[43] wrote Theodore Roosevelt to his son in 1903.

The same thing happened to Orrin Hatch in America's bicentennial year of 1976, when he came out of nowhere and captured his first and only political job—a seat in the United States Senate.

Orrin Hatch's beginnings were forged in conditions of Depression-era humility and struggle. "I was a janitor," Hatch once told a reporter. "I was a metal lather. I know what it is like to get my hands dirty. I'm one of the few senators to hold a union card. I won't take any crap. I'm a tough guy." He quickly added, "in an open-hearted way." To Stephen Wayne, political science professor at Georgetown University, Hatch is a person "who is constantly trying to prove something about himself to himself. Here's a guy who came from nothing to something. It's hard for him to stop achieving."[44]

Orrin Hatch was born on March 22, 1934, in Pittsburgh, Pennsylvania, the city that his Utah-born father, Jesse, had moved to with his wife, Helen Frances Hatch, so she could be closer to her mother. Both parents were devout members of The Church of Jesus Christ of Latter-day Saints, the Christian denomination that was founded by Joseph Smith Jr. in New York State in 1830 and gained a home in the promised land of Utah in the late 1840s. Jesse was branch president of the local church congregation, and while there weren't many members of the church in Pittsburgh, neighbors recalled a steady procession of visiting out-of-town church members flocking to the modest Hatch home as an oasis of fellowship and guest lodgings.

Jesse was also a skilled professional craftsman and metal lather, as well as a strong union man and longtime president of his local union chapter. Helen Frances, Orrin's mother, was a full-time homemaker who gave birth to nine children, two of whom, both boys, died within a year of their birth. Jesse hand-built the house Hatch grew up in, located in the hills and unpaved roads of the close-knit Baldwin Borough community. Three of the house's sides consisted of flame-damaged scrapyard wood salvaged from a building fire, and the fourth side featured a Meadow Gold Dairy sign. The children shared two bedrooms, while the parents slept on the living room couch.

For the first few years of Orrin's childhood there was no indoor plumbing, just an outhouse perched on a nearby hill. "I thought that was the neatest home until I realized that we were poor," Hatch once recalled. "I never pass by a bathroom. I always stop.

That 100-yard dash on the dirt path was no fun."[45] The family had a chicken coop, a vegetable patch, and an abundance of love. "I was raised in poverty in Pittsburgh," Hatch once explained. "I really had nothing but good parents who worked hard and taught me to love people from whatever walk of life and respect them."[46] Hatch recounted his regular childhood routine: "I would raise the chickens, feed the chickens, clean the stables, pick up the eggs, sell the eggs, deliver the eggs. I did all of that from six until sixteen."[47]

"That house had a lot of love in it," recalled Orrin's older sister Marilyn. "Every Sunday, we had groups of people in for dinner after church, between church." She explained, "It was Depression time anyway; a lot of people were poor. We didn't starve."[48] She remembered her brother Orrin as a serious and sensitive boy. His lifelong love of music was ignited with church singing, piano lessons, and discount student season tickets to the Pittsburgh Symphony his parents bought for him. "They bought a violin and I played violin all the way through high school and was concert master of our high-school orchestra and the all-state orchestra as well,"[49] recalled Hatch years later. Hatch's mother reported, "He could stand up and recite Scriptures at a young age. He sang from three years old on—country songs, church songs. 'The Old Rugged Cross'—he sang that over and over. He memorized it."[50]

Hatch described his father as a "big, husky tradesman" and an "intellectually profound artisan with his hands." He credited his mother with igniting a love of history and politics in him. She had an eighth-grade education, he recalled, plus the "equivalent of a Ph.D. in self-study." She spoke with her children constantly about American history and politics, and read them the Scriptures. "My parents taught me to seek answers to life's questions by studying the Scriptures, which has helped me gain a personal conviction of the doctrines and principles taught to me by my parents and church leaders," recalled Hatch. "This strong foundation has allowed me to easily live my religion no matter where I am or what I am doing."

When Hatch was a self-described "scrawny" fifth grader, a bully shoved him around a playground so badly he felt powerless to fight back. "I was too scared to do anything; I was humiliated,"[51] he remembered. "I made up my mind from that point on that nobody would ever do that to me again—nobody." He filled a duffel bag with sand and old rags, hooked it to a mulberry tree, and punched it every day for hours. "I got so that I had about as good a right cross and left hook as you could have," Hatch said. "I never backed down from a fight from that point on." Boxing became a metaphor for his life path. "My life has always been uphill," he noted. "I've had to fight for everything I have."[52]

When he was cut from the seventh-grade basketball team, Hatch spent the next year training furiously on a dirt patch in back of his house, shooting at a basket hammered into a tree. He became captain of the varsity team, playing with an aggressive style that included slamming opponents onto the floor during ball scrambles. "Some call it dirty,"[53] he later confessed. Though he weighed only 118 pounds, Hatch grew to his full height of six foot two early in high school, which gave him a big advantage on the basketball court.

A great tragedy struck the Hatch family during World War II, when a telegram arrived with the news that their oldest boy, Jesse Jr., who was flying missions as a gunner in a B-24 Liberator bomber in the 725th Bombardment Squadron, was missing in action. The ten-year-old Orrin idolized his older brother, and he took the news terribly hard. "When we received the news," Hatch later recounted, "I immediately got a white streak of hair on the right side of my forehead because it was such a shock to me."[54]

Four years later, Jesse's remains were found in an Austrian grave-yard and were returned for reburial in Pittsburgh. "They found a few bones, some teeth, bits of cloth—it was pretty pathetic,"[55] said Orrin, who later wrote two songs about Jesse and his fallen comrades: "Morning Breaks on Arlington" and "Someday I'll Fly (The Ballad of Jesse Morlan Hatch)." Orrin's sister Marilyn explained,

"It had a terrible effect on him. He always felt that he had to serve for two people rather than just one."[56]

Hatch himself described the death of Jesse Jr. as the driving force in his life. "Animating my public service has always been the desire to help those who could not help themselves,"[57] Hatch recalled. "Since that day I have pushed myself to pack the work and accomplishments of two lives into one—one for my brother and one for me. My brother's death taught me that life is short, and I wanted to make the most of it.[58]

"I decided I was going to fulfill a mission for my brother because he never got to,"[59] Hatch later explained. "I loved him. He was a good person. He always had a smile on his face. Everybody liked him. He would write and say if he was killed that he had an insurance policy. He had no qualms about giving his life for his country. I pray for him. He didn't have the privileges I have, like marriage and children. What a loss." Hatch explained, "It pushes me. I'm making up for my brother's death. I'm fulfilling a mission for Jesse. Every day I think about him, about being here for him and for my parents."[60]

When Hatch was twelve years old, his parents took him to experience the religious tradition of the "laying on of hands," in the form of a patriarchal blessing from a church elder, to anoint him as a deacon in the church's clergy and to help provide life guidance. The old Latter-day Saint patriarch, a farmer in the small town of Smithfield, Utah, told the boy, "Thou shalt be privileged to mingle with people of many types of character and learning, and shalt have contacts with men and women of educational attainments, and holding high and responsible positions of leadership among the people. These contacts will help thee to ripen in wisdom and judgment."According to Hatch, the words had a "simple yet profound" effect on him, and later directly inspired his career in politics.[61]

The Church of Jesus Christ of Latter-day Saints places America at the heart of Christian history, believing that a vanguard of Israelites left the Middle East hundreds of years before the birth of Jesus and became progenitors of Christianity, and that certain Native Americans descended from the Israelites. "The church that Joseph Smith set about building was almost achingly American," wrote McKay Coppins in 2020. "He held up the Constitution as a quasi-canonical work of providence. He published a new sacred text, the Book of Mormon, that centered on Jesus visiting the ancient Americas. He even taught that God had brought about the American Revolution so that his Church could be restored in a free country—thus linking Mormonism's success to that of the American experiment."[62]

While members of the faith hold many political beliefs, the Latter-day Saints church foundations of the nuclear family, thrift, and traditional values can be seen to connect easily to conservative thought. "It's deeper than politics; it's part of the culture," noted Ted Wilson, former Democratic Salt Lake City mayor. "Mormons don't vote conservative because of specific issues. Conservatism is closer to the church, or closer to God."[63]

When Hatch was sixteen, he followed in his father's footsteps and joined the Wood, Wire and Metal Lathers' International Union as an apprentice lather and learned to make partitions, suspended ceilings, and plaster molding. He worked his trade during the summers, often at his father's side, and developed the political views of a liberal Democrat and hardworking union man. Hatch especially admired President Harry Truman. "I thought he was a man of his word and a straight shooter with a lot of courage," Hatch later explained. "There was no half-truths and spinning. I have tried to be the same type of person."[64] As a teenager, Hatch read books about great American labor leaders and struggles, and was, in his words, "appalled at how the men were bullied and pushed around by some of the great industrialists."[65]

Hatch had thought about joining his father in the building trade, but one day a college scholarship appeared in the mail for him to attend Brigham Young University (BYU), the leading Latter-day Saints institution of higher education that was founded in 1875. Hatch never found out who arranged the award, but suspected his parents were behind it, and in 1952 he traveled to Utah to enter BYU, where, in his words, he "fell in love with learning."[66] In astronomy class, he met his future wife when he was alphabetically seated close to Elaine Hansen, a fellow church member from Newton, Utah.

One day while a freshman, Hatch got into a fistfight with a football player and slugged his larger opponent ten times in the face, rendering him unconscious. "He couldn't get up and I had blood all over me and my eye was bleeding," Hatch recalled years later. "That bothered me so badly. I worried for three days that I had killed him. I eventually saw him again and I was relieved he was all right. I vowed I never would get in a street fight again."[67] Hatch channeled his energy into amateur boxing, winning ten out of eleven bouts.

Hatch later explained that his instincts for compassion and leadership were sharpened at the age of nineteen, when he embarked on a two-year assignment as a missionary representative for his religion's Great Lakes Mission in Ohio, Indiana, and Michigan.

"My commitment was total," recalled Hatch. "I was going to be the best missionary in the church. Nothing was going to stop me. I had found the Lord at the age of seventeen, the first time I read and prayed about the Book of Mormon, and I was going to find him anew and preach him wherever I went."[68] He saw poverty in his missionary travels, in conditions that reminded him of his own childhood, and was moved by it. But he began to see differences between those poor people who seemed to give up and surrender to charity or public assistance, and those who, in his words, "struggled to stay independent and maintain their self-respect."[69] It was the start of Hatch's personal turn away from liberalism and toward a more conservative worldview that emphasized self-reliance and personal responsibility, but valued compassion for those who could not help themselves.

Hatch's mission work consisted of getting up early every morning in a low-budget communal apartment; dressing in a suit with tie and name tag; hitting the streets; knocking on doors; making friends with total strangers; and spreading the word of The Church of Jesus Christ of Latter-day Saints through informal conversations and formal lessons, quoting from memorized Scriptures he'd written on 3″ x 5″ cards. One Latter-day Saints missionary, McKay Coppins, described his own similar experiences decades later: "On slow days, we'd go door-to-door passing out pamphlets and copies of the Book of Mormon. This was not a particularly efficient method for finding future Mormons, but we looked for small victories. I skimmed an old copy of *How to Win Friends and Influence People*, and practiced jokes that I could deploy on strangers' doorsteps. We took consolation in these pleasant, fruitless interactions, telling ourselves that we'd improved the Mormon brand, however slightly. 'Planting seeds,' we called it."[70]

According to Hatch, he worked so hard at his mission that "I drove my companions crazy."[71] He felt he had to do the extra work on behalf of his lost brother, Jesse Jr. "His brother was a guiding light for him,"[72] said H. Bryan Richards, one of Hatch's missionary colleagues. "He worked very hard and was very successful. He baptized wherever he went. He led the mission in hours spent proselytizing. He's always had the energy." At the end of the two-year assignment, Hatch's mission president told him, "You have literally fulfilled two missions."[73]

To a large extent, Hatch's faith would define his life, as faith would for many of the Americans who belonged to the church. "I'm not fanatic about it," Hatch would explain years later. "But each senator's total makeup comes from a complex variety of experience, and religion is one of the more profound and worthwhile of those sets of experiences."[74]

After marrying Elaine and graduating from BYU in 1959, Hatch returned to Pittsburgh and experienced one of those random-chance events that can affect a person's life trajectory. He went to apply to the University of Pittsburgh law school but found the registrar's office unexpectedly closed. Hatch stood at the locked door, looking mournful.

A figure appeared from around the corner and asked, "Hey, can I help you?"

"Well, I don't think so," said Hatch. "I wanted to apply to the law school and it looks like the registrar's door is locked."

Evidently impressed by Hatch's earnest charisma, the man replied, "I can help you, I'm a professor here." He opened the door and gave Hatch the papers, saying, unexpectedly, "We want you here."

"You do?" asked a surprised Hatch, who explained he had attended Brigham Young University.

The professor asked, "You're a Mormon?"

"Yeah," said Hatch.

"Oh my gosh," said the professor. "I went to Arizona State law school. Those Mormons were the toughest competition we had. Why don't you apply for a scholarship?"

Hatch replied, "Well, I don't think I have good enough grades to really do it."

"Oh, I'm on the scholarship committee," reported the professor.[75]

Hatch filled out all the papers, and two weeks later a full honors scholarship to the University of Pittsburgh arrived in the mail for him. He moved his family back to his parents' house in Pittsburgh, where they lived in a chicken coop that his father had converted into a two-room apartment that Hatch recalled was "pretty pathetic," but "the only place we could afford."[76] While attending law school, he also worked as a lather, a janitor, and as the all-night desk attendant in an all-female dormitory, which was the only time he could study his lawbooks. "I was one of the few they trusted to do it," he said. "I was married with children and they knew I was religious."[77]

In law school, Hatch experienced a further political shift from left to right. "As a union worker, I heard only one side of things," he later explained. "Almost all the people I knew were working people and Democrats. But I found out later that some of the things I was proud of as a union man were wrong. The Democrats wanted to spend more, raise taxes, and force more government regulations on business. They believed in central control and less personal responsibility."[78] As Hatch was beginning to see it, an increasingly intrusive government was limiting freedom and harming individuals and businesses. Before long, his shift would go nearly a full 180 degrees.

After graduating from law school with honors, Hatch accepted a job at Pittsburgh's oldest law firm—Pringle, Bredin, and Martin—where he handled accident claims for insurance companies, property title searches, and small claims in county court. "He was a very good speaker," recalled Robert Grigsby, Hatch's colleague and mentor at the firm. "He was also extremely conscientious in preparing himself for his case." Foreshadowing a trait that would appear periodically in Hatch's career, Grigsby added that Hatch's strong religious and sheltered upbringing sometimes led to a tendency for him to "be very benign toward people." According to Grigsby, "He wants to see the best side of people. He's reluctant to see the seamier side."[79]

In 1969, Hatch accepted a job offer to join the law firm of his friend Walter Plumb III in Salt Lake City and moved his family to Utah. There, Hatch proved to be a brilliant trial attorney, specializing in commercial, liability, and tax matters for small businesses and individuals, racking up a winning streak of more than twenty consecutive cases. His partner recalled of one courtroom scene, "It was incredible. Orrin dominated everything. Three women on the jury had tears running down their faces." He added, "And he was defending a guy who hadn't filed his tax returns in five years!"[80] Another attorney reported that Hatch "never left a jury that wasn't crying."[81] After Hatch won five tax-fraud cases in a row, Plumb recalled contacting the Internal Revenue Service and saying, "Send your best team from Washington. We're going to kick your butt."[82]

Hatch's courtroom years sharpened his instinct for pinpointing the jugular of an argument, but he later spoke of the risks: "Sometimes, if you get too fierce and you get too combative, it can be a detriment to you." He added, "So you have to be careful that the skills you've refined in courts of law and arguments of law don't become the sole arena for all you do. You have to temper those things with a respect for other people."[83]

* * *

By 1976, Hatch enjoyed a comfortable life and a booming career as a thriving Salt Lake City attorney and Latter-day Saints church leader.

"I was involved in several business transactions that, if they turned out as I expected, would ensure my family a good income for some time," Hatch recalled. One of his promising side businesses was the production and sale of legal- and religious-themed audiocassette tapes. "My wife, Elaine, and I had six children, three boys and three girls, ranging from Brent, who was eighteen, to Jess, who was six. We had a wonderful home, a four-bedroom house on the East Bench of the Wasatch Mountains, and a spectacular view of the Salt Lake Valley below."[84]

At the same time, Hatch was increasingly disturbed at the state of American politics, to the point that he began to toy with the idea of running for a political office. "One could argue that I should have been content, but I wasn't," he explained. The United States was reeling from the shocks of multiple assassinations, racial turmoil, the Vietnam War, Watergate, an oil price crisis, and wars in the Middle East, and the American economy was tipping into rising inflation and unemployment. Hatch recalled, "I could not escape the powerful and persistent belief that my state and my country were in serious trouble, headed down a dangerous and destructive path, and that if given a chance, I could make a difference. I felt it was my duty, my responsibility, to run and at least give voice to my concerns and my ideas for remedying what was wrong. It was my obligation to give the voters another choice."[85]

In Hatch's view, many trends were converging to threaten the America that he loved, including the legalization of abortion, the expansion of welfare, increases in crime and drug use, the decay of the military, and cultural hostility toward religion. "Washington was governed by the belief that government was the answer to every question and the answer to every problem," Hatch explained. He thought "it was time for a different philosophy, a different kind of politician. I believed that the answer lay in lower taxes, less government, fewer regulations, less centralized power and a wiser use of the power that must be exercised on behalf of the people."[86]

The target of Hatch's increasing scorn was Utah's popular senior US senator Ted Moss, who, like Hatch, was a Latter-day Saint and an opponent of legalized abortion, but was also a Democrat who held many liberal views. At the time, Utah had a three-term Democratic governor who would be followed by another Democrat the next year, and there was only one Republican among the state's four-person congressional delegation, Senator Jake Garn, who was elected in 1974. According to Hatch biographer Lee Roderick, "Frank E. (Ted) Moss was a U.S. senator straight from central casting. Completing his third six-year term at age sixty-five, the native Utahn and former judge tooled around Washington in a yellow Mustang convertible, hair slicked back and flashing a million-dollar smile."[87] Moss had opposed the Vietnam War and written bills that banned cigarette ads on TV and sharply increased the power of the Federal Trade Comission to regulate business.

Hatch was, in his words, "constantly moaning and groaning"[88] to his friends about Moss and the state of national affairs, believing that Moss was totally out of step with Utah, a state that was gradually shifting toward more conservative politics. One day, an unusual suggestion was made to him by Grey Nokes, a fellow Salt Lake attorney.

"Look, Orrin, you're a good negotiator and one of the smartest guys I know," said Nokes. "You'd make a great senator yourself. Why don't you run against Moss?"[89]

Hatch recalled, "I was 42 by then, and the more I thought about it, I thought why should I stand on the sidelines? I knew I could win."[90] The trouble was, he had no money for a political leap so enormous, and no political connections or experience other than a stint as student body president during a university summer session.

At a church meeting, Hatch told his neighbor Frank Madsen, "I'm thinking about running for the Senate. What do you think?"

"You're crazy!" said Madsen. "Nobody knows you, you're not known as a Republican, and you don't have any money. It's crazy." Laughing at the audacity of the idea, Madsen added, "How can you possibly think that you could run for the Senate?" He quipped, "This is just nuts," stressing that Hatch wasn't even a Republican.

"Well, I am now," Hatch responded. "I'm going to do it and I can win."[91]

One person who did not approve of Hatch's candidacy at first was his wife, Elaine, who cried for three days straight when her husband told her of his determination to become a US senator. "It was a very tough decision for both of us," Hatch remembered. "She cried for three days. But I felt like I had to do it. I had the capacity, I had the background, the legal background—and I loved our country tremendously. So I was willing to do anything to help this country."[92]

Hatch sought the advice of three prominent Utah Republican power brokers, the first of which, Utah Republican Party chairman Richard Richards, told him he could win for the same reason Jimmy Carter would that year: "This is going to be an election year of anti-Washington sentiment."[93] The second, Ernest Wilkinson, was an attorney who had won Native American tribes tens of millions of dollars in compensation from the federal government for broken treaties, had served as president of Brigham Young University, and was a former Republican Senate candidate who lost to

Ted Moss in 1964. Wilkinson also encouraged Hatch and gave him a contribution to launch his campaign.

The third Utah power broker whom Hatch consulted was an outspoken anticommunist, former FBI agent, and ex–Salt Lake City police chief named W. Cleon Skousen. He was a Latter-day Saint who was friendly with the ultraconservative John Birch Society, which was widely viewed as an extremist (though nonviolent) organization. In the context of this era, such an association was not highly unusual—one senior church leader, Ezra Taft Benson, publicly expressed solidarity with the Birch Society in 1963, though that same year, then church president David O. McKay criticized the society for questioning the loyalty of elected officials and for seeking "to align the church or its leadership with (the society's) partisan views."[94]

As police chief, Skousen was a highly aggressive crime fighter who was fired by the mayor of Salt Lake City after Skousen raided a poker game where the mayor was in attendance. Hatch later recalled that "Cleon was one of the first people of political significance and substance who agreed to meet with me and discuss my candidacy. A few short years before this time, Cleon had organized a nonprofit educational foundation named 'The Freemen Institute,' to foster 'constitutionalist' principles including a drastic reduction in the size and scope of the Federal Government, and a reverence for the true, unchanging nature of our Constitution. I knew that he had strongly held beliefs and I was very interested in what he had to say. We found in each other at that first meeting many areas of common ground and a shared love for the principles that make America the strongest bastion of freedom on Earth. Cleon quickly agreed to help, and throughout the coming months he became a true champion of my candidacy."[95] Skousen lent Hatch his mailing list of thousands of supporters.

Hatch waited until the last possible moment—the day of the deadline with five minutes to spare—to file the paperwork to enter the Utah Republican nominating process for the Senate, which happened not in a primary election, but in votes in small meetings to elect delegates to a state party convention. A candidate would become the nominee if he or she won half the delegates to the party convention in August 1976; otherwise, there would be a runoff between the top two in September if no one won 50 percent. After filing the forms, Hatch faced the media, his knees buckling from nervousness, and declared he was a "non-politician," adding, "The old-line party professionals tell me I have no chance to win—to even come out of the party state convention. But I'm used to impossible odds. That's the story of my life."[96]

The article in the *Salt Lake Tribune* the next day noted that this was the first time Hatch had ever been mentioned in the paper. His novice campaign materials featured photos so unflattering that Hatch's own volunteers feared they made him look "like Beelzebub."[97] Working with a shoestring budget, Hatch packed his family into a van and campaigned across the state of Utah, rewarding his children with milkshakes for good behavior.

Hatch faced four opponents for the Republican nomination, including a former congressman, and each of them was Washington-experienced, well-financed, and well-known in Utah. The leading candidate, Jack Carlson, was a former Air Force fighter pilot and Harvard-educated economist who resigned his position as assistant secretary of the interior in the Ford administration to come back to campaign in Utah.

Hatch quickly made strong impressions with Republican delegates. At a party meeting near Provo, Utah, when asked whom he supported, the serving Republican president, Gerald Ford, or his conservative challenger, Ronald Reagan, Hatch triggered a loud ovation by declaring, "I give my unqualified support to Ronald Reagan, and I believe that, if he is nominated, he will be our next president!"[98]

Hatch's neighbor Frank Madsen, who was now serving in Hatch's fledgling campaign, watched Hatch square off against front-runner Jack Carlson, who was also Madsen's friend. "Jack was very bright but Jack was no debater and Jack was a slow thinker," Madsen recalled in an oral history years later. "They had debates and Orrin just tore him to shreds because Jack just couldn't respond quickly enough. Orrin just chewed him up and spat him out. And he destroyed my friend Jack. I'm just sitting there getting lower and lower in my chair because it's getting to be embarrassing because Jack cannot handle it."[99]

Carlson's wife, Renee, watched Hatch mingle with delegates and wrote down her own impressions of her husband's opponent. "Orrin was tall, physically attractive, however, and aware of this in an almost sensual way. Sometimes he seemed vain and egocentric; other times he displayed a forced testimony-bearing humility that left me either awed or disgusted," she wrote. "His rhetoric seemed to appeal to those who were slightly estranged from the general society."[100] In fact, Hatch was staking out positions that mainstream Republicans in Utah were shifting toward in great numbers, like opposing abortion except to save the life of the mother, opposing expanded power for labor unions, calls for deep federal spending cuts, and a constitutional amendment to balance the budget.

In the first of two campaign masterstrokes, Hatch used his office audiocassette-tape production equipment to record and mass-mail twenty-five hundred copies of a direct message to every prospective Republican primary delegate in Utah, using $3,000 in borrowed funds. On the recording, Hatch described himself as a champion of the people and a successful crusader against the federal bureaucracy through his legal career and criticized his opponents for their ties to Washington. "They believe they have the convention delegates all locked up. I don't believe that," Hatch concluded. "Please consider voting for me; then the Republicans will really have a choice." The Hatch campaign mailed the tapes in bicentennial red, white, and blue boxes and included a transcript of Hatch's message printed on American colonial-type parchment paper. It created a striking effect, and suddenly, every Republican who mattered for the nomination knew who the recently obscure Hatch was and what he believed. Hatch came in second at the state convention, netting 778 votes to Carlson's 930, qualifying for a two-man primary runoff.

The second maneuver by the Hatch campaign was equally brilliant, and it catapulted him over the top. Days before the primary, Hatch was within striking distance of Carlson, but still behind. Until then, Hatch and his aides had been kicking around the long-shot idea of asking for an endorsement from Ronald Reagan, who had just been defeated by Ford for the party's presidential nomination at the August national Republican convention. But Reagan was thought to adhere to his party's "eleventh commandment" of never speaking ill of a fellow Republican until a nomination is settled, besides which, he was then on vacation in Mexico.

Desperate and with little to lose, Hatch authorized his aides to contact Reagan's team and give it a try. As it happened, Reagan's own pollster, a Utah Latter-day Saint named Richard Wirthlin, was detecting a sharp conservative shift in his own Utah data and thought Hatch would have a very strong chance to win against incumbent Democratic US senator Frank Moss. Wirthlin's nephew, who was a fellow church bishop with Hatch, told his uncle, "You couldn't do better than Hatch." Reagan's aides spotted a promising future ally in Hatch and recommended that Reagan endorse him.

"Tell Hatch I will be happy to endorse," said Reagan in a call to the Hatch campaign.

"Say that again, sir?" asked the Hatch aide who answered the phone.

"Tell Hatch I'd be happy to endorse him!"

"Mr. Reagan, would you be so kind as to send us a telegram confirming our conversation for the press?"

"Well, yes, when do you need it?"

"The minute I hang up, sir."[101] On vacation, Reagan didn't have the time or equipment to record TV spots for Hatch, so the last-minute release of an endorsement telegram was all Hatch had to work with.

The Hatch campaign called a news conference to announce Reagan's telegram, which arrived with just minutes to spare, and read, "The time has come for me to do everything I can to endorse a man of quality, courage, discipline, and integrity; a man who believes in individual freedom and self reliance. With these qualities in mind, I enthusiastically endorse Warren Hatch for U.S. Senator from Utah."[102] Reagan had gotten Hatch's first name wrong. To clarify matters, Reagan called in to a news show on Saturday night and endorsed Hatch again, using his correct name. In the primary election on Tuesday, September 14, Hatch crushed Jack Carlson with 65 percent of the vote.

Hatch's meteoric rise continued in the general election, as the complacent Senator Frank Moss badly underestimated him. Hatch criticized Moss's long tenure in the Senate with the wisecrack "What do you call a senator who's served in office for eighteen years? You call him home." (In the years to come, as Hatch's own Senate tenure exceeded twenty and then thirty years, his political opponents would use this comment against him.) At a campaign debate before eight hundred Rotarians at the Hotel Utah in Salt Lake City, Senator Moss, dripping with contempt, fixed his eyes on Hatch and asked theatrically, pausing between each word to emphasize the message of his being a "carpetbagger" from a distant land: "Who is this young upstart attorney from—Pittsburgh?"[103]

Hatch uttered an ice-cool response that had the audience roaring with delight: "Senator," he said politely, "my great-grandfather, Jeremiah Hatch, founded Vernal and Ashley Valley in Eastern Utah. My great-uncle, Lorenzo Hatch, was one of the founders of Logan and Cache Valley in Northern Utah, and my great-uncle, Abram Hatch, helped to found Heber City and Heber Valley in Central Utah. They were all polygamists, and everywhere I go, people come up to me and say, 'You know, I think I'm related to you.' If you keep denigrating my Hatch family background, the Hatch vote alone is going to rise up and bite you in the ass."[104]

Moss was dumbfounded, and he seemed to lose momentum from that point on. His campaign was also crippled by a prostitution scandal involving a Moss associate. In a stunning upset, Moss lost to Hatch, 45 percent to 54 percent, in the general election.

Hatch later explained, "I won that election on sheer guts and sheer ability and ultimately by never quitting."[105]

The Chamber of History

I N HIS FIRST MOMENTS after being sworn in as a US Senator in the Ninety-Fifth Congress on January 3, 1977, Hatch was escorted to his assigned desk on the Senate floor.

Like all the desks assigned to Republicans, Hatch's desk was located on the right side of the chamber, on a multitiered platform of four concentric semicircles that faced an elevated central rostrum occupied by the Senate's presiding officer and assorted parliamentarians and stenographers.

Hatch absorbed the magnitude of his new job inside a small amphitheater that would be his stage for the next forty-two years— the US Senate chamber, located in the north wing of the US Capitol Building. In this room, Hatch would soon discover, in his words, that "the learning curve can be staggering."[106]

According to Kevin McGuiness, who was Hatch's chief of staff from 1988 to 1991, Hatch is "in many ways, an incredibly unknown, larger-than-life figure, and a man of contradictions." In 2020 McGuiness explained, "He came from nothing, grew up dirt poor, worked as a janitor, and lived as a grown man with his new bride in a reconverted chicken coop in back of his parents' house. He made it from there to what is arguably the most exclusive insiders club in America. I think he always had in the back of his mind the assumption that at some point the 'cool kids' would tell him to get out."[107]

Hatch's desk was in the front row. On his left was the desk of the longtime segregationist and 1948 Dixiecrat presidential candidate Strom Thurmond of South Carolina; and on his right was Wyoming senator Malcolm Wallop. One row back and one desk to the left sat conservative warhorse Barry Goldwater of Arizona, who had lost the 1964 presidential race in a landslide and was now physically and symbolically looking over Hatch's shoulder.[108] To Hatch, Goldwater resembled "a crusty, irreverent fighter, who lived by principle, was always anywhere and everywhere the same, with a coherent and consistent moral-conservative philosophy that never deviated from the high plane of his integrity." By now, however, Goldwater's national importance had largely evaporated, and he reminded Hatch of an "old wounded eagle."[109]

Opening the top of his hinged-lid mahogany desk, Hatch found plenty of room for books and papers, and he could see at the bottom of the desk several hand-scrawled autographs from previous twentieth-century senators who followed the schoolboy custom of signing their names right on the wood on their last day in office.

Over the coming years, Hatch would occupy three desks on the Senate floor, numbered 28, 40, and 90, and their previous occupants included giants from both parties, including Presidents John F. Kennedy and Harry S. Truman; former Republican majority leader Robert A. Taft Sr.; and former Senate president pro tempore and Democratic Georgia senator Richard Russell. Vice President Hubert Humphrey also previously occupied Hatch's desk. After his failed 1968 campaign for president, Humphrey had returned to the Senate and would soon become a very close friend to Hatch, who wrote, "Although we differ on many political matters, I can't help but say that this man has had a profound influence on my life. He is so optimistic, so sincere, so loving."[110]

Another previous occupant of Hatch's desk was former Senate pro tempore and Foreign Relations Committee chairman Arthur Vandenberg of Michigan, a Republican who in the 1940s gave the Democratic Truman administration critical bipartisan support for the Truman Doctrine, the Marshall Plan, and the formation of NATO. It was Vandenberg who coined the often-quoted invocation to a bipartisan foreign policy that "politics stops at the water's edge."

The US Senate chamber was a highly unusual, elite public work space, with one hundred individual desks, many separated by only a few inches, its occupants practically elbow-to-elbow in a cramped, windowless two-story chamber 113 feet long, 36 feet high, and 80 feet wide. It housed one hundred senators, ninety-eight men and two women, two from each state, supported by various aides and staff. An upper gallery for the public, diplomats, and the press provided seats for spectators to peer down from, creating a grand rectangular motif echoing that of a wraparound church, a sunken theater, or even—if you let your imagination really wander—a mini Roman Colosseum. Watching a Senate session one day in the twenty-first century, *New Yorker* journalist George Packer wrote that "from the press gallery, the senators in their confined space began to resemble zoo animals," with different senators reminding him of "a shambling brown bear," "a loping gazelle," and a "maddened grizzly."[111]

Above the chamber's four giant doors were gilt inscriptions that read "In God we trust"; "E pluribus unum" (Out of many, one); "Novus ordo seclorum" (A new order of the ages); and "Annuit coeptis" (God has favored our undertakings). In quaint connection to decades past, the desks of the Senate majority and minority leaders were still equipped with brass spittoons, and two tobacco snuffboxes were positioned on the rostrum, one for each political party. No one was sure when they were last used. The only food and beverages allowed on the Senate floor were water, milk (to soothe upset stomachs), and candy, so one senator's back-row aisle position on the Republican side, desk #80, which was near a busy exit door and a popular elevator bank, was designated by custom since the 1960s as the "candy desk," stuffed with sugary treats for senators of any persuasion to enjoy. In the new Ninety-Fifth Congress in January 1977, it fell to incoming New Mexico senator and former Apollo 17 astronaut Harrison Schmitt to honor the tradition of keeping the desk stocked with candy.

In 1966, longtime Washington journalist Mary McGrory described the work life of a senator in the chamber. "The two pencils in the groove on his desk are always finely sharpened," she wrote. "The points on the two old-fashioned pens are new, and the two inkwells are always full. Page boys quiver to serve him, they come bounding at the snap of his fingers. The chairs are comfortable and move smoothly on the carpeted floor. All around him are men he can talk to, men who understand his political problems, who will listen to his tales of foreign travel or his triumphs with rod and gun during the recess."[112] She described the phalanx of lobbyists outside who ached to have a word with senators and the parliamentary experts on staff standing by to help senators navigate the complex Senate rules contained in a sixteen-hundred-page book by Floyd M. Riddick called *Senate Procedure: Precedents and Practices*, which few people had ever read in its entirety.

For Orrin Hatch, a recently obscure young lawyer from a very modest upbringing, this was an entirely new and different world. "Enter the United States Senate and step back in time," wrote journalist Joyce Barrett in 1992. "Step into a world of marble, mahogany, leather and brass, a place of old-world deference and breeding and amenity. Take a steam. Swim. Dine in genteel company. Escape to hidden suites, salons, vaults and parlours. Leave most of life's inconveniences behind. Leave many federal laws behind, as well. And most women. Pray. Study. Give your word. Then call a car and driver when you must take your leave. Enter the senate and enter one of the world's last great gentleman's clubs—America's House of Lords."[113]

Senators were eligible for a wide range of perks and privileges, including VIP parking at capital-area airports; special license plates allowing parking anywhere in DC except in front of fire hydrants; subsidized haircuts ($3 for a razor cut, style, and shampoo); subsidized dining rooms serving entrées like "Chinese Low-Cholesterol Stir-Fried Chicken and Snow Peas with Crisp Water Chestnuts and Green Peppers over Rice" for just $2.50; free or heavily discounted medical care and life insurance; free use of mailing and audiovisual equipment to stay in touch with the folks back home; patronage jobs to divvy out to friends and constituents; free office decorations like potted plants and loaned artwork; free research and ghostwriting services from the Congressional Research Service of the Library of Congress; and even free funeral planning and management, courtesy of the Senate sergeant at arms.[114]

Hatch's new profession was created 190 years before he arrived in the chamber, the product of a "Great Compromise" reached at the Constitutional Convention of 1787, in a deal brokered by a widely respected delegate from Connecticut, Roger Sherman. He negotiated with delegates from highly populated states who wanted proportional representation in the new government, as well as those from small states who were happy with the equal representation they experienced under the Articles of Confederation. Sherman's Solomon-like solution was simple—power would be shared between a state-appointed Senate with equal representation and a popularly elected House of Representatives with proportional representation. With enactment of the Seventeenth Amendment in 1913, the Senate would be elected by direct popular vote too.

The Senate, with staggered six-year terms of office, was designed to act as a check against bad or hasty decisions both by the president and by the much larger House of Representatives, whose members faced reelection every two years. Even as a freshman senator who ranked ninety-eighth out of a hundred in seniority since Frank Moss had denied him the customary courtesy of resigning a few days before his swearing-in, and despite being initially assigned to a dingy basement office with exposed ceiling pipes in the Russell Building, as a senator, Hatch immediately commanded a strong potential arsenal of power in the US government.

In effect, Orrin Hatch or any other senator had the power to instantly bring the business of American government to a crashing halt, simply by raising a hand and objecting to a motion, threatening to filibuster, or adding endless amendments to a proposed piece of legislation. As Senate parliamentarian emeritus Robert B. Dove and scholar Richard A. Arenberg noted in 2010, two powers that define the Senate are "the right of its members to unlimited debate and the right to offer amendments practically without limit."[115]

In his 1897 farewell address, then vice president Adlai Stevenson noted the logic of the arrangement, stating, "Great evils often result from hasty legislation; rarely from the delay which follows full discussion and deliberation."[116] Martin B. Gold, a historian of the Senate, has pointed out that "a single senator can block legislation that is desired by ninety-nine others because the requirements to overcome his objection are so cumbersome that there may not be time to address them," an arrangement that "will strike the average person as being tremendously anti-democratic and tremendously unfair, but that's the nature of the Senate."[117] Gold wrote that "Senate rules grant substantial power to individual members, coalitions, and the minority party. Senators knowing procedure—and willing to employ it—can wield influence far beyond their single vote."[118]

The framers of the Constitution structured the Congress so that both bodies had to agree on legislation to be passed, and with enough votes they could together override a presidential veto. The House would largely control the purse strings, while the Senate would approve treaties and federal appointments proposed by the president and hold the ultimate power, following impeachment action by the House, to put on trial and remove the president and other federal officials. It was a unique power-sharing scheme; no other nation had one like it. Most everyone was happy with the arrangement, including Founding Father James Madison, who saw the Senate as a "necessary fence"[119] against the potentially dangerous whims of a hot-tempered majority in the House, a body that could "protect the people against the transient impressions in which they themselves might be led."[120] Twentieth-century journalist Russell Baker noted that the Senate was also created "to prevent presidents from governing recklessly and to bring them to their senses when they persisted in governing recklessly anyhow."[121]

The Senate's treaty-ratification function gave it huge history-shaping power. On October 20, 1803, under President Thomas Jefferson, the Senate approved a treaty with France that doubled the size of the nation by authorizing the purchase of the Louisiana Territory. In 1919, President Woodrow Wilson campaigned for Senate approval of the Treaty of Versailles, but he managed to offend his archenemy Republican senator Henry Cabot Lodge and his allies by ignoring their suggestions and calling them "contemptible," "narrow," "selfish," "poor little minds that never get anywhere but run around in a circle and think they are going somewhere."[122] The Senate rejected the treaty and killed Wilson's dream of the United States joining the League of Nations.

From the start, senators had strong individual power when compared with members of the House of Representatives. "The House is an institution whose rules, precedents, and parliamentary mechanisms enhance majority party power," noted historian Gold. "As the House has evolved over time, it has become ever more so a majority-dominated institution. The Senate is opposite. Its rules, precedents, and the absence of procedural mechanisms enhance individual and minority power."[123] A standard Senate procedure is "unanimous consent," which requires all senators to agree to a measure, and contributes to the atmosphere of extreme consensus and collegiality, sometimes forced, that suffuses the walls of the Senate. Sarah Binder, a congressional scholar at George Washington University, once observed, "To have a chamber that rules by unanimous consent—it's nutty!"[124]

The Capitol Building has witnessed some of American history's most dramatic events and fiercest debates, its most soaring oratory and colorful personalities, such as the legendary Senate giants of the "Great Triumvirate" of Henry Clay of Kentucky, Daniel Webster of Massachusetts, and John C. Calhoun of South Carolina, who together dominated American history for several decades of the nineteenth century. Writing of his 1831 visit to the Capitol in his classic book *Democracy in America*, French aristocrat Alexis de Tocqueville marveled, "The Senate is composed of eloquent advocates, distinguished generals, wise magistrates, and statesmen of note, whose arguments would do honor to the most remarkable parliamentary debates of Europe."[125] The Senate played host to statesmen and stateswomen, heroes and geniuses, and—occasionally—scoundrels, dullards, and slobs.

The Senate's moment of birth occurred on April 30, 1789, when the towering figure of former general George Washington swept into the original Senate chamber on the second floor of Federal Hall in New York City wearing a brown broadcloth civilian suit bedecked with fancy gilt buttons. He briefly greeted the assembled senators and representatives, stepped onto the exterior balcony to take the oath of office as America's first president, and returned to the chamber to proclaim his inaugural address, while according to one witness, "all the bells in the city rang out a peal of joy."[126] The American government was born and immediately got down to business. The new Congress convened in New York for a year before relocating to a second-floor chamber in Congress Hall in Philadelphia in 1790.

In 1793, President Washington personally laid the cornerstone of the US Capitol Building, but the precise position of that stone has been lost to history. Two years later, bowing to public pressure, the Senate decided to open its proceedings to the public to avoid charges of conspiracy and secrecy.

In November 1800, the Senate and the rest of the federal government packed up from the temporary national capital of

Philadelphia and moved to the brand-new District of Columbia, which was located in a brackish, malarial swamp that suffered blast-furnace heat and humidity through the summer. There, the Senate convened in a dark and cramped temporary hall on the first floor of the unfinished Capitol, now known as the Old Supreme Court Chamber.

The following year, Vice President Thomas Jefferson put together a "Manual of Procedure" for the Senate that borrowed from ancient books of parliamentary procedure used by the British House of Commons. Of the Senate's first twenty rules, ten of them warned against rude behavior, including: "No one is to disturb another in his speech by hissing, coughing, spitting, speaking or whispering to another; nor to stand up or interrupt him; nor to pass between the Speaker and the speaking member; nor to go across the [Senate chamber], or to walk up and down it, or to take books or papers from the [clerk's] table, or write there." Most of these rules endure to this day, in the form of forty-four Standing Rules of the Senate.

On January 2, 1810, the Senate moved to an ornate second-story hall in the Capitol Building designed by architect Benjamin Latrobe that is now called the Old Senate Chamber. In 1814, British troops used torches and gunpowder paste to set the Capitol on fire, forcing senators to convene in temporary locations, and when the repaired Senate chamber was finally reopened five years later, forty-eight new mahogany desks were supplied by a New York City cabinetmaker. When Orrin Hatch arrived in 1977, all of those desks were still in service, plus fifty-two more that had been commissioned over the years.

On April 3, 1850, while presiding over a Senate debate, Vice President Millard Fillmore ruled Missouri senator Thomas Hart Benton to be out of order. This triggered a fracas between Benton and Mississippi senator Henry Foote. The burly Benton ominously marched up the center aisle toward the diminutive Foote, and pandemonium erupted when Foote pulled out a pistol right on the Senate floor to defend himself. Benton exclaimed theatrically, "I have no pistols! Let him fire! Stand out of the way and let the assassin fire!"[127] Other senators stepped into the line of fire to break up the imminent bloodshed, and Fillmore hastily adjourned the proceedings.

On May 19, 1856, the threat of bloodshed on the Senate floor became very real for a crusading abolitionist Republican senator from Massachusetts named Charles Sumner, who was working through a pile of outgoing mail at his back-row desk. Representative Preston Brooks of South Carolina, upset over a fiery anti-slavery speech Sumner had given three days earlier, slipped onto the Senate floor and crept up to Sumner brandishing a thick metal-tipped cane. Brooks swung the weapon onto Sumner's head and proceeded to give him a savage beating as an accomplice, South Carolina representative Laurence M. Keitt, held off would-be rescuers with a pistol. It took Sumner three years to recover from the attack and return to the Senate, where he served another eighteen years. Brooks, his attacker, was hailed as a hero in the South and reelected to the House.[128]

The Capitol Building underwent major expansions in the 1850s, and in 1859 the Senate moved into its final home, or "new chamber," a larger and grander room that would be the nerve center of Orrin Hatch's professional life from 1977 to 2019. As soon as the senators moved into their new quarters, however, they complained about bad lighting, poor acoustics, stuffy air, boiling heat and freezing cold, and the relentless noise of rain crashing onto the glass-paneled ceiling. Senator John P. Hale of New Hampshire groused in 1861 that the Senate chamber was "the worst, the most inconvenient, uncomfortable, and unhealthy place that ever I was in all my life."[129] The complaints continued for decades, and the acoustics were not straightened out until the 1940s.

For seven decades, the US Senate was a death trap, a "broiling death-dealing business for elder Congressmen," according to one reporter. Between 1916 and 1928, thirty-four incumbent senators died in office, and Senator Royal Copeland of New York, a practicing physician and former commissioner of the New York City Board of Health, blamed the fatality rate on dirty, humid air that circulated common illnesses during winter and heat sickness in summer. Major relief didn't come until the 1930s when proper air-conditioning was installed.[130]

On the cold morning of January 21, 1861, the Senate witnessed perhaps the most momentous moment ever to occur in chamber when the skeletal, defiant figure of Democratic Mississippi senator and slave master Jefferson Davis rose from his chair to announce that his state had "declared her separation from the United States."[131] Amid a burst of applause and weeping by onlookers, Davis strode out of the chamber with several Southern colleagues to take charge of a bloody rebellion that tore the nation apart for four years and cost the lives of at least six hundred thousand soldiers and an unknown number of civilians. A kind of poetic justice unfolded nineteen years later, when Mississippi's Blanche K. Bruce, a former slave, became the first African American to serve in the Senate.

During the Civil War, the US Capitol became a barracks for Union troops defending Washington, DC, and the new Senate chamber served as dormitory, mess hall, and medical office, while seventy brick ovens in the basement churned out eight hundred loaves of bread per day for the troops. The violence on the battlefields nearly spilled onto the Senate floor one day in 1863, when an apparently drunk antiwar Democratic senator, Willard Saulsbury, verbally lashed out at President Abraham Lincoln, who was not present, in what one commentator called "language fit only for a drunken fishwife."[132] Vice President Hannibal Hamlin told Saulsbury to stop and sit down, but to no avail, so the Senate's sergeant at arms approached to eject the inebriated Saulsbury. The senator produced a revolver, aimed at the officer, and announced, "Damn you, if you touch me, I'll shoot you dead!"[133] Saulsbury soon regained his senses, backed down, and apologized.

On March 4, 1865, the day of President Lincoln's second inauguration, when his newly elected vice president, Andrew Johnson, rose to address the Senate, witnesses were shocked to realize that Johnson was completely drunk and uttering gibberish; he was soon hustled out of view. Three years later, the chamber was the scene of the nation's first presidential impeachment trial—that of Andrew Johnson, who avoided conviction by a single vote.

Physical violence on the Senate floor broke out on February 22, 1902, between two Democratic senators from South Carolina. Junior senator John McLaurin burst into the chamber and announced that senior senator Ben Tillman was guilty of "a willful, malicious, and deliberate lie." In response, according to the Senate historian's office, "the 54-four-year-old Tillman jumped from his place and physically attacked McLaurin, who was 41, with a series of stinging blows," and "efforts to separate the two combatants resulted in misdirected punches landing on other members."[134] The Senate censured both men and added a rule that survives today: "No Senator in debate shall, directly or indirectly, by any form of words impute to another Senator or to other Senators any conduct or motive unworthy or unbecoming a Senator."

Orrin Hatch would become a clean-living, fastidious, physically fit, polite, and proper senator, and if he had been on the Senate floor eighty years earlier, he would not have been favorably impressed by the sight of Pennsylvania senator Boies Penrose, one of the most inelegant people to ever serve in the job.

Senator Penrose was "a graceless hulk of a man" according to his biographer and historian John Lukacs, and "a gargantuan devourer of oysters, the bigger the better," who "drank cheap gin and whisky in low dives" and dismissed President Theodore Roosevelt as "a cock-eyed little runt." For breakfast, Penrose was reported to consume a dozen eggs, twelve rolls, a quart of coffee, and a half-inch-thick slab of ham, while for lunch he favored an entire stuffed turkey. According to one witness, reported the historian, the senator "ordered reedbirds for dinner; the waiters brought a chafing dish containing twenty-six, which he proceeded to devour one by one, finishing the wild rice and drinking the gravy out of a cup, all of this after having drunk nine cocktails and five highballs." Unsurprisingly, Senator Penrose's fine English suits were often coated with food stains.[135]

Penrose was just one of many devotees of unhealthy living on Capitol Hill, and for many decades the Congress was populated by hard-drinking, heavy-smoking elected officials, most of them older white men, whose lifestyles must have damaged their decision-making as well as their morality. According to historian Ira Shapiro, "The culture of alcoholism that pervaded the Senate through much of the twentieth century took its toll in the form of diminished judgement, erratic behavior, and recurrent health problems."[136]

To provide some measure of fitness, a tiny pool and steam room were included in the construction of the Russell Building in 1909; the facilities were for senators only, who over the next decades were usually naked except for a towel. Exercise equipment and massage tables came later. Senate historian Don Ritchie recounted in 2021, "A former page told me that when they delivered something to the gym and encountered a naked senator they were instructed to avert their eyes."[137] The Senate was an all-male preserve until the first female US senator, Rebecca Latimer Felton of Georgia, was appointed by the state governor to serve for just a single day in 1922; and the first woman elected to the Senate, Hattie Caraway from Arkansas, arrived in 1932. When Orrin Hatch arrived in 1977, the Senate never had more than two female senators serving at the same time.

If you sat in the Senate visitors' gallery on a day in the 1950s, you might have witnessed the spectacle of a tall, commanding Texan prowling the floor like a big-game hunter, pulling senators aside, grabbing them by the lapels, pushing his face into theirs, hugging, shaking, and slobbering on them to vote a certain way on an upcoming piece of legislation. It was Lyndon Baines Johnson, the barnyard humorist and human bulldozer who served as Democratic Senate majority leader from 1955 to 1961 with equal measures of intensity and repulsiveness.

According to Florida senator George Smathers, Johnson was a "real tyrannical, tough, disagreeable dictatorial fellow," but "when it came to getting things done, there was nobody that was equal to Lyndon, before or since as far as I could see."[138] Journalist Ben Bradlee described the Texan in action: "When Johnson wanted to persuade you of something, when you got the Johnson treatment, you really felt as if a St. Bernard had licked your face for an hour, had pawed you all over. When he was in the Senate especially as majority leader, it was like going to the zoo. He never just shook hands with you. One hand was shaking your hand, the other hand was always someplace else, exploring you, examining you."[139]

A close aide who later served Johnson in the White House, Horace Busby, considered Johnson "an insufferable bastard, a bully and a sadist,"[140] while Democratic "Wise Man" Dean Acheson, who served as secretary of state under Truman, dubbed LBJ "a real centaur—part man, part horse's ass."[141]

The writer Robert Caro christened LBJ as "Master of the Senate" in his biographical trilogy of the man, but Johnson's chief accomplishment as majority leader was the passage of the toothless and quickly forgotten Civil Rights Act of 1957. "In the history of the institution," wrote historian Lewis Gould, "Johnson did not change the Senate or create an enduring new role for the majority leader. Johnson enjoyed a brief period when an evenly divided upper house and a fractured Democratic party allowed his special abilities to flourish. Once these circumstances shifted, after 1958, the chamber reverted to a more individualistic style, and Johnson's methods lost their power."[142] Johnson's successor, Mike Mansfield of Montana, who retired the day that Orrin Hatch was sworn in, was the polar personality opposite of LBJ, and he led Senate Democrats with a low-key, hands-off style. Correspondent Saul Pett of the Associated Press wrote of the tight-lipped Mansfield: "Often, he wears the anxious look of an undertaker who fears that the casket won't fit through the door; at other times, the pained look of a school teacher waiting and wondering why the hell the kids can't return faster from recess." Mansfield's favorite phrases were said to be "Yep. Nope. Maybe. Can't say. Don't know."[143]

When he became a senator in 1973, twenty-nine-year-old future president Joe Biden was given a tour of the private Senate gym by Massachussetts senator Edward "Ted" Kennedy, who told Biden it wasn't a hard-core fitness center, but "an old-guy gym, a place to get a massage or have a steam bath." The two of them opened the gym doors and ran into a group of legendary senators, including New York Republican Jacob Javits and Missouri Democrat Stuart Symington.

"They were standing there, two feet away from me, reaching out to shake my hand," recalled Biden. "And they were all naked as the day they were born. I tried hard to keep eye contact, but I didn't know what the hell I was supposed to say. They were perfectly at ease, but for me it was like one of those dreams where you look down in class and realize you aren't wearing any pants."[144] During Orrin Hatch's early years in the Senate, in the late 1970s and 1980s, the gym was gradually expanded into a proper health center for both male and female senators, with gym clothes required, and Hatch became an early-morning workout regular.

*   *   *

The history of the Senate is often one of polite but bare-knuckled political combat, but it is also a story of negotiation, compromise, dealmaking, and a concept that would come to define some of Orrin Hatch's greatest achievements in office—bipartisanship.

Some bipartisan milestones contributed to American progress, while others delayed it or even pushed the nation backward. The Senate ratified a series of multipartisan compromises on the issue of slavery that held the young nation together until 1861, but at a horrific cost—for more than three generations, millions of human beings within the borders of the United States were condemned to the threat of legally sanctioned physical bondage, hard labor, torture, rape, and murder, making the American South a de facto racial dictatorship. The Capitol Building was built in part by slave labor, and in the early 1800s, some members of Congress came to Washington accompanied by their personal slaves. According to Senate historian Betty Koed, slavery was "a constant presence in the Capitol in Washington D.C. right up until 1862 when it was finally abolished in the District of Columbia."[145]

When the Senate approved the bipartisan Compromise of 1877, the era of Reconstruction ended, federal troops were withdrawn from the South, and a dark age followed of Ku Klux Klan white terrorism in the South and Supreme Court–sanctioned national segregation of the races.

In the 1930s, many Republicans in both the House and the Senate endorsed President Franklin Roosevelt's New Deal programs, and the vast majority of them voted for the landmark Social Security Act of 1935. Passage of President John F. Kennedy's 1963 Nuclear Test Ban Treaty was facilitated by support from prominent Republicans like former president Dwight Eisenhower and Senate majority leader Everett Dirksen.

The supreme moments of bipartisanship in the twentieth century occurred on the Senate floor when the Civil Rights Act of 1964 and Voting Rights Act of 1965 were passed into law, both with strong Republican and Democratic support. But simultaneously, overwhelming bipartisan support for President Johnson's Gulf of Tonkin congressional resolution plunged the United States into the disastrous Vietnam War.

Bipartisan landmarks continued into the decades that Orrin Hatch served as a senator. The 1973 Endangered Species Act was supported by President Richard Nixon and leaders of both parties. The sweeping reforms of the Food Stamp Act of 1977 were the product of common ground that was forged by President Jimmy Carter, Republican senator Bob Dole, and Democratic senator

George McGovern. The Social Security Act of 1983 that President Ronald Reagan signed into law resulted from an alliance between Dole and Democratic senator Daniel Patrick Moynihan, and the Reagan-backed Tax Reform Act of 1986 was a bipartisan compromise between President Ronald Reagan and congressional Democrats that created the most sweeping reform of the tax code in postwar history to that date.

Some bipartisan legislation was followed by thoroughly ambiguous results. In 1996, for example, passage of the welfare reform legislation known as the Personal Responsibility and Work Opportunity Reconciliation Act was backed by President Clinton, most Senate Democrats, and nearly all House and Senate Republicans, including Orrin Hatch. The US poverty rate, which was already falling, fell to 11.3 percent by 2000, then climbed to 15.1 percent by 2010, which was where it was in 1993, but by 2019 it had fallen to 10.5 percent.[146] The impact of bipartisan welfare reform was difficult to disentangle from other powerful economic and social factors. Similarly, the net effects of bipartisan reform legislation on criminal justice, campaign finance, and financial institutions have been controversial and unclear.

One massive bipartisan project, the 2001 No Child Left Behind Act, championed by Republican president George W. Bush and Democratic senator Edward Kennedy and voted for by Hatch, subjected American education to incentives based on data generated by the universal standardized testing of children. But well into its second decade, the federal scheme and its successors were widely considered to have failed to achieve their objectives of stimulating sustained positive effects in math or reading scores or in reducing racial achievement gaps, despite the spending of tens of billions of dollars.[147]

Along with Senators Joe Biden, Hillary Clinton, and twenty-one other Democratic senators, Orrin Hatch voted to authorize President George W. Bush to order the invasion of Iraq in 2003, but in hindsight the war was considered by many to have been a mistake.

The year after the invasion, Hatch signed off on a blistering Senate Intelligence Committee report[148] condemning the Central Intelligence Agency for abusing its position in the intelligence community by mischaracterizing Iraq's program for weapons of mass destruction, the major justification for that war. The 2002 vote to authorize America's military intervention in Afghanistan, which Hatch joined, was even more bipartisan, but in 2020 and 2021 the war ended in total failure for the United States.[149]

Hatch could, however, be proud of many major victories that would come for him during his forty-two years in office on a host of issues, some of them highly partisan and others intensely bipartisan. His first big success was intensely partisan, and it would unfold against near-impossible odds.

It began in 1978, when Hatch volunteered to take charge of a seemingly lost cause.

It was, he thought, nothing less than a life-and-death mission to rescue the Republican Party and the American economy itself.

CHAPTER 4

When Titans Clash

H E HAD TWELVE MINUTES to change the course of history.
At 9:38 a.m. on May 15, 1978, Senator Orrin Hatch walked into the Oval Office of the White House to meet with President Jimmy Carter.

The two men were on a collision course over an issue that was going to detonate on the Senate floor the next day—labor law reform.[150]

President Carter was supporting a proposed pro-union law that had passed the House of Representatives and was backed by organized labor and most of the Democrats in Congress. Senator Hatch, backed by much of American business, was determined to stop it. Huge amounts of money and political power were at stake.

Carter and Hatch had much in common. They were both devout Christians, longtime Sunday school teachers and students of Scripture, and both were family men intensely devoted to their wives. Both were elected to national office in the same year, 1976, as Washington, DC, outsiders from seemingly nowhere. They both were former businessmen, Carter as proprietor of a Georgia peanut farming operation and Hatch as partner of a small law firm. They were both very hard workers and early risers: on that day, Carter went to the Oval Office at 5:30 a.m., a time when Hatch was usually awake and on his way to Capitol Hill. On a wide range of big issues, however—like unions and labor law—the two were diametrically opposed.

Both men were national leaders of opposing forces in the battle, but Carter, advised by his staff that "the less visible you are on this divisive issue, the better,"[151] was relatively disengaged, while Hatch, though seemingly outgunned in probable final votes in the Senate, was impassioned and as focused as a laser-guided missile. He had volunteered to lead the fight because no other senator wanted to take on such a daunting task. The odds looked impossible.

This meeting was supposed to be a discussion of congressional authorization of Carter's proposals for the sale of advanced F-15 and F-16 fighter aircraft to Israel and Saudi Arabia, so Carter brought his national security adviser, Zbigniew Brzezinski, into the room, along with Frank Moore, his assistant for congressional affairs. Hatch was a fervent, vocal supporter of Israel, and his approval was important for the president's plan.

But Hatch pulled a last-minute surprise on the president—he wanted to focus instead on the proposed labor law, at least for a few of the tightly allotted twelve minutes. Hatch viewed the bill in near-apocalyptic terms, fearing that if it passed, it would give Democrats a hammerlock on Congress for the foreseeable future by sharply boosting union membership and dues, which would flow into Democratic campaigns.

Hatch handed Carter an alarming report from a New York economist named Pierre Rinfret that predicted the labor reform law would hit small businesses hard, would add 3 percent to the consumer price index, and would increase inflation, which was already trending upward in a dangerous direction.

The Republican Party was in a death spiral. That's what it looked like to many political pundits in 1976–1978—the

Republican Party was about to die. On the surface, the party did resemble a mortally wounded beast. Richard Nixon's presidency had collapsed in disgrace a few years earlier, and his successor, Gerald Ford, triggered his own demise by pardoning Nixon and presiding over a slumping economy that saw unemployment rise to 9 percent, the highest level since 1941.

The Democratic Party seemed to be on an unstoppable victory march, in which it was supported by most of the nation's unions. After the 1976 election, the Democrats controlled the White House, over 90 percent of state governments, plus a 149-member majority in the House of Representatives, and a seemingly filibuster-proof 61–38 majority in the Senate. Democrats had controlled the Senate for the last quarter century. Only 20 percent of the electorate identified as Republican. *Fortune* magazine ran an article proclaiming "The Unmaking of the Republican Party" and detected signs that big business was defecting to the Democrats.[152] In an article titled "Ailing GOP May Not Recover," *Wall Street Journal* Washington bureau chief Norman C. Miller declared, "Even party professionals no longer regard the death of the GOP as an impossibility."[153] Prominent Republicans joined the deathwatch. John Deardourff, an official of the failed Ford campaign, said the party's outlook was "a choice between a slow, painful death and a mercy killing."[154] The Republican National Committee's political director stated, "Anyone who says we are not potentially at the sunset of the Republican Party is kidding himself."[155]

But in fact, the opposite was happening. Just below the surface, America was becoming more conservative, and so was the Republican Party. There had been networks of conservatives and conservative think tanks, funders, intellectuals, and media figures ever since Franklin D. Roosevelt's administration, but in the Carter years they were rapidly blossoming and expanding, often quietly and behind closed doors. White Southern conservatives were migrating from their traditional home in the Democratic Party to the Republican side. Far from defecting to the Democrats, many businesses and industry groups, alarmed by what they saw as the threat of a resurgent national labor movement and antibusiness legislation, began beefing up their grassroots organizing and lobbying efforts in Washington, DC, with millions of dollars in new funding. They were greatly helped by the Federal Election Campaign Act Amendments of 1974 that made it easier to form political action committees (PACs) to collect political contributions—measures originally championed by unions who wanted to pool donations from their members but wound up being used by companies and trade groups to channel campaign money from stockholders and employees. "New Right" conservative strategists linked up with impresarios of computer-assisted direct-mail campaigns like Richard Viguerie to feed blizzards of cash into an alphabet soup of multi-issue think tanks and PACs, creating interconnected organizational structures that one observer wrote "look like an octopus trying to shake hands with itself."[156]

Representative Philip Crane, a Republican, reported sensing "a tangible resurgence of conservative ideas" at the time. He argued, "What is in fact occurring is a rebirth. The core of the Republican Party—conservatism—is reasserting itself. This strong base, submerged during the unrealistic groundswell attempt to gather every American into the GOP fold, is now coming into its own." James Buckley of New York, the first and only member of the Conservative Party to serve as a US senator (from 1971 to 1977), recalled in 2021 that "the country was ready to listen to conservatives. You could make the argument, and people listened. It was a reaction to the hideous things that happened in the late 1960s, with students throwing bombs around and burning flags. There was the ability to appeal to the socially conservative Democrats, what became known as the Reagan Democrats."[157]

Increasingly, one man was near the center of all this action. "Conservatives may have found a new national leader in Utah's freshman Senator Orrin G. Hatch," announced *US News & World Report* on February 7, 1977, just one month into his first term. "Today conservatives across the nation are taking his measure as a potential successor to Barry Goldwater and Ronald Reagan." The National Conservative Political Action Committee called Hatch "one of the most attractive political newcomers in many years. He is a seasoned debater and a born leader."[158] And *Congressional Quarterly* dubbed Hatch "one of the most intriguing new figures in the Senate," "a born campaigner, with unusual stage presence and oratorical skill," and reported that some conservative groups "were even talking about him as a possible presidential candidate in 1980."[159]

In his first year as a US senator, Hatch was a young man in a hurry with a talent for getting himself booked on TV news shows, triggering headlines, and launching high-profile initiatives to ban abortion, balance the federal budget, and block the Equal Rights Amendment. He was assigned to three committees: the Judiciary Committee, the Joint Economic Committee, and the Labor and Human Resources Committee, the latter of which placed him, as the ranking Republican member, at the center of the imminent labor law fight.

But Hatch's hard-charging ambition was so strong that he sometimes rubbed colleagues the wrong way. "Orrin had a save the world complex," remembered Paul Laxalt, a Republican senator from Nevada and one of Ronald Reagan's closest friends. "He wasn't malicious, just very ambitious," and "he rode pretty roughshod and I was put out with him at first." After Laxalt's dressing-down, Hatch privately wrote, "I must accept the fact although I don't intend to be pushy, aggressive, arrogant or irritating, I apparently am and he's right."[160]

According to Hatch biographer Lee Roderick, Jake Garn, then the senior Republican senator from Utah, was also initially put off by Hatch, and told him, "You've got to approach things differently if you want to get along back here." Garn counseled Hatch to stop saying "I" so much, and stop any speculation that he might run for the presidency someday, at least until he was reelected to a second term and had achieved a record in the Senate.[161]

Inside the Oval Office on this late spring day in May 1978, Hatch noticed that President Carter had an "almost wild" look in his eyes, the result, he speculated, of Carter's being under "tremendous stress."[162] As if to illustrate the point, perched on the old presidential oak desk and made from the timbers of the lost British Arctic exploration ship HMS *Resolute* was a little sign, which Queen Victoria had sent as a gift to President Rutherford B. Hayes in 1880. Last used in the presidential office by John F. Kennedy, the sign read "OH, GOD, THY SEA IS SO GREAT AND MY BOAT IS SO SMALL."[163]

In fact, Carter often seemed in-over-his-head since being sworn in to the presidency the year before. His term fell in a transitional era between the decline of the New Deal and imperial presidency eras and the coming age of an assertive Congress and rising public sympathy for fiscal and social conservatism, lower taxes, and limited government.

When Carter took office, the country was suffering the worst natural gas shortage in history, and his single term would end with oil shocks and a hostage crisis, both triggered by upheavals in the Middle East and Iran, as well as runaway inflation. As a moderate pragmatist, Carter faced the intractable challenge of forging a centrist governing coalition with a sharply rebellious Congress as parties were polarizing toward extremes—Republicans toward what would soon be called the New Right and Reaganite Right; and Democrats in two directions, one toward the remnants of the McGovernite Left and the other toward "Watergate babies," or relatively conservative Democrats elected in suburban districts that had previously voted Republican.

A chronically poor public communicator as president and an infamous fetishist for molecular detail, Carter wasted precious time early in his presidency not only by comanaging the White House tennis courts schedule on his secretary's desk, but by repeatedly poking his nose into staff expense accounts, newspaper and magazine subscription lists, and even the pay scales and staffing procedures of the White House barbershop. "At times," noted national security adviser Brzezinski, "I thought he was like a sculptor who did not know when to throw away his chisel."[164] Each man, Jimmy Carter and Orrin Hatch, personified the Latter-day Saints maxim "If we are prepared, we have nothing to fear," but Hatch marshaled details and facts like a skillful trial attorney, while Carter often increasingly seemed to be crucified by them.

Years later, Orrin Hatch described Jimmy Carter as "a very fine man but he was not qualified to be president in my eyes, in the sense of the times that we had."[165] Carter's own secretary of agriculture, Bob Berglund, described the White House congressional relations team as "an unmitigated disaster," and Capitol Hill insiders of both parties dismissed Carter and his staff as inept, arrogant, uninformed, and disorganized. When Democratic House majority whip John Brademas was blindsided by Carter's staff in a foreign policy matter, he accused the White House of having "all the finesse of an alcoholic hippopotamus." One disillusioned Carter aide quipped that his White House was "like a movie set for a Marx Brothers picture, only except instead of four brothers, there were about a dozen."[166]

On this day, however, Jimmy Carter was savoring a recent political victory, one of the rare happy triumphs he ever experienced in the Oval Office—the Senate's approval for ratification of his cherished Panama Canal Treaties, upon which he had risked much political capital. Orrin Hatch had been a fierce public opponent of the treaties, which he felt surrendered a strategic piece of American sovereignty, but sixteen Republicans, including Senate minority leader Howard H. Baker Jr. of Tennessee, joined fifty-two Democrats to approve the treaty, just barely, with sixty-eight votes. It was just one vote more than the necessary two-thirds majority. After the historic Panama Canal Treaties roll-call vote on the night of April 18, a jubilant Carter called his point man on the Senate floor, Majority Leader Robert C. Byrd of West Virginia, and told him, "You're a great man—it was a beautiful vote."[167] Byrd, no doubt mindful of the Carter staff's ineptitude in congressional dealings, had asked the White House to stay out of the way during the final Senate maneuverings that led to victory.

Orrin Hatch wanted Jimmy Carter to stop Byrd from bringing Senate Bill 2467, the Labor Law Reform Act, onto the Senate floor, since he feared it would cause untold damage to business, the economy, and the two-party system. It looked like Hatch didn't have the votes to stop it on the floor, so this encounter was Hatch's last-minute chance to get Carter to call off the vote. It was an extreme long shot.

Unions and other supporters of the proposed law saw it as a way of closing what they viewed as unfair promanagement loopholes in the governing document of federal labor law, the National Labor Relations Act of 1935, also known as the Wagner Act, which guaranteed workers the right to organize and established the National Labor Relations Board (NLRB) to implement their rights.

Labor supporters argued that businesses had exploited weaknesses in the existing laws that allowed them to delay contract negotiations, fire employees who tried to unionize, and delay NLRB enforcement with prolonged legal action. The cost of doing this, they argued, was lower than allowing a union in the first place. Also, according to the *New York Times*, union leaders viewed the proposed Labor Law Reform Act "as the key to unionizing the South and the rest of the Sunbelt states, where unions have always been weakest and where most of the nation's future economic growth is likely to be."[168] Supporters of the law saw it as a way of restoring balance to business-labor relations.

But Orrin Hatch took the diametrically opposite view, considering the Labor Law Reform proposal to be "reprehensible" and a "monstrosity"[169] that was heavily weighted in favor of union organizers. It could, he thought, force employees to join unions, inject the federal government into all aspects of labor negotiations, and conflict with the "right-to-work" state laws in Utah and nineteen other states. It would give union organizers a wide range of weapons to tip the scales against management in negotiations, including "quickie" or "push-button" union elections with tight deadlines, punitive financial penalties on business, "packing" the five-member National Labor Relations Board with two extra pro-union members, imposing restrictions on employers' free speech rights, and enabling union organizers to talk to employees during working hours on company property. The act would empower the NLRB to set wages for newly unionized workers if an employer was deemed not to have bargained in good faith, which would represent a major injection of the federal government into the free enterprise system.

Hatch feared the bill was a dagger aimed at the heart of both American business and the two-party system. If passed, he predicted, it would boost union control of the American labor market from 20 to 50 percent. Assuming a new tidal wave of union political contributions to Democrats, there would be one-party domination of the Congress for decades to come, as there already had been for forty-one of the last forty-five years. The law was unnecessary, Hatch declared, because "of the over 37,000 unfair labor practice cases (reviewed by the NRLB) last year, less than 25 required contempt proceedings. That is less than one-half of one percent."[170] No doubt remembering his recent work for small businesses in Utah as an attorney, Hatch argued, "I think that business is tired of all this liberal legislation that has just made it impossible to do business in our society, and certainly small business people are sick of it."[171]

President Carter's congressional relations deputy, Frank Moore, who was in this Oval Office meeting, was impressed by Hatch's warm, helpful personality whenever he visited him on Capitol Hill. "Hatch was always very friendly to us and very receptive; whenever we asked him for a meeting, we'd get it," Moore recalled in 2021. "Hatch was fun to be around. He was always such a pleasure to visit with. He was a very personable guy. You'd go to his office and he'd ask if he could get you a glass of water and he'd pour the water himself and give it to you very graciously. He and I were always talking about contemporary country music. He would lead you up to the point where you thought he was going to vote with you, whatever the subject was. And then he wouldn't."[172]

In political terms, the Carter White House had good reasons to be wary of Orrin Hatch. In his first speech on the Senate floor in January 1977, Hatch spoke out against the nomination of Ray Marshall to become Carter's secretary of labor, arguing that Marshall was too pro-labor, was opposed to states' right-to-work laws, did not rule out unions in the military, and supported "common situs picketing," or the right of unions to close down an entire construction site over a dispute with a single subcontractor or contractor. "Dr. Marshall is an obvious captive of the big union labor bosses in this country,"[173] Hatch told the *Salt Lake Tribune* just before the Senate confirmed Marshall by a 73–20 vote. Hatch opposed many Carter administration policies, including its support for the proposed new Labor Law Reform Act, and he had adamantly opposed the Panama Canal Treaties. In the case of one Carter official, the feeling was one of abject fear. "There's nothing funny about Orrin Hatch," an anonymous White House lobbyist told the *Washington Post*. "He's scary—really."[174]

Orrin Hatch was a former blue-collar union worker in the construction trade for ten years and went through a formal apprentice training program. He believed in unions. "The union movement has been responsible for the growth of the middle class," he said, "which I think has been very, very healthy." He asserted that "unions have made valuable contibutions to American society, and the right of any American to join a union if he so wishes should be defended." He favored the existing system of federal labor laws, which he felt was slightly slanted in favor of unions. "I didn't find that repugnant," he explained, "having read many books about the terrors of early unionizing attempts by courageous men and women who wanted working people's rights in a society slanted in favor of powerful businesses."

But Hatch strongly believed in employees' explicit right to *not* join a union, and in 1977 he introduced legislation, backed by business and industry organizations, for an Employee Bill of Rights that would further strengthen and guarantee that right, as a counterproposal to the Labor Law Reform Act. Hatch also believed that unions should not have more power than they already had. This was a mainstream idea at the time, evidenced by the fact that President Carter's own opinion pollster Pat Caddell reported that the American public thought unions should have less power, not more.

Organized labor was not that popular among its own prospective members either—unions were losing fully 50 percent of employee representation elections for their formation. Union membership in the United States had been on a sharp decline for decades, from 34 percent of American workers in 1956 to 25 percent in 1978. How much, if any, of this was due to unfair management pressure is unknown. But the world economy was transforming rapidly, and union strength was diluted by many trends, including the rise of American deindustrialization, global competition, and the networks of satellite communications and container shipping that powered it.

There was also a beast in the room, and its name was the Mafia.

Unions, Hatch believed, were thoroughly penetrated by organized crime.[175] As Hatch argued in an editorial opinion piece, antiunion sentiments were the result of "pension fund embezzlements, extortions to obtain dues, union racketeering, misuse and unpopular political use of union dues, beatings and even deaths." The vast majority of rank-and-file union members were decent, hardworking, and law-abiding citizens, but labor leaders, Hatch argued, "earn kingly ransoms for a few hours' work each day, travel the world in private luxury jets, ride to work in chauffeured Cadillacs and Lincolns, and enjoy French cuisine prepared by chefs at their offices."[176] Here again, the public agreed with him. A 1977 Harris poll revealed that by a margin of 64 to 13 percent, the public believed union leaders were connected to organized crime.[177]

The facts were on Hatch's side. At that point in American history, the nation's "big four" unions—the International Longshoremen's Association, the Hotel Employees and Restaurant Employees International Union, the International Brotherhood of Teamsters (IBT), and the Laborers' International Union of North America— were, in the words of an FBI report, "substantially influenced and/ or controlled by organized crime." Labor history scholars James B. Jacobs and Ellen Peters reported, "For decades, the IBT, the nation's largest and most powerful union, was controlled by organized crime. Indeed, from the 1950s on, Cosa Nostra bosses chose the union's general president. Organized crime used its influence to loot the pension and welfare funds, extort employers, and place its own members and associates in high-paying jobs. Through their influence in the IBT, the organized crime families were able to exert political and economic influence at the local, state, and national levels."[178]

Hatch knew, as did other federal officials, that in many parts of the nation, gangsters ran major sections of the trucking, construction, meat processing, garbage carting, shipping, hotel, restaurant, casino, and other industries. An FBI undercover investigation of the International Longshoremen's Association launched in 1975 uncovered systemic criminality and labor racketeering along the entire Eastern Seaboard and Gulf Coast, in the ports of New York City, Wilmington, Miami, Charleston, and Mobile.[179] At a Senate hearing in 1978, a Justice Department official testified that in excess of three hundred union locals were dominated by organized crime.[180] Mafia gangs took in hundreds of millions of dollars from skimming union dues, and from bid rigging, price-fixing, fraud, intimidation, patronage, sweetheart deals, threats of illegal strikes and work stoppages, and workplace sabotage. In 1984, federal judge Harold Ackerman described criminals in the longshoremen's union as engaging in "a multifaceted orgy of criminal activity."[181]

Beyond sporadic congressional hearings in the late 1950s and a short-lived campaign by Attorney General Robert Kennedy in the early 1960s, combating labor racketeering did not become a high priority or well-coordinated federal effort until the early 1980s. The AFL-CIO, the national union umbrella organization, had the authority and the responsibility to police its members. But according to labor history scholars Jacobs and Peters, "After the early 1960s, the ethical practices committee never met, and the AFL-CIO ceased playing any significant role in opposing corruption and racketeering in its affiliated unions."[182] In the context of 1978, Orrin Hatch's skepticism of "union bosses" was a very legitimate one.

In Jimmy Carter, the labor movement thought it had a friend, but he was a lukewarm ally at best. He was a moderate, pragmatic Southern Democrat, not a strident union supporter. "We didn't try for revolutionary things; we pushed for things we thought we could get broad support for,"[183] said Ray Marshall. With the White House's support, the House of Representatives passed its version of the Labor Law Reform Act in October 1977 by a comfortable vote of 257–163, with 33 Republicans supporting it, and sent it to the Senate for consideration. The Senate's Labor and Human Resources Committee approved the bill in January 1978 by a 13–2 vote, with only Hatch and one other Republican voting against it.

By now, business groups and their conservative allies were in a flat-out panic. Ironically, key provisions of the proposed law had been based on recommendations of a presidential labor-management committee advisory panel that included CEOs of giant "blue-chip" American companies like General Motors, General Electric, Alcoa, Bechtel, and Sears. But by early 1978, fearing worst-case scenarios, many business leaders decided the Labor Law Reform Act had to be stopped. Some corporate economists were predicting that over 50 percent of the nation's workforce would be compelled to join a union if the bill became law. As Hatch feared, the Democratic Party would be flooded with union cash passed through from increased dues, and an avalanche of anti-business legislation could follow.

A well-funded National Action Committee of business and industry groups was formed to lobby against the bill, backed by the US Chamber of Commerce, the National Association of Manufacturers, the Business Roundtable, and the Associated General Contractors of America, and it joined forces with small businesspeople and conservative groups. They looked for a champion among Senate Republicans. "Not surprisingly, everyone turned them down," recalled Hatch. "No one wanted to stand in front of a runaway train. Having run out of options, they turned to me."[184]

Hatch quickly became a formidable legislative field commander. He told the coalition that he would agree to lead the campaign, but only on two conditions: the business community had to stay united, and it had to follow his leadership in public and in private. When Hatch heard that one big company was considering leaving the coalition and supporting the Labor Law Reform bill, he called an emergency meeting at the National Association of Manufacturers and laid down the gauntlet, announcing, "I'm going to be here for thirty years or more, and whoever does that will be one sorry company."[185] The defection didn't happen.

The only way Hatch and his allies could stop the bill on the Senate floor was to use the procedure of a filibuster, a parliamentary procedure that was the equivalent of a legislative blockade. "Our strategy was simple," Hatch later explained. "We could not stop the bill just by voting, since more than a majority of the Senate favored the legislation. Our only hope was to filibuster the bill, taking advantage of the Senate rules to talk it to death. Under a filibuster, a senator or a group of senators use a member's right to speak as long as physically possible, to talk endlessly about virtually anything, in order to delay or prevent a bill from passing. The key is endurance, not persuasiveness."[186] A filibuster, Hatch pointed out, can be dangerous: "Not only can it tie up a bill but it can stop the Senate from moving on to other issues, raising the possibility of offending not only the proponents of the bill being filibustered but also the supporters of completely unrelated legislation."[187]

At the moment Carter and Hatch faced off in the Oval Office, both sides had unleashed what journalist Marilyn Berger called "the most extensive lobbying on Capitol Hill in the history of this country."[188] Under the leadership of its grizzled, crotchety, cigar-chomping eighty-three-year-old president, George Meany, a former plumber who had never walked a picket line in his life and whose leadership was blamed by some union members for declining union power, the AFL-CIO and its allies were flooding the Senate with millions of postcards, telegrams, and letters. Business groups did the same, outspending the unions by more than 2 to 1. Small businesses would eventually be exempted from key provisions of the bill, but the business coalition used the "slippery slope" argument to keep small business owners engaged in the fight by meeting with their hometown newspaper editorial boards, and by descending upon Washington, DC, by the busload to buttonhole their senators into opposing the bill.

On the morning of May 15, 1978, the big grandfather clock on the Oval Office's northeast wall ticked off the minutes as Senator Hatch tried to talk President Carter out of putting the labor law to a Senate vote the next day, but time was running out.

Carter would hear nothing of it. He wanted the bill to pass, and Hatch wasn't going to change his mind.

The president changed the subject back to the original purpose of the meeting—Middle East arms sales. Nine minutes into the meeting, national security adviser Brzezinski left the meeting, and three minutes later, at 9:50 a.m., Hatch left the Oval Office, too, empty-handed.

"This bill," declared Orrin Hatch, "is going to attack every basic fiber of the free-enterprise system."[189] Jesse Helms, the ultra-conservative firebrand senator from North Carolina, charged that the legislation "is designed to unionize the South by federal force."[190] Republican senator Strom Thurmond from South Carolina declared, "We will fight this bill, and fight it to the last."[191]

Now, Hatch would have to do battle in the Senate chamber with one of the most skilled parliamentarians in Congress, Democratic majority leader Robert C. Byrd.

The odds looked nearly insurmountable.

The Senate comprised sixty-two Democrats, many elected with union support; and thirty-eight Republicans, some of whom joined Democrats on pro-union votes. "The task," recalled Hatch, "was more difficult than convincing three Democrats to join the filibuster. In the 1970s there was far more diversity in both parties than today. I knew I could count on some Democrats, but I couldn't count on all the Republicans."[192] Some Republicans, Hatch knew, would vote with him a few times, but they would eventually switch sides and vote for "cloture" to end the filibuster.

At 8:55 p.m., President Carter called Senator Byrd to review their plans, and the die was cast.

Debate would begin the next morning on the Senate floor.

* * *

Senator Robert C. Byrd once had a terrible secret.

As a politically ambitious young butcher in West Virginia, he belonged to America's oldest terrorist organization, the Ku Klux Klan. Not only was he a member and a recruiter for the white supremacist cult, but he also was the founder and chief officer of a "Klavern," or local Klan chapter, and he held the title "Exalted Cyclops."

As the Democratic Party's Senate majority leader beginning in early 1977 and its assistant majority leader or "whip" for six years before that, Robert Byrd had earned a reputation as a cold, methodical organization man who mastered details and parliamentary procedure, ran the day-to-day operations of the Senate, and "made the trains run on time."

But three decades earlier, Byrd had put his organizational talents to work recruiting 150 friends and acquaintances to a new Klan chapter in his hometown of Sophia, West Virginia, collecting the $10 per Klansman membership fee and charging $3 for each regulation Klan-branded robe and hood.

Byrd was born in 1917 into poverty in North Carolina, the fifth child of a woman who died in the great influenza epidemic within a year of his birth. He remembered his adoptive family surviving on meals of "a little lettuce and butter and sugar."[193] A Christmas gift was an orange or an apple, and ice cream and soda pop were savored just once a year, on July 4. As a boy, Byrd watched his adoptive father walk in a Klan parade.

One day in the early 1940s, Byrd wrote to Joel L. Baskin, the Klan's "Grand Dragon of the Realm of Virginia, West Virginia, Maryland, and Delaware," who promised to help Byrd set up a chapter if he could recruit and organize 150 people. When Byrd did, Baskin was impressed. "You have a talent for leadership, Bob," he wrote to Byrd. "The country needs young men like you in the leadership of the nation."[194] Byrd later recalled, "Suddenly lights flashed in my mind! Someone important had recognized my abilities! I was only 23 or 24 years old, and the thought of a political career had never really hit me. But strike me that night, it did."[195]

When Byrd ran for the United States House of Representatives in 1952 and news of his Klan dealings was revealed, he claimed that "after about a year, I became disinterested, quit paying my dues, and dropped my membership in the organization,"[196] and that he had never since been interested in the Klan. Byrd spent the rest of his life apologizing, sometimes nebulously, for what he described as a "youthful mistake." In 2005 he said, "I know now I was wrong. Intolerance had no place in America. I apologized a thousand times."[197] Byrd and his fellow local Klavern members were never connected to acts of violence.

But Byrd's racist passions persisted well into his later twenties—in 1944, Byrd wrote a fan letter to Mississippi Democratic senator Theodore Bilbo, a rabid white supremacist, proud Klansman, and fervent supporter of FDR's New Deal programs, who publicly called for the murder of Black citizens who tried to vote. "I shall never fight in the armed forces with a negro by my side," Byrd wrote to Bilbo. "Rather I should die a thousand times, and see Old Glory trampled in the dirt never to rise again than to see this beloved land of ours become degraded by race mongrels, a throwback to the blackest specimen from the wilds."[198] In 1946, Byrd wrote to a Ku Klux Klan official, stating, "The Klan is needed today as never before, and I am anxious to see its rebirth here in West Virginia and in every state in the nation."[199] Soon, encouraged by another Klan boss, Byrd won his first political office, a spot in the Virginia House of Delegates.

Byrd knew how to run a Senate filibuster. As a US senator in 1964, Byrd filibustered against the Civil Rights Act for a record fourteen hours and thirteen minutes, arguing that whites had heavier brains than Blacks. "Men are not created equal today and they were not created equal in 1776, when the Declaration of Independence was written," he declared on the Senate floor. "Men and races of men differ in appearance, ways, physical powers, mental capacity, creativity and vision."[200] He opposed the 1965 Voting Rights Act and its extention in 1970, and in 1968 he called the Reverend Martin Luther King Jr. a "self-seeking rabble-rouser."[201]

By the time he took command of the forces opposing Orrin Hatch over the Labor Law Reform bill in 1978, Byrd was a well-respected parliamentarian and historian of the Senate who had a near-fanatic approach to his work, which included channeling huge amounts of federal money to his home state of West Virginia. He was described in the press as vain, petty, and abusive to his staff, and he had not taken a vacation in more than twenty-five years. Byrd was said to be a dark-tempered, distant and brooding figure known for browbeating aides and nitpicking their work.

On May 16, 1978, the Senate floor debate on the Labor Law Reform Act began.

Majority Leader Byrd decided to let Hatch and the opposition proceed with its announced filibuster without trying to break it until after the Memorial Day recess. This way both sides would get a fair hearing and a chance to fully express their positions. Pro-union Democrats were confident of victory and decided with Byrd to let Hatch's side win the first two cloture votes, and then the filibuster would be stopped on a third vote. As majority leader, Byrd was in charge of fixing the chamber's schedule. He could keep the Senate in session around the clock, requiring Hatch's team to never leave the floor.

Beyond his own passion and energy, Orrin Hatch had four powerful assets to deploy in the struggle on the Senate floor, the goal of which was clear: to prevent the pro-union side from gaining sixty votes for cloture which would end the filibuster and put the bill to a simple majority vote. The filibuster rule had recently been changed to require just sixty cloture votes to cut off debate, compared with the previous sixty-seven-vote requirement, making the job significantly harder for Hatch's team.

Hatch's first asset was fellow freshman Republican senator Richard Lugar from Indiana, a former Eagle Scout, Rhodes Scholar, mayor of Indianapolis, and president of the National League of Cities. The low-key, efficient Lugar signed on as Hatch's deputy for the filibuster. Hatch and Lugar organized three rotating teams of five or six senators each to stay on the floor to protect against surprise maneuvers to shut the filibuster down, and they kept the teams tightly organized with daily strategy meetings, charts, bulletins, briefings, and conference calls with business groups and other allies.

The second asset was the Senate's widely respected Republican minority leader, Howard H. Baker Jr. of Tennessee, who wasn't sure the bill could be stopped but agreed to help Hatch. "He did so knowing that by working with us, he was jeopardizing the fragile relationship he had built with the AFL-CIO," Hatch remembered. "At the time, the unions considered him a moderate Republican, an assessment that was critical, given his presidential aspirations."[202] Hatch could count on the support of most Republicans and Southern Democrats, and a few Democratic senators from the right-to-work states of Nevada and Nebraska, but this might not be enough to sustain a filibuster. The gravitas and popularity of Howard Baker could be a "force multiplier."

Hatch's third asset was Ernest "Fritz" Hollings, a Democratic senator from South Carolina and a staunch defender of his state's giant textile industry. Hollings, like Hatch, believed that the proposed law was an unreasonable "power grab" by unions. His state was the site of a big production facility owned by New York City–based textile giant J. P. Stevens, a company that was held in contempt multiple times by the National Labor Relations Board for violating labor law, but Hollings pointed out that no other textile company in South Carolina had ever been held in contempt.

Finally, Hatch had a largely secret weapon in the form of James Browning Allen, a hulking, sleepy-eyed, second-term Democratic senator from Alabama, who was just as formidable a parliamentary warrior as Robert Byrd, but was an ultraconservative who agreed with Hatch on labor law reform and many other things, and briefly became a father figure to Hatch. Allen was, in Hatch's words, "one of the most remarkable men I've ever known."[203]

The now long-forgotten Jim Allen was a towering sixty-four-year-old former Alabama state legislator and former lieutenant governor to George Wallace. Like Hatch, he avoided the social scene in Washington, DC; unlike the fitness-conscious Hatch, however, Allen scrupulously avoided exercise and healthy eating, preferring hamburgers, desserts, and deep-fried Southern cooking. "He loves to eat his grits and eggs, and he can't pass an ice cream store or a Burger King to get a Whopper,"[204] noted one aide. Columnist George Will described Allen's perpetual demeanor as "that of a man who has been prematurely aroused from a summer snooze to which he hopes to return soon."[205]

He may have resembled a giant sloth with slicked-back red hair parted in the middle, but on the Senate floor Jim Allen was a master martial artist. According to Senator Edward Kennedy of

Massachusetts, Allen was "perhaps the greatest parliamentarian ever to sit in the United States Senate."[206] The press called Allen "a man who could out-talk or outmaneuver many of the wisest and most experienced politicians in Washington,"[207] and the "wizard of the rulebook."[208] According to a report in the *National Journal* on December 25, 1976, Allen's knowledge of Senate rules "has led to bitter struggles with Byrd as the Alabaman has sought to halt legislation and Byrd has tried to move it along."[209] Most recently, Allen had joined forces with Hatch to unsuccessfully block the Panama Canal Treaties.

A profile by journalist Spencer Rich of the *Washington Post* on September 30, 1976, reported that Allen "put the Senate into a position where almost no action could be taken without his assent." Rich reported, "He so wound the Senate into parliamentary knots that a whole series of major pieces of legislation—air pollution, lobbying regulation, export control and anti-Arab boycott bills—were threatened with death in the final days before Saturday's adjournment, simply by a single objection." Then Senate majority leader Mike Mansfield complained about Allen's tactics and accused him of abusing the rules, but Allen explained, "To debate and discuss can't do anything but good."[210]

Allen had a history of strong support for racial segregation, which was typical of many Southern Democrats of the time, and it was not unusual for Republicans and liberals in the Senate to form alliances and even bonds of affection with them when conditions warranted. Democratic US senator Joe Biden from Delaware, for example, had decades-long cordial working relationships and friendships with segregationist and former segregationist US senators like Bob Byrd, James Eastland of Mississippi, and Strom Thurmond of South Carolina.

Early in Hatch's first term, Allen sensed a powerful potential ally in the Utah novice Republican and took him under his wing. Hatch recalled, "Allen was especially helpful, taking the time to walk me through some of the more arcane parliamentary rules that governed the floor: the order of amendments, the amendment trees, and other procedures that can dictate not only when language can be debated but whether it will even be considered."[211] Hatch added, "Most important, he showed me that a legislative fight on the Senate floor, especially if it was close, was very much like a chess match. Without a thorough understanding of both rules and strategy, one could lose despite having a majority of the votes." Allen had created an ingenious new delaying tactic, called the "post-cloture filibuster," where a single senator could tie up the Senate for weeks or even months, even after cloture had been invoked, with maneuvers like introducing multiple amendments, asking that they be read, and calling for time-consuming roll call votes.

According to Hatch, Allen was a master of slowing down legislation to win concessions, but not at fully stopping proposed laws he opposed. "He did filibuster quite a bit, but he never won anything," Hatch noted in a 2020 interview. "He couldn't win because the Democrats screwed him every time he turned around. With me, he saw for the first time somebody who could win, and who had the guts to take people in his party on. He would have made a great Republican."[212] In the buildup to the Labor Law Reform Act debate, Hatch consulted quietly with Allen in private at Allen's office in order to not provoke Allen's Democratic colleagues.

One day, to Hatch's surprise, Allen said, "Orrin, you've got to take over. I'm not going to be here much longer. You're really going to have to take over now." Hatch thought to himself, *What are you talking about? You just got reelected!* But he was too bewildered to ask Allen what he meant.[213]

As the debate began, the stakes were clear: AFL-CIO boss George Meany called the showdown a "holy war," while the national chamber of commerce declared that "freedom is at stake."[214] Other Senate business ground to a halt as Hatch supervised the filibuster, working eighteen-hour days, drafting speeches for colleagues, conducting strategy meetings, making speeches on the floor, reviewing Senate rules with Senator Allen, lunching on yogurt from an office refrigerator, and doing fifty laps in the Senate pool every day to stay sharp.

Then, on June 1, 1978, Hatch received a shock.

Senator Allen had died of a heart attack in Alabama over the Memorial Day weekend. "Jim was the one senator, more than any other, who had gone out of his way to make me feel welcome and befriended in the Senate," Hatch later explained. "No one would ever take his place. Moreover, I had lost my parliamentary trump card, the one person I knew who could come close to matching wits with Robert Byrd. I had no idea whether we could win without him."[215]

The first vote to shut down Hatch's filibuster came on June 7. It failed by a whopping eighteen votes, but senators often voted no to cloture on the first vote, like a batter avoiding a first pitch, and to appear magnanimous to fellow senators. A handful of key senators, all of them moderate or conservative Democrats from the South or Midwest, were supporting Hatch but possibly on the fence, and it was widely believed that the final vote might come down to them. One of them, Senator Russell Long of Louisiana, offered Hatch a compromise amendment, which would further reduce the bill's impact on small business, in exchange for stopping the filibuster. Hatch declared it cosmetic and rejected it. He was intent on total victory, and he appeared prepared to stop the Senate in its tracks for weeks or even months to kill the bill.

The next day, on the second cloture vote, the margin against Hatch narrowed by two votes, which inched the tally up to forty-nine for cloture, forty-one against. Several senators, including Byrd, offered further concessions to Hatch, who rejected them. He was playing a dangerous game—if his gamble didn't pay off, he might be considered a reckless firebrand, to whom the stench of failure would attach.

On June 9, Hatch was thrilled to hear the news that The Church of Jesus Christ of Latter-day Saints made the decision to allow non-white men to become members of the clergy. "This is really, really wonderful," he wrote in his journal. "I had been praying for a long time for this change. I was so excited and so buoyed up by this event that I floated all day long. I think I could have stood losing labor reform today."[216] While Hatch had voiced support for civil rights and for voluntary affirmative action, he did not yet have a substantial record on civil rights, a subject that in his home state of Utah was less visible than in many other states due to its very low nonwhite population. But he was jubilant at this news, as he knew that the historic decision brought his church closer to its proper destiny.

The third cloture vote on June 13 saw Hatch's opponents reach fifty-four votes, and the next day they won fifty-eight votes, just two short of victory, a tally repeated the next day on a fourth attempt to stop the filibuster, and again on an unprecedented fifth attempt on June 15. Never before had there been so many attempts to stop a filibuster on a single piece of legislation, and by now some moderate Republicans had defected to the other side. Very little other Senate business had occurred for a solid month. "At this point, labor law reform had become a monster, dominating nearly every moment of the day," remembered Hatch. "No one could escape the lobbying campaigns being run by both sides. It seemed that proponents and opponents were everywhere. Nerves were beginning to fray, and it was increasingly difficult to maintain a united front."[217]

Hatch assigned Senator Fritz Hollings to body-shield a potential swing voter, the seventy-eight-year-old John Sparkman, a Democrat from Alabama, by sitting next to him and repelling anyone who tried to get him to vote for cloture. But when Majority Leader Byrd came over to make an attempt, Sparkman himself pushed Byrd off, exclaiming, "Get away from me!"[218]

Byrd scheduled a final floor vote for Thursday, June 22. The media predicted the filibuster would be broken and the bill would pass, handing unions an epic triumph. Sensing victory, President Carter sent his secretary of labor, Ray Marshall, to the scene on Capitol Hill to prepare to bask in glory and congratulations. "You have to admire Senator Byrd," remembered Hatch. "The old fox almost had us trapped. Almost."[219]

Hatch strode through the Capitol parking lot with a suitcase containing a list of five hundred new amendments he was ready to introduce, saying he had twenty-five hundred more ready to file if needed.

A pessimistic Minority Leader Howard Baker urged Hatch to accept the various compromise revisions and amendments that the other side had offered so he could claim a victory and call off the filibuster. Hatch thought it would still be a terrible bill and declined. Baker said, "Orrin, you know you're going to lose today."[220] The re-mark hit Hatch like a punch in the stomach. He rushed out of Baker's office to the Senate floor and filed his five hundred amendments with the reporting clerk. With this pile of paper, even if he lost the vote on cloture, Hatch could tie up the Senate indefinitely. This could backfire, of course, and widely cast Hatch as an unreasonable obstructionist. A furious Senator Bob Byrd scowled at him.

The five swing votes had so far held for the filibuster, but Senator Russell Long was wavering, and Hatch's team feared he would flip to Byrd and the pro-cloture side in exchange for some pro-business amendments. This seemed to leave the outcome of the entire drama in the hands of a single midwestern Democrat, Edward Zorinsky of Nebraska, who was also wavering. Byrd had worked hard on him overnight. If he flipped, all was lost for Hatch.

"They promised me everything," Zorinsky told Hatch.

"Ed, you didn't give in, did you?"

Zorinsky replied in the negative, but said he was "mushy," add-ing, "If I change my mind, I'll call you."[221]

The final vote was scheduled for 3:00 p.m., and everyone assumed this would be the last attempt to break Hatch's legislative blockade. Any more failed cloture votes were unsustainable, and the Senate had to get back to its normal business.

When debate began, Senator Russell Long bolted up to make an angry speech about how the will of the Senate was being frustrated, and declared that he would change sides to become the fifty-ninth vote for cloture. Now just one more vote was needed to force the drama to end.

When Zorinsky came onto the floor, fellow Democrats begged him to join Long and break the filibuster.

Hatch's and Zorinsky's eyes met. Hatch nodded hopefully. Zorinsky's face was blank, then he nodded to Hatch, just once.

Jubilant, Hatch raced over to Hollings and said, "We have Zorinsky." Hollings smiled.

The slenderest of threads remained. If a single senator decided to join Senator Long and defect at the last minute, Hatch's crusade was doomed.

The room fell silent.

Suddenly, a disgusted voice in the chamber announced, "If Senator Long is going to cross over, then I'm crossing back." Heads turned and a buzz erupted. It was Republican senator and minority whip Ted Stevens of Alaska, who had voted twice for cloture, and would now withhold that vote. Without warning, he was flipping to Hatch's side.

Senator Byrd was checked on the Senate chessboard. Desperate now to push off a vote he knew he would lose, Byrd stood and asked for unanimous consent to take the bill off the floor for further revision.

A still-smiling Ernest Hollings rose up and uttered two words that denied Byrd the necessary unanimous consent and forced the cloture vote to occur: "I object!" This was a great symbolic turning point in American business and labor history.

Byrd was checkmated. After five weeks, Hatch's filibuster held together, the cloture attempt collapsed, and Labor Law Reform was dead.

The sixth and last cloture vote was just fifty-three in favor, seven short of the necessary sixty. Several senators decided to join Hatch's winning side in the final vote, and Byrd himself decided to vote against cloture in a futile attempt to scramble the conclusion and argue that the tally didn't reflect the true sentiment of the Senate. The measure was sent back to the Senate Human Resources Committee, where it died.

That night, Hatch came face-to-face with AFL-CIO boss George Meany during a reception at the home of Senator John Sherman Cooper.

"I know who you are!" exclaimed Meany.

To Hatch's surprise, Meany was courteous and gracious and congratulated him on his victory.

Then Meany's grizzled face turned hard and cold. "We respect you, Orrin, no hard feelings," he growled, "but even if it costs us $4 million in 1982, we're going to get rid of you."

"If you spend that much money in Utah to get rid of me," quipped Hatch, "it will double our gross state product and make me a great hero."[222]

The two men laughed and parted cordially.

George Meany died in 1980. The AFL-CIO did spend heavily to defeat Hatch in 1982, but Hatch won reelection to his second term.

According to labor historian Taylor E. Dark III, professor of political science at California State University in Los Angeles, there is debate among scholars over what the actual impact of the defeat of Labor Law Reform in 1978 was. "There are some who view it as a major turning point," Dark explained in 2021. "They believe that the bill had a real chance of passing, and that if it had, it would have allowed a major improvement in the capacity of unions to organize new members and engage in collective bargaining. In this view, the defeat sealed the fate of organized labor as a weaker force in both politics and the economy. Conversely, success would have allowed a substantial turnaround. In 1976, unions represented 24.5 percent of the private sector workforce; today that number is 7.4 percent."[223] One expert who agrees with this view is Joseph A. McCartin, professor of history at Georgetown University, who concluded that "unions' ability to project their influence with enough senators to overcome a filibuster deteriorated sharply after 1978," and "it is difficult to overstate how consequential the filibuster of labor law reform in 1978 was."[224]

An alternative view, according to Professor Dark, is that this was just one episode in a long series of legislative failures for organized labor, like the defeat in 1966 of the effort to repeal the right-to-work provision of the 1947 Taft-Hartley Act, and later attempts under Presidents Carter, Clinton, and Obama to reform labor law and boost union power. "The whole economy was restructuring," Dark noted, "and unions faced great challenges completely separate from the details of labor law."

In the mind of Orrin Hatch, the results were clear. He and his colleagues had saved American business, the economy, and the two-party system, from incalculable damage. "Small business has won the biggest victory in its history,"[225] he said. "Instead of being a crowning moment for the AFL-CIO," Hatch wrote, "the Labor Law Reform Act represented the last comprehensive attempt by the unions to rewrite federal labor laws, and its defeat prevented a massive upheaval of the delicate balance between labor and management."[226]

Hatch saw it as the first major victory in years for conservatives in Congress, and a vital stepping-stone for Republicans to capture control of the Senate two years later, as he put it, effecting "a change in power that would help us set a different course for the United States for the remainder of the century."[227]

"That was an all-important battle," asserted Hatch. "If we hadn't won it, the country would be gone today, in the sense that we know it. It would have given Democrats absolute control."[228] Never again would organized labor enjoy a major victory in Congress.

Today, American unions operate under largely the same structure bequeathed to them by FDR and the Wagner Act in 1935 and its successors, which was successfully defended by Orrin Hatch's dramatic victory in 1978.

The Labor Law Reform Act drama thoroughly stunned

Washington, DC, insiders and instantly solidified Orrin Hatch's position as a rising Republican superstar. The election of Ronald Reagan in 1980 ushered in a decade of intense productivity and influence for Hatch. To a large extent, Hatch owed the start of his political career to Reagan's 1976 endorsement of his Senate campaign, and as president, Reagan was, in Hatch's memory, "like an older brother who was always there for me."[229]

Hatch became a reliable, trusted congressional executor of the Reagan agenda. The two men were kindred spirits on a wide spectrum of issues, including protecting the free market economy, stimulating growth through tax reform, supporting individual liberties and promoting limited government, opening up foreign markets to American exports, opposing judicial activism, entitlement reform to ensure the long-term sustainability of Social Security and Medicare, and prevailing in the Cold War global competition with the Soviet Union.

In the process, Hatch accumulated a powerful arsenal of political capital, legislative skill, and personal gravitas that enabled him to attempt a series of bipartisan achievements that would shape American history.

The highly partisan clash over labor law reform in 1978 cemented Orrin Hatch's reputation in national Republican politics. It was a textbook example of one measure of legislative effectiveness—the ability to block big legislation that a senator believes would hurt the national interest.

But it also earned Orrin Hatch so much influence among conservatives and Republicans that it enabled him, in "Nixon goes to China" and "Reagan goes to the Soviet Union" fashion, to regularly reach across the political divide over the decades that followed and forge great bipartisan achievements with his political opponents.

CHAPTER 5

Summer of Glory Part 1 The Americans with Disabilities Act

THE GREATEST CIVIL RIGHTS bill since the 1960s was about to die.

It was going to die on live TV, on the floor of the US Senate.

There was one person who could save it, and his name was Orrin Hatch.

It was early afternoon on Capitol Hill. The date was July 11, 1990. A Senate staff lawyer named Bobby Silverstein spotted Hatch stepping into an elevator in the subbasement of the Senate side of the US Capitol Building and raced over to plead with Hatch to stage a last-minute, seemingly impossible rescue.[230]

The hopes, dreams, and daily lives of America's forty-three million citizens with disabilities hung in the balance.

Hatch had been working with Silverstein for a solid year on this landmark piece of legislation, the Americans with Disabilities Act (ADA).

In a strong bipartisan alliance with leading Democrats like Senators Edward "Ted" Kennedy of Massachusetts and Tom Harkin of Iowa, and Republican senators including Minority Leader Bob Dole of Kansas and John McCain of Arizona, Hatch, Silverstein, and their colleagues ran the twenty-two-thousand-word law through a maze of five congressional committees and seven subcommittees. They steered it through hundreds of hours of public hearings and closed-door negotiations with disability activists, attorneys, George H. W. Bush administration officials, business delegations, and dozens of members of Congress and their staffs.

Orrin Hatch was the lead Republican sponsor of the bill, and Silverstein was its chief legal and technical author in his role as chief counsel for the Senate Subcommittee on Disability Policy and staff director for Harkin, the ADA's lead Democratic sponsor in the Senate.

The bill was scheduled for a roll call vote in the Senate in a matter of hours. If the bill passed, it would be one of the proudest moments of both men's careers, and the nation's citizens with disabilities would receive their own "Emancipation Proclamation" to fully join American life. The ADA would be the most consequential civil rights measure produced by Congress since the Civil Rights Act of 1964 and the Voting Rights Act of 1965. For the first time, citizens with disabilities would be given federal civil rights protection.

But it looked like the ADA was about to be torpedoed by one of the most powerful and controversial personalities in the federal government—former archsegregationist and longtime conservative Senator Jesse Helms, a Republican from North Carolina. He was preparing to deliver the coup de grâce on the floor of the US Senate.

The instrument of the ADA's imminent execution was, at first glance, a relatively innocuous item known as the "Chapman Amendment," which was named for its author, Democratic representative James Chapman of Texas. The amendment, if attached to the final version of the ADA, would allow restaurant managers to reassign employees who handled food to other jobs if they had a contagious disease like the HIV/AIDS virus. Supporters of the amendment conceded that there was no evidence that AIDS could be spread through food handling, but they believed the amendment was needed to shield business from public panic about AIDS.

Until now, it seemed to be a relatively minor item among a host of other issues that had been successfully hammered out in the months of grueling negotiations on the ADA.

The Chapman Amendment had a formidable army fighting for it. The measure had already been approved by the US House of Representatives on May 17 in their version of the ADA, and it was backed by Senator Helms, by small business lobbyists of the National Federation of Independent Businesses, and by the powerful National Restaurant Association, which represented America's biggest employer, the food services industry. Until now, Senator Hatch himself had supported the amendment as something that seemed to make basic common sense by protecting restaurants and other food service businesses against customer fears and misperceptions of HIV/AIDS that could hurt their business. If customers heard that a restaurant food handler like a chef or a cook had the condition and the restaurant didn't transfer the employee, so the theory went, the public might boycott the business and shut it down.

Senator Helms was arguing that the Chapman Amendment was necessary as "a matter of staying in business" for restaurants, even though there was no known evidence that AIDS could be transmitted through food, drink, or casual contact. Since the operation of restaurants was dependent largely on "public perception," Helms argued, if "the public is led to perceive that there will be a health risk to those coming into the restaurant and eating the food, rightly or wrongly, that business could be destroyed."

Earlier that day, however, disability rights activists issued a stark challenge at a press conference outside the Capitol Building, with civil rights icon Coretta Scott King standing by their side:

they were going to withdraw their support for the ADA over the Chapman Amendment, and, in effect, kill the legislation.

Their leader was Patrisha Wright, who was such a tough negotiator and skilled organizer that her nickname was "the General." She headed the Disability Rights Education and Defense Fund, a national pro-ADA coalition that included wounded Vietnam veterans and people with HIV/AIDS, spina bifida, cerebral palsy, vision and hearing impairments, Down syndrome, and intellectual and mental health conditions. The coalition also included organizations as diverse as the Women's Legal Defense Fund, the National Association for the Advancement of Colored People (NAACP), the National Congress of American Indians, the Leadership Conference on Civil Rights, the American Civil Liberties Union, and no fewer than one hundred other businesses and civic and medical organizations. On paper, people with disabilities were a powerful voting bloc, representing 1 out of every 5 Americans.

The Chapman Amendment, the disability activists believed, would codify built-in discrimination against people with HIV/AIDS and, indirectly, against members of the LGBTQI+ community. It would also, they feared, establish a "slippery slope" precedent that could later exclude other groups from protection. At the press conference, Wright announced that if the Chapman Amendment were attached to the ADA, the coalition would immediately pull their support from the ADA, meaning that it would unravel for an indefinite period of time.

Suddenly, with a Senate vote coming in a matter of hours, the Chapman Amendment was a deal breaker.

Even before Silverstein intercepted him, Orrin Hatch was having second thoughts about his previous support for the Chapman Amendment. But Senator Jesse Helms, who was an ideological compatriot with Hatch on many other issues, was adamant that the Chapman Amendment stay attached to the ADA, and it had already been approved by both Democrats and Republicans in the House of Representatives in their version of the ADA. In the Senate, Helms would not give an inch, and he was prepared to deliver the death-blow in the Senate chamber that afternoon on C-SPAN live TV.

The man who approached Hatch in the Capitol basement, Bobby Silverstein, was an idealistic, methodical attorney of forty-one and a proud liberal who, behind large eyeglasses and tousled hair, resembled a much younger graduate student. He grew up in a Jewish family in New York City, and the biblical exhortation to "do justice and pursue acts of love and kindness" inspired him to devote much of his life to advocating for people with disabilities. In his work with Hatch, he had come to admire the Utah senator's skill as a lawmaker and his dedication to the cause of helping America's citizens with disabilities through bipartisan action. Hatch had already become a reliable ally in backing legislation to support people with disabilities.

Silverstein came face-to-face with Hatch and began his pitch. "Senator, if this Chapman Amendment is included, it will kill the bill," he stated. "We're not going to pass a civil rights statute that has built-in discrimination against people who are HIV-positive, and your advisory committee [of disability advocates and experts] in Utah agrees. This could potentially undo years of our work together for the disabled. All that you've worked for is not going to happen.

"You've got to help us out here," Silverstein implored Hatch. "You've got to do something, because the rights and lives of people with disabilities are going to fall to the side if this [Chapman Amendment] isn't taken down."

Appealing to Hatch's impulses to build legislation upon facts and not fear, Silverstein concluded, "Reconsider. Think about it. You're a man of science. You're one of the strongest supporters of the NIH [the National Institutes of Health]. You've been very positive in terms of HIV issues. You really support the principle—let science decide."

This chance meeting in the subbasement of the US Senate represented a potential "turning point within a turning point" of postwar American history, as it opened up the door for Orrin Hatch to attempt to rescue the Americans with Disabilities Act. As disability scholar Jonathan M. Young explained, "Silverstein and Hatch had worked together on disability policy for many years, and both agreed that the disability policy should not, generally, encourage business decisions to be made on unfounded fears. Silverstein, however, emphasized to Hatch that it was dangerous to use a different standard for a single constituency of the disability community—persons with contagious or communicable diseases. Supporting the Chapman amendment, said Silverstein, by allowing prejudice to prevail in one area, would create an internal chasm within the disability community."[231]

This conversation was having a crucial impact on Hatch, who called it "the key to my own evolution on the Chapman amendment."[232]

Silverstein wound up his pitch by asking, "Can't we try to reach an agreement to have an amendment that will clarify the law, by saying let science decide?"

Hatch said, "Yes, Bobby, I'll look at this issue. Let's get the staffs together and see if we can reach an agreement. I'll see what I can do. Let's talk again."

But Hatch had no idea how to solve the predicament. Neither Helms nor the disability activists looked like they would give an inch.

Hatch took the elevator up to the main Senate floor, where senators and their staffs were preparing for a final series of "showdown" votes on the amendment.

Before Hatch could reach the Republican cloakroom just off the Senate chamber, he was intercepted in the hallway by "the General" herself, Pat Wright, and a small group of disability rights leaders. They would normally not be allowed in this restricted area, but senators were allowed to bring guests in, and this enabled Senator Kennedy's chief AIDS adviser, Michael Iskowitz, to escort a team of disability advocates into a nearby conference room, which they now occupied as their strategy room within arm's reach of senators passing in the hallway.

Now, standing in the hallway, Wright, Iskowitz, and their compatriots buttonholed Hatch, just as Silverstein had done moments earlier. Wright recalled, "As fast as we could, we threw out every fact and argument we could think of. We encouraged him to champion an alternative to the Chapman Amendment."

"Only you can bring the Republicans around on this issue," Wright implored Hatch. "You've done so much work on AIDS. We all know there's no way you can get AIDS from food handling." This was true and had been publicly known since as early as September 9, 1983, when the Centers for Disease Control and Prevention confirmed that "there has been no evidence that the disease was acquired through casual contact," and "AIDS is not known to be transmitted through food, water, air, or environmental surfaces."[233] But public biases and ignorance over AIDS persisted. According to scholar Young, when Wright and her colleagues met with Hatch in the Senate hallway, "They urged the senator not to allow fear and prejudice to prevail. Rather, they argued, let available medical evidence be the deciding factor. They also made an impassioned plea that the bill was on its way to dying unless Senator Hatch helped resolve the conflict—only he had the stature to shoulder a compromise."[234]

Thirty years after the drama unfolded, Patrisha Wright recalled her impressions of Hatch at the time: "I came to see he was a very serious legislator with an incredible staff. We knew we were dealing with a very sophisticated, smart person in Senator Hatch and it was reflective of the staff he had as well. Nothing was going to get past Senator Hatch and his staff. We knew the only way to be able to work with him and his staff was to be 100 percent up-front honest and transparent, and if there were issues with what we were proposing, we would make sure that they knew about it."

Wright added, "At the same time we knew him to have a really personal, heartfelt commitment to enhance opportunities for people with disabilities, based on his work with Senator Kennedy on other issues. He understood that public policy needed to address the systemic discrimination, isolation and segregation, and denial of opportunity that disabled Americans faced."[235] Two years earlier, as the two top party leaders of the Senate Labor and Human Resources Committee, Hatch and Kennedy had teamed up to sponsor an AIDS research and information spending bill, which authorized $665 million for state and federal AIDS programs. Hatch was the only Republican sponsor of the bill.

By now, Wright was preaching to the choir—Hatch knew that he had to find a way to stop the Chapman Amendment and save the Americans with Disabilities Act.

The question was how to do it.

The success or failure of a lawmaker often depends on the quality of his or her staff, and Orrin Hatch had the reputation of having a very smart, loyal group of staffers. Once he made it to the cloakroom, he turned to one of them for help by placing a call to his top aide on health affairs.

At that moment, thirty-two-year-old Nancy Taylor was lying down on a sofa in her office in the nearby Hart Senate Office Building, managing the thirty-eighth week of her pregnancy with twins. She was working on Senate business by day and a law degree at night. "I was feeling pretty miserable, but I was still coming to work every day," she recalled. She felt like she could go into labor at any second.

"Are you good enough to come over?" asked Hatch. "I need you."

"Of course I can," said Taylor. She boarded the subterranean Senate subway for the short ride to the Capitol, and, approaching the chamber, she made her way through a throng of cheering disability activists who assumed she was on their side. She also spotted a group of business and restaurant industry lobbyists, and they, too, seemed thrilled at the sight of a very pregnant woman coming to try to break the legislative deadlock.

When she entered the Republican cloakroom, Hatch told her the ADA was about to collapse if they didn't think of some way of saving it. It was a hectic scene, with senators and their staffs coming and going, and Taylor stepping out to confer with aides to the ADA's top two Democratic sponsors, Senators Kennedy and Harkin. Taylor and Hatch fell into an intense discussion of legislative and legal options, maneuvers and complexities, synthesizing a year of work by hundreds of people into a fifteen-minute burst of thinking.

Then, at about the same time, a lightbulb went off in their minds.

Both Hatch and Taylor realized that there might be a way of addressing the concerns raised by the Chapman Amendment while at the same time guaranteeing that people with HIV/AIDS would not be discriminated against.

It was an idea that would be sure to gain the support of the disability community and an idea that Hatch might be able to persuade a majority of senators to accept as a replacement for the Chapman Amendment.

It might offer Hatch a chance to beat Helms in a debate on the Senate floor.

The answer, they both realized, lay in a simple phrase that had been floating around in many ADA discussions in these last intense hours: "Follow the science."

Taylor sat down in the most comfortable chair she could find, grabbed a pencil, and began sketching out their idea on a piece of paper, periodically joined by Wright, Iskowitz, and Chai Feldblum, an American Civil Liberties Union attorney and key ADA advocate.

Taylor paused to sip from a quart-carton of fresh milk that the Kennedy aides had generously rushed in to her, since she looked to be both exhausted and on the absolute verge of giving birth to her twins right there in the Republican cloakroom of the US Senate.

Orrin Hatch towered over Nancy Taylor as she scribbled away.

He liked what he saw.

"That's it," he said softly. "That could work."

* * *

For over two hundred years, Americans with disabilities had no federal civil rights protection.

Wounded soldiers came home from America's wars to face severe obstacles to their employment, family lives, and daily lives. Their struggles were shared by multitudes of other Americans with physical and mental challenges who often suffered in shrouds of silence, segregation, and shame imposed by society.

In early America, people with disabilities were often supported with compassion as the "worthy poor" by their communities, but the upheavals and dislocations triggered by urbanization and industrialization shattered this tradition and led many to be treated as social outcasts.

In the nineteenth and twentieth centuries, some American cities enacted so-called ugly laws that banned from public places people who were, in the words of one such edict, "diseased, maimed, mutilated or in any way deformed, so as to be an unsightly or disgusting object."[236] Chicago's "ugly law" was on the books for a full ninety-three years. In the words of pioneering disability rights advocate Justin Dart Jr., "People perceived as having significant disabilities have been treated as sub-humans." He noted, "At worst they were killed or left as beggar-outcasts to die, at best they were cared for through subsistence welfare, out of sight and mind in institutions and back rooms."[237]

For generations, Americans with disabilities were often treated with widespread indifference, rejection, avoidance, neglect, and outright disgust. The attitudes extended to the US Supreme Court, which ruled, in the words of Justice Oliver Wendell Holmes in the notorious *Buck v. Bell* decision in 1927, that it was "better for all the world, if, instead of waiting to execute degenerate offspring for crime, or to let them starve for their imbecility, society can prevent those who are manifestly unfit from continuing their kind," and "three generations of imbeciles are enough." That ruling, which has never been formally overturned by the court, upheld the legality of the forced sterilization of people deemed intellectually unfit, which resulted in nearly seventy thousand forced sterilizations that continued into the 1970s.[238]

These prejudices persisted well into the twentieth century. As of early 1989, according to President George H. W. Bush, "the statistics consistently demonstrate that disabled people are the poorest, least educated, and largest minority in America."[239] Americans with disabilities faced staggering levels of poverty, unemployment, and social isolation. The large majority did not go to movies, did not attend theater or musical performances, and did not go to restaurants, sporting events, houses of worship—or even grocery stores. Office buildings, transportation, sidewalks, and schools were fiendishly ill-designed in ways that locked people with disabilities out of much of society. Their job prospects were bleak. In 2020, Orrin Hatch recalled, "Although hard to imagine now, in the summer of 1990, the doors of opportunity were quite literally closed to millions of persons with disabilities. There were few laws on the books requiring reasonable accommodations in the workplace and almost nothing to protect these individuals from discrimination."[240]

In 1971, a New York judge reported that people with disabilities were "the most discriminated [against] minority in our nation." Many American children with disabilities were systematically denied a public education, and conditions in state-supported institutions for people with disabilities were often horrific. According to a New York court report, conditions at the notorious Willowbrook State School for people with mental disabilities were, as of 1972: "horrible," "dreadful," "sub-human," "a blot on the conscience," "appalling," and "frightful," in a place where "the most helpless and defenseless of our citizens were left living on a thread of life," "rotting in inadequate warehouses, the living among the dead, the dead among the living."[241]

The years since World War II saw a huge influx of veterans with injuries and disabilities returning to society, and they and other people with disabilities began to organize and demand treatment as full American citizens. These efforts began as tentative, individual, and small-group actions in scattered cities and towns and slowly gathered strength.

In the 1950s, disability advocates proposed "independent living" and personal attendant care as a more affordable and effective alternative to institutionalization. In 1962, students with disabilities at the University of Illinois at Urbana-Champaign and the University of California, Berkeley, launched parallel actions to improve campus accommodations for people with disabilities, which were practically nonexistent in American education. In the 1970s, acts of civil disobedience by activists in New York, San Francisco, Denver, and Washington, DC, drew attention to the abysmal conditions in public transportation and public accommodations for people with disabilities. While the 1964 Civil Rights Act made no reference to persons with disabilities, a "baby step" in federal law was passed by Congress in 1968 in the form of the Architectural Barriers Act, which decreed that buildings designed and constructed by the federal government be made physically accessible to people with disabilities.

Five years later, a strong civil rights enforcement provision for people with disabilities was written into the Rehabilitation Act of 1973, which was signed into law by President Richard Nixon. The measure prohibited discrimination against people with disabilities in federally funded programs, marking the first time that segregation of persons with disabilities was explicitly defined as stemming from discrimination. Two years later, another incremental step occurred with passage of the Education for All Handicapped Children Act of 1975, which gave children with disabilities the right to a free, appropriate public education in "the least restrictive environment."

The Americans with Disabilities Act was the product of years of advocacy by disability rights activists that, combined with a sudden burst of interest by the federal government, began to coalesce in early 1988. That January, the National Council on Disability (NCD), an independent federal government agency, issued a report titled *Toward Independence*, which proposed a comprehensive law prohibiting discrimination on the basis of disability. The report suggested that the law, which was intended to provide full opportunities and empowerment for people with disabilities, be called the Americans with Disabilities Act.

Then, in June 1988, President Ronald Reagan's HIV/AIDS commission released a report on the growing epidemic that also recommended a comprehensive civil rights law that would protect people with the condition as persons with disabilities. Both candidates for president that year, Republican vice president George H. W. Bush and Democratic Massachusetts governor Michael Dukakis, were eager to court the huge vote of people with disabilities, and both men pledged strong action toward a federal civil rights law for people with disabilities.

Momentum for a law quickly reached Congress and the jurisdiction of the Senate Committee on Labor and Human Resources, of which Orrin Hatch was a member, Senator Edward "Ted" Kennedy was chairman, and Senator Tom Harkin of Iowa, a fellow Democrat, had just become chair of the subcommittee on disability.

Together with Republican senator Lowell Weicker of Connecticut and Democratic representative Tony Coelho of California, Kennedy and Harkin took the lead in drafting the ADA into early 1989. Staffer Bobby Silverstein served as the point person, and Orrin Hatch eventually agreed to be the lead Republican cosponsor. Hatch was concerned about the costs of any such large-scale federal intervention in American society, and he was especially concerned about potentially severe cost impacts on small businesses.

The ADA, as it took shape, would restrict preemployment medical and disability questions, prohibit discrimination against Americans with disabilities, and require employers to reasonably accommodate people with disabilities. It would also require that a wide range of public and private buildings, services, transportation, and telecommunications be made more accessible to people with disabilities.

From the start, the bill was a model of bipartisan debate, negotiation, and compromise. But it was such a fragile and complex proposition that it could easily unravel at any point.

The ADA was designed to do nothing less than legally and physically "reengineer" major portions of American society.

Nothing like it had ever been attempted before.

*   *   *

It seemed that the stars of history were aligning for the Americans with Disabilities Act in 1989 and 1990. One major reason was the strong personal connections that many key political players felt with the issues of disability.

In Orrin Hatch's case, the connection was through his beloved brother-in-law Raymond Hansen, a fellow member of The Church of Jesus Christ of Latter-day Saints, who contracted two forms of polio as a young man in college. The disease forced Hansen to sleep in an iron lung machine every night of his adult life, but he managed to complete a master's degree in electrical engineering and work until the day he died. "During Raymond's twilight years his body was so weakened by the effects of polio that he asked me to carry him from room to room at a special temple service for our faith," Hatch recalled. "He and I had always shared a close bond, but it was made even closer by this spiritual experience. So when the going got tough on ADA, I reminded myself why I was fighting: for Raymond and for others like him."[242]

According to Professor Lennard Davis, a historian of the ADA, Hatch's dedication to the cause of people with disabilities was also the product of his faith. "As a Mormon, Hatch would follow his church's teaching that holds people with disabilities in high regard and sees disability not as punishment resulting from sin, but as an opportunity, a benefit, and a learning experience," wrote Davis.[243] Hatch explained that his instincts for compassion and leadership were also sharpened at the age of nineteen, with his two-year assignment as a missionary representative for his church. Such missions are a rich tradition for many Latter-day Saints, and Hatch's mission involved religious outreach and community service at locations across the American Midwest. "Of all the experiences I've had, that's probably the most important experience of all," he remembered. "It was the highlight of my life, it really was. I was able to meet a lot of really outstanding people, including congregations of other faiths and poor people who were really having a rough time."[244]

By 1990, some observers detected what they saw as an evolution in Hatch from hard-line, doctrinaire conservative to an increasingly pragmatic seeker of legislative action and compromise. In March of that year, Neil Lewis of the *New York Times* wrote a profile of Hatch, reporting that the senator had "baffled and enraged many old allies in his party's right wing as he has associated himself with a variety of bills sponsored by liberal lawmakers."[245] Lewis pointed to Hatch's lead role in several battles, including providing federal funds for child care, curtailing the use of polygraphs, requiring the Justice Department to compile statistics on bias crimes against homosexuals, and pushing for the ADA. Some conservatives reportedly thought Hatch was being bewitched by the spell of his friend Ted Kennedy, the modern "lion of liberalism." But Hatch explained to Lewis that he had simply matured as a legislator. "I think the Orrin Hatch of 1977 might have come to a different conclusion about many of these issues," he said.[246]

The article noted that Hatch seemed to be fighting on the Senate floor with fellow conservative Republican Jesse Helms as much as with Kennedy. In March 1990, Hatch debated Helms over a bill requiring statistics for crimes committed against people because of their sexual orientation, race, or religion. On the Senate floor, Hatch described how, as a Latter-day Saint, he knew the impact of hate crimes based on religion. When Senator Helms attacked the proposed bill as furthering "the homosexual-lesbian agenda," Hatch declared that violence against homosexuals was "wrong and against everything that we as Americans stand for." Hatch said that he "always felt sympathy for the downtrodden, those who get the short end of the stick."[247]

According to disability advocate Pat Wright, "Hatch had always been critical in identifying a Democrat opposite in his view, to talk to them and find middle ground. Senator Hatch comes from the time that Congress was really Congress. It was a deliberative body, not a body that totally depended on what your political view was. As a result of that he really was instrumental in the passage of the ADA."[248]

By the time the ADA was being debated in Congress in 1989 and 1990, Orrin Hatch had established himself as a truly "compassionate conservative" who had fully integrated his strongly held conservative values into his strong support for biomedical research, public health, child care, AIDS funding, and the rights of people with disabilities. By now, Hatch had backed a wide range of federal legislation to help disabled and sick Americans, and he had played key roles in steering through Congress the 1983 Orphan Drug Act to promote drug development for rare diseases, the landmark 1984 Hatch-Waxman Act that created the modern American generic drug industry and saved consumers hundreds of millions of dollars, and the 1984 National Organ Transplant Act that helped create a national transplant registry.

In the case of President George H. W. Bush, his strong support of the ADA was informed by his own family's deep personal experience with disabilities. Bush's daughter Robin died from leukemia at the age of three. His son Neil was born with severe learning disabilities; and another son, Marvin, had a bowel disease that required use of a plastic ostomy bag. Additionally, Bush's uncle John M. Walker suffered from polio.

Bush's attorney general, Dick Thornburgh, a former two-term Republican governor of Pennsylvania, was the father of a child with traumatic brain damage. The wife of Democratic congress-man Steny Hoyer of Maryland, ADA's chief sponsor in the House of Representatives, had epilepsy. Democratic senator Tom Harkin of Iowa, the bill's chief sponsor in the Senate, had an older brother who was hard of hearing and a nephew who was a paraplegic. Senator Lowell P. Weicker Jr. of Connecticut, the original Republican lead sponsor of the ADA until he lost his seat in the 1988 election, had a son with Down syndrome.

The Republican leader in the Senate, Bob Dole of Kansas, was a wounded US Army veteran whose disability was highly visible to all—a right arm that had been paralyzed by a sniper's bullet in Italy in 1945. His first speech in the US Senate on April 14, 1969—the anniversary of his injury—was devoted to Americans with disabilities, which he called "a minority group whose existence affects every person in our society and the very fiber of our Nation." On every April 14, Dole gave a speech about disability on the floor of the Senate.

Senator Ted Kennedy, Hatch's ideological adversary and friend, had an older sister named Rosemary who was born with an intellectual disability. On the secret orders of her father, the master financier Joseph P. Kennedy, she was subjected to a barbaric, botched brain operation called a "prefrontal lobotomy," which was sometimes called an "ice-pick lobotomy," and spent the final sixty-three years of her life with the IQ of a very young child and requiring round-the-clock care. Also, Senator Kennedy's son Edward Jr. contracted bone cancer at age twelve and endured a leg amputation and chemotherapy.

All of these life experiences combined in 1988 and 1989 to form a team of congressional and White House leaders who were poised to create a civil rights bill for Americans with disabilities.

At first, Orrin Hatch declined to sign on as a cosponsor of the version of the ADA that Kennedy and Harkin were putting together with the help of disability advocates. As Senate hearings on the bill, now designated "S. 933," began in the Dirksen Senate

Office Building on May 9, 1989, Hatch declared, "I support a comprehensive civil rights bill for persons with disabilities." However, he said he harbored "serious concerns." Hatch thought the bill was too broad, and he wanted exemptions for small businesses. This echoed the increasingly dire warnings from business lobbyists that the costs associated with the ADA would do untold damage to their earnings and to the American economy.

Senator Hatch even prepared to introduce his own, more business-friendly, alternative ADA bill. This was a very strategic move by Hatch. In fact, according to ADA scholar Jonathan Young, Hatch's maneuvers were "ultimately designed to aid in the ADA's passage." Young wrote, "A quick endorsement of the Harkin bill might have alienated other Republicans, whose support was necessary for effective implementation.[249]" Senator David Durenberger of Minnesota, a fellow Republican and cosponsor of the ADA, explained that Hatch "in effect had to stay off of the original bill in order to leverage Republican support for the final product." By threatening to push for his own ADA bill, Hatch paved the way for achieving a broader base of consensus and helped prevent filibustering on the Senate floor. Pat Wright noted, "By not coming on as original sponsor, and because of his ranking role and experience in the disability community, [Hatch] was able to play with Kennedy a more integral role in the negotiations than if he had cosponsored the original drafts of the bill. I think it was a real strategic move on his part."[250]

At the Senate committee hearings, as he watched Orrin Hatch meticulously question witnesses and challenge the myriad details of the draft bill, Bobby Silverstein realized that Hatch was playing a very sophisticated game. Rather than creating roadblocks for the ADA, what Hatch was in fact doing was pretesting and "blow-torching" the details of the legislation to smooth the process later on as it traveled through a maze of other committees, conference reports, and votes in the House and Senate. Coming from one of the most conservative members of the House and Senate, Hatch's painstaking review would provide "cover" for other conservatives and Republicans to join him in supporting the final version of the ADA. With the support of both Hatch and President Bush, as well as that of Democratic leaders like Senators Kennedy and Harkin, the ADA would be seen as a truly bipartisan piece of legislation.

Getting the ADA through the US Congress was "an overwhelming strategic nightmare"[251] according to disability rights advocate Arlene Mayerson. In the Senate, the bill was reviewed by just one committee and one subcommittee. But in the House, it had to proceed through no fewer than four committees and six subcommittees and endure a byzantine procedure of review by scores of elected officials and technical experts on public works, transportation, commerce, employment, education, tourism, telecommunications, and small business.

Each review threatened to slow progress of the ADA—or get it stuck in a quagmire.

*   *   *

Before he faced the final battle over the Chapman Amendment in July 1990, Orrin Hatch had already "saved" the ADA on three separate occasions.

The first time was when he decided to withdraw his alternative ADA proposal in favor of joining forces with Kennedy, Harkin, Bush administration officials, disability advocates, business lobbyists, and pro-ADA legislators in the House and Senate to try to craft a compromise bill that would gain the widest support. In the process, Hatch extracted concessions in the bill that he felt made it fairer to businesses.

The second time was when an angry debate erupted over how to define "disability." Republican senators William Armstrong of Colorado and Jesse Helms of North Carolina believed that the definition of "disability" in the ADA was too wide, and Helms worried that homosexuality would somehow be protected and promoted by the bill unless some conditions were "carved out" from protection.

Helms feared that employers would no longer be allowed to maintain "moral standards" in their businesses unless the ADA spelled out a series of conditions that were expressly not covered by the law. Senators Kennedy and Harkin didn't want to unduly limit the definitions of "disability," but Hatch realized that the bill was in danger of failing unless something was done.

Hatch took a piece of paper, fed it into a typewriter, and led a marathon negotiation session with disability activists and various senators and their staff members.[252] They hammered out a list of conditions that would not be covered by the ADA, including pedophilia, exhibitionism, gambling, kleptomania, pyromania, and psychoactive substance use disorders.

The Senate approved Hatch's list by a voice vote, and the ADA survived and continued its journey through the pipeline of congressional review.

The third time Hatch saved the ADA was on July 28, 1989, when he witnessed the ADA nearly fly off the rails.

It happened at a summit meeting between Bush administration officials and congressional representatives that unfolded around a polished walnut table in the air-conditioned Capitol conference room of Senate minority leader Bob Dole.[253]

The meeting was called to try to break a deadlock over what some conservatives—led by President Bush's pugnacious chief of staff John Sununu, who was also a former governor of New Hampshire—thought would be the ADA's excessive negative impact on small businesses. Around the table were Sununu; Attorney General Richard Thornburgh; Secretary of Transportation Samuel Skinner; Senators Hatch, Kennedy, Dole, Harkin, and Durenberger; and various Senate and administration aides. Also at the table was Bobby Silverstein, Senator Harkin's ADA adviser.

After ten weeks of staff-level negotiations between the White House and Congress, progress had been made, but a deadlock loomed. Sununu was going to launch a verbal assault on the bill; everyone in the room knew it and braced themselves. Sununu was widely perceived as the arrogant, abrasive "bad cop" of the Bush administration, and he had a reputation for bluntness and confrontation.

At the start of the meeting, Senator Hatch whispered to his aide Mark Disler, "You watch—in fifteen minutes, Kennedy is going to turn red, stand up, and start yelling at Sununu. That's how strongly he feels."

As expected, Sununu launched into a series of objections to the latest version of the ADA. According to observer Bobby Silverstein, the objections ran along these lines: "What if there's a barbershop in New Hampshire that occupies the second floor of an existing building? Is that small business barbershop supposed to pay for an expensive new elevator installation to accommodate wheelchair customers looking for haircuts? How about a ski lift in Vermont? How are they supposed to accommodate the handicapped?"

At this, a frustrated Senator Kennedy grumbled out loud at Sununu, "You're flyspecking the bill." Bobby Silverstein stepped in to calmly answer Sununu's objections by pointing out details in the legislation that he pulled from a pile of big black binders in a luggage trolley. A back-and-forth ensued between Sununu and Silverstein, who, as a relatively junior "staffer," was now leading the conversation in a room filled with more senior "principals."

Suddenly, Sununu, his face twitching, lashed out at Silverstein, exclaiming, "How dare you correct me? Every time I say something, you always bring something up. I don't want to hear from you anymore—you're staff!" Now, in the words of Silverstein, Sununu was "screaming at the top of his lungs."

Sununu demanded, "Get the staff out of this room!"

By now, Ted Kennedy had had enough. He exploded in rage. According to ADA scholar Lennard Davis, Senator Kennedy "jumped to his feet, his bulky frame creating seismic jolts as it crashed against the table."

Slamming his hand on the table with room-shaking force, Kennedy unleashed a barrage of screams of his own, aimed straight at Sununu, their faces inches apart.

Kennedy pointed his finger at Sununu's face and bellowed, "Who do you think you are? You don't treat our staff that way! If you want to yell at anybody, you yell at me, or you yell at Senator Harkin. You don't go after the staff! You go after the big boys. You got something to say, you say it to me. You yell at me, Sununu! You want to yell at me? You go right ahead and yell at me!"

Just as Hatch had predicted, Kennedy was yelling at full force, his neck tendons bulging, his face red with outrage.

Pointing out that White House chief of staff Sununu himself was "staff," and wasn't elected by anybody to his appointed post, Kennedy declared, "*You* get the hell out of here! *You're* staff! *You're* not elected!"

At this point, just as Senator Harkin was afraid Kennedy was going to grab Sununu by the collar and punch him, and split seconds from when it seemed key players were going to storm out of the room in anger, Orrin Hatch stepped in to defuse and salvage the out-of-control meeting.

"Ted, Ted, Ted," Hatch pleaded, placing his hand on Kennedy's arm. "Relax, relax! You're going to have a heart attack! Let's work this out." Hatch calmed his friend down and urged everyone at the table to come to a solution that would address the White House's concerns as expressed by Sununu, who slumped back in his chair.

"Sununu suddenly became pale and quiet and backed down," recalled Silverstein. "Hatch calmed everybody down, including Kennedy, which helped facilitate us getting back on track to discuss things on the merits, and break the logjam and get it through committee."

Within moments of Hatch's taking charge, the dynamics of the meeting shifted, the discussion went back on track, and an agreement in principle was reached to address all of the outstanding issues. In the words of scholar Young, "A grand consensus was reached, with major concessions from both sides: the [ADA] enforcement scheme and remedies would parallel those of the Civil Rights Act of 1964, the scope of public accommodations would be broad, and very small buildings would not require installation of an elevator."[254] Based on the results of the meeting, a few days later, the sixteen-member committee voted unanimously to move the ADA forward to the floor for its first full Senate vote.

On September 7, 1989, four months after it was introduced, and with Orrin Hatch now on board as the lead Republican cosponsor, the latest Senate version of the ADA passed by a vote of 76 to 8, with sixteen senators "not present." The ADA then went to the House of Representatives, where many hoped for a quick passage. But instead, it got slowed down and stuck there for the next eight months, winding its way through a myriad of hearings, backroom negotiation sessions, and committee meetings.

A striking image unfolded on March 12, 1990, when sixty impatient disability activists gathered on the grounds of the Capitol Building, abandoned their wheelchairs and crutches, and began to literally crawl on their hands and knees up the eighty-three marble steps that led to the building's West Front. A bystander asked one of the activists, an eight-year-old girl with cerebral palsy named Jennifer Keelan, if she wanted to take a rest. Keelan declined the offer, raised her head from the steps, and exclaimed, "I'll take all night if I have to!"[255]

When the House version finally passed by a vote of 403 to 20 on May 22, 1990, there were so many differences with the Senate version that congressional leaders, following standard legislative procedure, sent the bill to a joint conference committee, whose members were known as "conferees," to hammer out a compromise bill to be sent to the Senate for final passage. Hatch successfully insisted on protections for small businesses with fewer than fifteen employees.

There remained a single, potentially fatal point of controversy—the Chapman Amendment, which would enable restaurant owners to move food handlers with HIV/AIDS to other jobs so long as the transfer entailed no loss of pay or benefits. It had been proposed by a Southern Democratic member of the US House of

Representatives, it was included in the version of the bill passed by the House, it was backed by Senator Jesse Helms, and it was at first supported by Senator Hatch. But even though the amendment was rejected by the final report of the House-Senate conferees, lawmakers in both the House and the Senate were now trying to reattach the amendment to the ADA by getting it voted into the Senate version.

Many ADA advocates passionately opposed the amendment, believing that, as Senator Harkin put it, the provision would "codify ignorance" and strike at the heart of the ADA by sanctioning discrimination based on "unfounded fear, prejudice, ignorance, and mythologies."[256]

Realizing that the ADA was on the verge of collapsing over the Chapman Amendment, Orrin Hatch, as the lead Republican sponsor of the ADA in the Senate, prepared for the final battle. Hatch had science—and the White House—on his side. The Bush administration issued formal statements on the medical facts of food handling and AIDS, and the secretary of Health and Human Services (HHS), Louis W. Sullivan, and director of the Centers for Disease Control (CDC), Dr. William L. Roper, wrote letters affirming that people diagnosed with HIV/AIDS did not pose a health risk in food handling.

*   *   *

In the Senate's Republican cloakroom on the afternoon of July 11, 1990, Orrin Hatch took a final look at the handwritten notes prepared by his adviser Nancy Taylor and asked an assistant to immediately make scores of photocopies for each member of the Senate and their staffs.

There was no time to have the document typed up—the debate was already starting a few feet away on the Senate floor.

The handwritten notes represented the "Hatch Amendment" to the Americans with Disabilities Act, and it was designed to reflect and replace the Chapman Amendment in a way that would not discriminate against people with HIV/AIDS, and therefore rescue the ADA now—at the eleventh hour and fifty-nine minutes.

Hatch and Taylor had hit upon a simple, intriguing solution to do this. Their proposed amendment would authorize the US secretary of Health and Human Services to prepare a list of those communicable and contagious diseases that were scientifically known to be transmitted through food handling, to update the list as necessary every year, and to distribute it widely. The amendment would allow restaurant operators to remove anyone with a disease on the list from food handling positions. Hatch and Taylor knew that given the latest medical and scientific knowledge, there was little to no chance that HIV/AIDS would appear on that list. The solution was so eminently sensible that it might attract wide support among the majority of senators.

On this day, a series of procedural nuances unfolded on the Senate floor over the Chapman Amendment deadlock. They involved conference reports, motions to recommit the issue back to House-Senate conferees, and a duel over which "perfecting amendment to the pending motion" should be adopted—Helms's or Hatch's. Senate majority leader George Mitchell, a Democrat from Maine, announced that the conflict could be settled only in open floor debate.

It had now been ultimately reduced to a showdown on the Senate floor between two sheets of paper—the Chapman Amendment and the new Hatch Amendment—and a battle between two Senate titans—Jesse Helms and Orrin Hatch.

At 3:39 p.m., Hatch took the floor with Nancy Taylor sitting directly behind him. The Senate chamber was packed. Scores of senators looked on, including those who had led the two-year fight to bring the ADA to this point—Kennedy, Harkin, Dole, Durenberger, and McCain. A future vice president was in the room, Tennessee Democratic senator Al Gore, as was a future president, Delaware Democratic senator Joe Biden.

"I am proud to have played a part in crafting this legislation,"

Hatch began, then read out the key points of his amendment from his handwritten sheet. Hatch stressed that his amendment placed "a premium on science" as the guiding foundation.

"I think education can reduce fear," Hatch declared. "This amendment is geared to do away with fear and prejudice that can be utilized against certain citizens where there's no justification at all for the fear." Turning to the overall ADA bill, he explained, "I think that if we would rely on science and less on some of the fears that some of us have that we would be better off as a society, as a nation, and there would be less prejudice, there would be less unfounded fears, and there would be less people hurt in the final analysis and more people would be better off in our society." He added, "The real purpose of this bill is to take away the discrimination that's been given against those with disabilities from time immemorial. The real purpose of this bill is to give them a chance to warrant their right and their franchise to be equal human beings. The real purpose of this bill is to give them the opportunity to participate like anybody else, and to be able to earn their living, and to be able to support themselves. And to be able above all to be independent."

Next, Senator David Durenberger took the floor to support the Hatch Amendment, praising Hatch for coming up with "another miracle." He said that while Hatch was not an original sponsor of the ADA, "the bill would not be here today as the civil rights bill for people with disabilities if it weren't for the senator from Utah."

It was now Jesse Helms's turn to speak, his voice growling in a thick baritone. "Now, then," Helms began. "I was very interested in listening to my dear friend from Utah—and he is my friend, Senator Hatch—when he identified three things which he said his amendment would do. But he neglected to mention a fourth thing his amendment will do. *It will gut the Chapman Amendment!* For the purpose of emphasis let me repeat it. It will gut the Chapman Amendment and render it totally nugatory!"

Helms now launched a verbal assault that his supporters might interpret as homespun, commonsense wisdom, but could also be considered a blatant appeal to fear, prejudice, and outright hatred. "Let me pose a question," he said. "If you knew that the chef of a restaurant you have been patronizing had AIDS, would you go there? Rightly or wrongly, would you stop going there?" He continued, "Just suppose that the chef in a restaurant who has AIDS or is HIV-positive, he's chopping up a salad and he cuts his finger. Do you want to eat that salad? I'd like to poll the people in this chamber and see whether they would or not. Restaurants have closed [in such circumstances] because the patronage dropped to zilch."

Helms admitted, "Now, you can call it hysteria all you want to. But you'd better believe that the vast majority of people who eat in restaurants don't want to have their food prepared or handled by people who have AIDS or are HIV-positive."

Orrin Hatch would not give an inch to Helms's arguments, and at 4:27 p.m., he took the Senate floor in a final attempt to save the Americans with Disabilities Act. In a cinematic performance worthy of Gregory Peck as Atticus Finch in *To Kill a Mockingbird* or Jimmy Stewart in *Mr. Smith Goes to Washington*, Hatch launched a volley of arguments, pacing around the lectern, speaking extemporaneously without notes, his arms chopping the air to make his points.

A former chief of staff for Hatch, Michael Kennedy (no relation to Senator Kennedy), once recalled, "I think there were different sides of Orrin; there's 'Grandpa Orrin' or 'Uncle Orrin,' the avuncular, bipartisan guy who could put his arm around Ted Kennedy and be the guy that's very humorous and warm and inviting and would never hurt a fly—and then there's Prosecutor Hatch, who could sit on the edge of the dais and point his finger and put the fear of God into people."[257]

This was "Prosecutor Hatch" in action on the Senate floor now, taking Senator Helms head-on. Hatch cut to the heart of the matter, asking, "Why should people be discriminated against if they are not a health hazard?

"Let us use science. Let science govern. Which is the only way to do it," Hatch said.

Hatch built his argument up to a final, emotional crescendo: "I think of Elizabeth Glaser. She got it from a blood transfusion." Glaser was an actress, AIDS patient, and pediatric AIDS advocate whom Hatch had befriended and then helped to stage a major fund-raiser in Washington, DC, that raised $1.3 million for her new foundation. Glaser had contracted HIV through a contaminated blood transfusion and passed the virus to her infant daughter through breast-feeding. The young daughter died in 1988, and Glaser would die in 1994. Recalling another patient, Hatch stated, "I think of the beautiful lady that Senator Helms's office had me meet. She got it because a doctor didn't tell her that her husband was bisexual and he had AIDS and he could have told her. Should she be discriminated against? Should Elizabeth Glaser be discriminated against? Should some teenager who got it because his mother got it through a blood transfusion be discriminated against? And yes, *should a homosexual be discriminated against*? And the answer to that is no!"

In that moment, at 4:34 p.m., with angry, irrefutable logic, Orrin Hatch symbolically won the moral high ground, clinched the argument, and saved the Americans with Disabilities Act, by convincing more than enough senators to vote for his amendment, not Helms's. "At the eleventh hour," wrote disability rights scholar Robert L. Burgdorf Jr., who wrote one of the earliest drafts of the ADA, "conservative Senator Orrin Hatch stepped forward to become the surprise hero of ADA passage." It was a great moment in US Senate history, and one of the finest moments in Orrin Hatch's forty-two-year Senate career, but it was visible only to those people in the Senate chamber and whoever happened to be watching C-SPAN on this weekday afternoon.

He was beaten, but Jesse Helms still wouldn't give up. Grasping at straws, he veered into nonsensical free association: "Scientists may make any contention they wish, that, 'Oh, you cannot transmit AIDS by food.' I know the story of a very prominent political figure who, years ago, worked in a restaurant and he said he used to spit in the salads that he made because he didn't like his job all that much. Now just suppose he was HIV [positive]. He wasn't. That was long before this came about, but suppose. Are scientists prepared to tell me that somebody with AIDS, or HIV, who is bitter about the fact that he is sick, if he expectorates into a salad that he is making, will that not transmit the disease? How do they know? Do we want to take that risk with AIDS? With the AIDS terrorists like ACT UP?" This was an activist group known for dramatic public media actions that later fashioned a giant condom out of a latex balloon, hired a cherry picker truck, and stretched it over Helms's home in suburban Virginia.

Minutes after this outburst, Senator Kennedy took the floor and noted, "I come from a state where men feared witches and hanged women. That was in the 1690s. This is the 1990s and I hope the Senate is mature enough and civilized enough to reject the appeals to witchcraft we have just heard and do the right thing."

When the amendments were put to a vote early that evening, Hatch won an overwhelming victory. The Senate rejected the Helms amendment by a vote of 61 votes to 39—and passed the Hatch amendment by 99 to 1. Only Jesse Helms opposed it.

On the next day, July 12, 1990, the House of Representatives passed the final version of the Americans with Disabilities Act by a vote of 377–28, with twenty-seven members not voting. The act contained the Hatch Amendment, not the Chapman Amendment. On the following day, July 13, 1990, the Senate passed the same version of the ADA by a vote of 91 to 6, with three members not voting. Applause broke out in the chamber, and delighted shrieks and commotion could be heard from disability advocates in nearby hallways and conference rooms.

The final deliberations on the Senate floor that day brought Senator Hatch, Senator Kennedy, Senator Harkin, and many others to tears. Harkin delivered part of his speech in sign language, the first time anyone remembered this happening on the Senate floor. On C-SPAN, the broadcast also featured a first-time-ever panel showing a simultaneous sign language translation, and the impact on the nation's tens of millions of Americans with hearing challenges can only be imagined. "I suspect that every senator in this chamber will feel the floor shake as thunderous applause breaks out all over America following our approval of the conference report on the Americans with Disabilities Act," Hatch predicted. "I just want to say that my heart is with every disabled American in this celebration. This is a victory which has taken many long years and much hard work in an effort to bring to fruition.

"The real victory," Hatch pointed out, "belongs to each and every one of the forty-three million disabled Americans who benefit from the ADA. In the final analysis it was the courage and dedication of each and every disabled American that made this day possible. And I am proud to have played a part in this legislative effort. And I am delighted that this bill will now go to the president for his signature and that it will now become the law of the land."

Hatch then turned to his family's connection to disability. "I want to pay tribute to my brother-in-law, who contracted both types of polio as a college student undergraduate. This young man went through unholy hell. But he finished his baccalaureate degree and then went on to get a master's degree in electrical engineering and worked right up to the day he died going into an iron lung every night to be able to survive." Choking back tears, Hatch continued, "I personally carried him in my arms all the way through the Los Angeles temple of my faith. And he was probably—sorry to feel so emotional about this—but he was probably, without question, other than my own brother who was killed in the Second World War, the greatest inspiration of dogged determination to do what is right and to make his life worthwhile of anybody in my life. And I feel very, very deeply about this bill, and all those who have worked on it, and I just want to personally dedicate all of the efforts that all of us have made to my brother-in-law Raymond Hansen and for the type of life he lived and the type of person he was.

"This is a banner day," Hatch declared. "This is a major achievement. And I believe it is a very, very important day in the lives of all Americans who have to be proud that in this great country of freedom we're going to the farthest lengths we can to make sure that everybody has equality and everybody is free and everybody has a chance in our society."

Moments after the bill's passage, an emotional Hatch stepped off the Senate floor with other lawmakers and entered a nearby anteroom packed with jubilant disability rights advocates, many of whom—including activist Justin Dart Jr., a major organizing force behind the bill—were weeping with joy. Hatch leaned down to embrace Dart in his wheelchair, and thinking of his brother-in-law Raymond Hansen, the man who had died at the age of thirty-five and inspired his crusade for the ADA, Hatch let his tears flow as the room blossomed in hugs and kisses.

The Americans with Disabilities Act became the law of the land on July 26, 1990, when it was signed by President George H. W. Bush in a sun-drenched, emotional ceremony on the South Lawn of the White House with more than three thousand people attending, including Orrin Hatch. It was the largest signing ceremony ever held at the White House.

In his speech, Bush compared passage of the ADA to the collapse of the Berlin Wall, calling it "a sledgehammer to another wall," "one which has, for too many generations, separated Americans from the freedom they could glimpse, but not grasp." Declaring, "We will not tolerate discrimination in America," Bush added, "Let the shameful wall of exclusion finally come tumbling down."

For disability advocates, it was a day for rejoicing. "Having been told for so long how powerless we were," said disability activist Judi Chamberlin, "here we were with the president of the United States signing this document that was our Emancipation Proclamation."[258] Justin Dart Jr. commented, "It is the world's first declaration of equality for people with disabilities. It will proclaim to America and to the world that people with disabilities are fully human; that paternalistic, discriminatory, segregationist attitudes are no longer acceptable; and that henceforth people with disabilities must be accorded the same personal respect and the same social and economic opportunities as other people."[259]

* * *

In a very real sense, the ADA championed by Orrin Hatch, Tom Harkin, and their allies reshaped the United States, and eventually much of the Western world.

Since the act's passage in the summer of 1990, many thousands of new and existing American buildings, malls, shopping centers, airports, train stations, stadiums, theaters, parks, playgrounds, parking lots, and garages have been redesigned or constructed with ramps, flat entrances, wheelchair lifts and elevators, disability parking spaces, automatic door buttons, and signage using braille and raised characters. Ramps and curb cuts on sidewalks are now commonplace throughout the nation.

Thanks to the ADA, bus, rail, water, and air transportation have been made accessible to people with disabilities. Telecommunications networks provide closed captioning, and telephone services include relay services for people with hearing or speech disabilities. Discriminatory practices against people with disabilities in the public and private sectors have been wiped out in the legal sense, and workplace and public accommodations have been sharply improved. The US Supreme Court's interpretation of the ADA in the 1999 *Olmstead v. L.C.* case triggered the expansion of community-based residential treatment and care services instead of unnecessarily segregated big state institutions. The ADA has helped better provide for veterans with disabilities who served in Vietnam, Iraq, and Afghanistan, supporting them as they reenter the civilian workforce and become active members of their communities.

In a shining example of poetic justice, the ADA has also paid huge dividends for the Americans whom Orrin Hatch defended with such passion on the floor of the US Senate when it looked like the bill was about to die—people with HIV/AIDS. According to disability rights scholar Robert L. Burgdorf Jr., "The ADA has proven to be the principal civil rights law protecting people with HIV from the sometimes egregious discriminatory actions directed at them, and has been so applied by the Supreme Court."[260]

Hatch's strong commitment to the ADA endured in the decades that followed. In 2008, after the US Supreme Court issued a series of decisions that narrowed the scope of the ADA to cover only those people most severely afflicted by their disabilities, Hatch helped lead a bipartisan coalition of lawmakers—including Democrats Tom Harkin in the Senate and Steny Hoyer in the House—to pass the ADA Amendments Act, which strengthened the scope and intent of the original civil rights bill. The act was strongly backed by most national disability organizations and advocacy groups, as well as the US Chamber of Commerce and the National Association of Manufacturers.

The Americans with Disabilities Act inspired the world.

In the years that followed its enactment in the United States, the ADA directly inspired similar measures in the United Kingdom, Japan, Australia, Brazil, Italy, Chile, and other nations. Beginning in 2006, 157 nations adopted the United Nations Convention on the Rights of Persons with Disabilities (CRPD), which was modeled on the ADA and identified protected rights for 650 million people with disabilities around the world. According to Susan Sygall, cofounder of the nonprofit global disability training organization Mobility International USA, people around the world see "the magic of the Americans with Disabilities Act." She explained, "You can see that, yes, people with disabilities should and can ride the public buses. Yes, people with disabilities can and should be at high schools, at the universities. Yes, people with disabilities can be employed, can be leaders, can participate in recreation and sports, can basically have the same rights as everybody else."[261]

Ironically, one of the few nations not to ratify the CRPD is the United States, where some lawmakers—including Orrin Hatch—argued that an international treaty should not supersede US laws, especially when the ADA is so effective to begin with. "We should continue to lead by example," Hatch argued in an opinion piece in the *Salt Lake Tribune* on August 29, 2014. He warned that since treaties become, according to the Constitution, the "supreme law of the land," the CRPD would place America's performance under the authority of a "compliance committee" of international experts, and thus "endorse an ongoing role for the U.N. in evaluating and telling us how to conduct virtually every area of American life."[262]

On July 26, 2015, Hatch cowrote a *USA Today* op-ed celebrating twenty-five years of the ADA. "It gives countless children and young adults with disabilities hope that their dreams of college and careers will not have to be set aside, as was once the norm," Hatch noted with coauthors Steny Hoyer, Tom Harkin, Bob Dole, and Steve Bartlett (a former Republican US representative from Texas). "The ADA has also helped America fulfill its responsibility to returning service men and women who bring with them the physical and mental scars of war, sustained in defense of our freedom and way of life."[263]

The ADA did not originate with Orrin Hatch, and it was the product of many years of work by a host of courageous, dedicated disability advocates and their allies. But at several critical moments, Hatch stepped in and rescued the ADA and enabled it to be born through the force of his conviction, passion, and skill.

"If it wasn't for Senator Hatch," contended disability rights leader Pat Wright in 2020, "we would still be fighting the ADA and there probably wouldn't be final passage of the ADA." As of the afternoon of July 11, 1990, she remembered, "the ADA was about to go down the tubes."[264] In 2020, her colleague Bobby Silverstein agreed: "But for Orrin Hatch, I am not sure we would have ever passed the ADA."[265] In the words of Professor Ruth Colker, constitutional law professor at Ohio State University, "Hatch was crucial in holding the line against AIDS hysteria."[266]

At almost exactly the same time that Orrin Hatch and his allies were battling for disability rights on the Senate floor in the summer of 1990, Hatch was helping to create another epic moment in Senate history—to apply the full power of the American government to conquer the AIDS epidemic itself.

CHAPTER 6

Summer of Glory Part 2
The Ryan White
CARE Act

T HE STAGE WAS SET for the second triumph coengineered
by Orrin Hatch to unfold in the Senate chamber in the summer of 1990, just weeks after the passage of the Americans with
Disabilities Act.

It was a story that symbolically began on June 5, 1981, the day
that the Centers for Disease Control and Prevention (CDC) first
described the illness that came to be known as HIV/AIDS.

On the same day, a woman arrived in Salt Lake City, Utah, to
start a new medical practice. Over the next decade, that woman,
Kristen Ries, an MD and lifelong Republican, became Utah's
"AIDS Doctor" by treating over 90 percent of people with HIV/
AIDS in the state during the epidemic's initial years.

Forty years later, she recalled, "In the first nine years I had a
solo medical practice and I had almost all the [HIV/AIDS] patients
in Utah, Wyoming, Nevada, and Idaho." No other doctors would

see these patients. Working with her nurse and physician's assistant Maggie Snyder and a team of Roman Catholic nuns at Salt Lake City's Holy Cross Hospital, she was often the only doctor in those four states who would even accept appointments with HIV/AIDS patients.[267]

The 1980s were a time of widespread ignorance, fear, and prejudice among many Americans over both AIDS and homosexuality, and Dr. Ries said she was treated as "a pariah of the medical community" for her work. These attitudes extended into religious communities, and in this respect, the intensely conservative state of Utah was no different from many other locations and religious denominations in the nation. Utah journalist Gillian Friedman noted that at the time, "the cause of the epidemic was still unknown and public fear of needles and blood, of touching anyone who might have the virus and of the gay community in general, was running rampant."[268]

"Very early on in the epidemic," recalled Dr. Ries, "some of the local bishops of the churches encouraged the parents and families of people with HIV—or even gay [people]—to disown their children. Some of them did. But that didn't last too long. Finally, some of the mothers stood up, and now they have Mama Dragons [a community of Latter-day Saint mothers with LGBTQI+ children]. It's come really almost 360 degrees around in the last number of years. But back then, many of these patients died almost alone. Some of 'em, they didn't have friends."

In the first decade since its emergence in 1981, the HIV/AIDS pandemic killed tens of thousands of gay and straight Americans, primarily through blood transfusions and sexual contact. As Senator Edward Kennedy recalled in a 2007 oral history, "The kind of discrimination against gays during this period, and the vehemence and the vitriol directed towards them, was just extraordinary. The disease was obviously the result of gay sexual behavior, but it was also the result of the use of needles and of the blood supply being contaminated. People who were hemophiliacs were getting AIDS and were suffering this extraordinary discrimination. In school, parents would be yelling at children not to play with other children. It was a very volatile, hate-filled moment."[269]

Both Kennedy and Hatch were confronted with the AIDS epidemic early in the 1980s through their senior positions on the Senate Education and Labor Committee, which in 1999 became known as the Health, Education, Labor, and Pensions Committee. An unusual and powerful alliance began to develop between the two men on some major issues, driven both by a surprising personal chemistry and by pure realpolitik. "One of my motivations for coming to the Senate was to fight Ted Kennedy," Hatch explained. Then, in 1981, when Hatch became chairman of the Senate Education and Labor Committee and Kennedy was the ranking Democrat, Hatch was compelled to work with Kennedy to get anything passed. Hatch explained, "Even though I was chairman, Kennedy had a 9–7 ideological edge on votes because two Republicans kept voting with Democrats."[270] In 1988, Kennedy became chairman and Hatch became the ranking Republican.

Both Hatch and Kennedy became devoted to understanding the blossoming AIDS epidemic and seeing what the federal government could do about it through hearings, countless meetings with experts and advocates, and legislative action through the 1980s. In 1982, Chairman Hatch authorized the first Senate hearings on AIDS. According to his then committee aide and medical adviser Dr. David Sundwall, "This first hearing started the ball rolling and we quickly enacted legislation authorizing AIDS Education and Training Centers [ETCs] to be established in the cities with the highest prevalence. It took almost a decade but antiretroviral drugs against the HIV virus were identified, that when used in combination were effective, which essentially changed AIDS from an inevitably fatal disease to a chronic illness that can be managed over time."[271]

Hatch recalled in 2020, "AIDS came along and people were frightened to death. I knew that these people didn't choose to be homosexual. They were born that way. So it was not for me to judge them in a despicable manner, which is what a lot of others did. I knew that if we didn't get on top of working on this problem, we would have an immense problem not only in this country but around the world. I wanted to make sure that these people were not only helped but that they were treated fairly."[272]

Hatch's belief that people may be born gay and do not "choose" to be so, which he also stated on the Senate floor at the time, put him sharply at odds with many religiously conservative Americans, including members of his own faith, many of whom believed that homosexuality was a self-selected, severe aberration that could be "cured" through outside intervention or "conversion." In the early 1980s, Hatch had no deep public history on gay issues, and he sometimes made statements of personal aversion to homosexuality that were typical of many other Americans' beliefs at the time. Over his years in office, Hatch would sometimes exhibit contradictions on issues of interest to gay Americans. On some occasions he made ill-chosen remarks that angered gay advocates and that he fully apologized for.

During 1977, his first year in the Senate, Hatch made an off-hand comment that gay people have a "psychological deficiency," saying that he wouldn't want them teaching school any more than members of the American Nazi Party. He later bluntly dismissed these utterances as being "stupid on my part." Similarly, in 1988 he was quoted as calling Democrats "the party of homosexuals." Again, he apologized for the comment. "That was a dumb thing for me to say," he affirmed. "I deserve to have fault found with me because I said it."[273]

But despite a national climate of widespread ignorance and hostility toward AIDS victims and homosexuality in the 1980s, Orrin Hatch's early and steady support for congressional AIDS research funding was guided by a personal sense of compassion, an instinct to rely on science rather than fear, and an almost libertarian view of personal sexual behavior. In 1990, he unambiguously told the

New York Times, "I feel very deeply about people's heartaches and problems, and I don't care what their sexual preferences are." He added, "That's their business and I'm not going to judge them by my standards or what I think is right." In the context of being a conservative Republican in this era, in fact, Hatch's record on AIDS-related issues, while little-known and underappreciated, is striking, and even heroic.

On February 9, 1984, Hatch introduced and sponsored the Senate's first AIDS legislation, included in the Preventive Health Amendments of 1984, which was signed into law by President Reagan later that year. The law authorized funding for the CDC to "make grants to public and nonprofit private entities for information and education programs on, and for the diagnosis, prevention, and control of, acquired immune deficiency syndrome." It was a modest but historic first step in the fight against AIDS.

In a dramatic gesture that was years ahead of its time, one day in 1986, Hatch embraced an AIDS patient in his Senate office after the man testified at a committee hearing. It came at a moment in time when the illness was still becoming understood publicly, and usually as a deadly, possibly highly contagious "gay disease," and many people then assumed that the disease could be contracted through a simple touch. Hatch approved the public release of a photo of himself with his arm around the man, a fellow Latter-day Saint who was a hemophiliac who contracted the disease through a blood transfusion. The photo, startling for its time, gained widespread attention and played a role in the long process of shifting public attitudes toward the then mysterious condition. "People were scared to death to even be in the presence of people with AIDS," Hatch remembered in 2020. "I gave him a big hug. That opened the door to a lot of kindness toward some of these people."[274]

Hatch's instinct to welcome the man to his office was automatic, but Hatch quietly double-checked with his Senate aide and medical adviser, Dr. David Sundwall, just before the meeting on whether it was safe to do so. "As long as you don't tongue-kiss him, Senator," deadpanned Dr. Sundwall, "you'll be just fine."[275] Sadly, the man died just a few months later. In 1987, Diana, the Princess of Wales, was photographed shaking hands—without gloves—with an AIDS patient at Middlesex Hospital in London. That gesture and the photo caused a worldwide sensation and helped transform Diana into an icon of compassion. One year earlier, Orrin Hatch, one of the most conservative figures in American politics, had done exactly the same thing.

By 1987–1988, the HIV/AIDS death rate was rising exponentially to alarming levels, and Senators Hatch and Kennedy teamed up to craft and fight for S. 1220, the Acquired Immunodeficiency Syndrome (AIDS) Research and Information Act, a major first step toward establishment of a comprehensive federal AIDS policy. The bill authorized nearly $665 million in education and research funds to be channeled through the National Institutes of Health (NIH) and the CDC to state and local governments, national and international organizations, and community-based groups, focusing on educating people at increased risk of contracting AIDS. The bill also directed the US secretary of Health and Human Services to declare AIDS a public health emergency, authorized a national clearinghouse on AIDS, a twenty-four-hour telephone hotline, advertising campaigns, and funds for clinical trials on pharmaceutical and other treatments for AIDS and for care and treatment programs including home care, a concept that Hatch had strongly advocated for other health issues as being humane and cost-effective.

On April 27 and 28 in 1988, an emotional debate unfolded on the Senate floor over Senator Jesse Helms's objections to the bill, which he said would "promote sodomy." Standing a few feet away from Helms, Hatch carefully dismantled Helms's objections, in an often-unscripted oration that in its forcefulness presaged his rescue of the Americans with Disabilities Act that would occur two years later.

"We are talking about the number one public health problem in

America," Hatch said. "The fact that it affects homosexuals ought to make us that much more interested in at least trying to help those people who are being devastated by it, in spite of their sexual preferences. But that does not mean I do not have compassion for them; that I am just going to write them off and tell them to forget it, go ahead and die, because they differ from me.

"I am not sure that homosexuals chose to be the way they are or that anybody else fully chooses to be who or what they are," Hatch continued. "And I am not sure that I should stand here on the floor of the US Senate and pass judgment on anybody."

Invoking the words that Jesus Christ uttered in John 8:7 when he came across a woman accused of adultery who was about to be stoned to death, Hatch asked his fellow senators, and by extention all Americans watching on the C-SPAN live feed, "Who are we to judge anyway? Let him who is without sin cast the first stone."

Hatch then referenced his own work as a Latter-day Saint bishop who had conferred spiritually with gay members of his church, saying, "We have to tell homosexuals more than simply to become heterosexuals. I am not sure if we tell them to become heterosexuals that it will make any real difference. In fact, my experience in having counseled a few in my day is that it will not make any difference at all." He added, "And if we do not educate them as to how to avoid it and what to do about it, and some of these funds will go for that, then my gosh, what are we doing here? We are just going to subject this whole country to a widespread pandemic or epidemic of AIDS?"

One could argue that Hatch was delivering "a pitch for the angels," in the words of a character in an episode of *The Twilight Zone* from long ago. "I swear to God," remembered Thomas Rollins, chief counsel of the Senate Labor and Human Resources Committee, "I think it was the first gay rights oration given in the Senate, and it was done by Orrin Hatch of Utah, and it was because every now and then they get under enough pressure that they stop being politicians and they turn into themselves."[276]

The pitch worked. Hatch and Kennedy successfully neutralized Helms's arguments and proposed amendments, and on April 28, 1988, the Senate passed S. 1220, the Acquired Immunodeficiency Syndrome (AIDS) Research and Information Act, by an over-whelming vote of 87 to 4. President Reagan, who was criticized by many for not becoming deeply engaged in the AIDS crisis through much of his presidency, signed it into law. Later that year, Hatch cosponsored a bill sponsored by Kennedy, S. 2889—the Health Omnibus Programs Extension Act of 1988, which further expanded and strengthened the federal government's wide-ranging programs to combat the HIV/AIDS epidemic. The two bills sig-nificantly increased AIDS education, research, and prevention activities; and both bills, Hatch recalled, were passed only with "tremendous difficulties."[277]

In 1990, the AIDS crisis continued to rage, and effective treat-ments were still not widely available. As of July 30, 1990, accord-ing to the US Public Health Service, there were 143,286 reported cases of AIDS in the nation, 87,644 of those people had died, and some one million Americans were infected with HIV.

*   *   *

A hero stepped forward to capture this moment in American his-tory, in the form of a boy from Indiana named Ryan White who loved skateboarding, comic books, and toy cars, and contracted HIV/AIDS in 1984 at the age of thirteen when he was treated for hemophilia.

Despite assurances from public health experts who testified that he posed no threat to his peers, his school expelled him, his community shunned him, and his family was forced to move to another town. When he was diagnosed, doctors estimated that White would live only three to six more months, but he survived for another five and a half years before dying on April 8, 1990, at the age of eighteen. In that time, he testified before Congress and the Presidential Commission on AIDS; joined President Reagan's

Academy Awards party; spoke to ten thousand teachers at the Louisiana Superdome; met with Senators Hatch, Kennedy, and other
congressional leaders; and became a powerful national symbol of
the HIV/AIDS epidemic.

Inspired by Ryan White and countless other people grappling
with HIV/AIDS, Hatch and Kennedy painstakingly fashioned an
expanded, highly comprehensive federal attack on the AIDS epidemic, with special attention to top urban and rural areas struck
by the crisis. As he invariably did when preparing legislation, Hatch
worked to get the legislation in shape to be feasible to conservatives
and Republicans by maximizing the efficiency and accountability
of results, containing costs as much as possible, minimizing the
creation of big new federal bureaucracies, and channeling funds
through states and localities.

In February 1990, Senators Hatch, Kennedy, and twenty-six
other initial Senate cosponsors introduced S. 2240, the Comprehensive AIDS Resources Emergency (CARE) Act of 1990. The
actress Elizabeth Taylor joined Hatch and Kennedy for a widely
publicized hearing and press conference to announce the bill and
urge its quick passage in Congress. "In terms of pain, suffering and
cost, AIDS is a disaster as severe as any earthquake, hurricane, or
drought,"[278] said Kennedy. After Ryan White's death, Hatch and
Kennedy suggested that the bill be named the Ryan White Comprehensive AIDS Resources Emergency (CARE) Act of 1990, and
White's mother agreed. The boy was well-known and admired,
and the use of his name as a tribute made it easier for broader audi-
ences to support the bill, including those in Congress who strongly
opposed homosexuality and tried to attach restrictions on the
legislation. With the conservative Hatch as the bill's Republican
defender, its chances improved.

On May 14, 1990, Hatch took the lead in introducing the legislation on the Senate floor. Using charts, statistics, and sometimes
choking back tears, Hatch made his case for the Ryan White CARE
Act as powerfully as he would two months later for the Americans

with Disabilities Act, resembling a trial attorney making a masterful final summation to the American people:

> We are talking here about children who contracted this deadly virus through no fault of their own. We are talking about children who have AIDS because they received HIV-infected blood, or because their mothers were carriers of the virus. We are talking about children like Ryan White and Ariel Glaser. We are talking about the 2,200 children who have contracted AIDS and the over 1,000 children who have died from this dreadful disease.
>
> This bill also begins to recognize that the AIDS epidemic has not escaped rural America. When we think of AIDS, we may see images of New York City, or Los Angeles, or San Francisco. But the fact is that AIDS is in the rural North, it is in the rural South, rural Midwest, in the rural New England and rural West of the United States, and every other part of the country.
>
> This bill also comes to grips with the adverse ramifications that the disease has on our Nation's health care system. Health care providers, particularly urban hospitals, have been stretched to the limit to provide treatment for AIDS patients who are largely low income.
>
> Mr. President, there is not a single Member of the Senate, Republican or Democrat, who would not jump into the water to save someone who is drowning. I do not think any of us would fail to get in there and do our best. We would do it without first asking how he or she happened to fall into the water or happened to lose their confidence to swim. We would jump in and help.
>
> This bill is not a debate about factors causing individuals to contract AIDS. It is not a debate about the efficacy of education programs. This bill is simply an effort by those of us in this body who want to do something to heal all the victims of this terrible disease. It is a terrible, debilitating, worrisome, outrageous epidemic disease. This bill provides humane care.

Mr. President, I do not want to condemn to death any person who has AIDS in this country. I do not care, in all honesty, what it was that caused them to contract the disease in the sense of wanting to help. I just want to help them....

Oddly enough, any of us who may stand by and criticize better look at ourselves. We better look into our own hearts and our own minds and our own lives and if anybody, even in this body, does that, they are going to have to conclude that there are lots of things they can improve upon. We have some very wonderful people in this body, but we all make mistakes. We all do things that are wrong. We all have problems. And, I would hate to think that if people anywhere in this world or this country had diseases, and we could maybe find a cure, that we would not take the time or the effort or spend the money or do the things necessary to get a cure.

Should we just let the disease run rampant because we do not agree with the morals of certain people? For one, I, do not. I do not condone homosexual activity, but that does not have a thing to do with this bill. AIDS is a public health problem. It is hurting our country and hurting people who really should never have had to come in contact with this disease. It is hurting children, and mothers, and families and a lot of people.

Mr. President, I have only been in this world 56 years, but I can say that I know there are a lot of good people who have made mistakes in their lifetime. There are a lot of good people who are infected with the AIDS virus who make contributions to our society. We should provide them compassion and care.

The reason this Nation is great is because of diversity, because of our great laws, because of the great freedoms that we have. This Nation is great because of the rights that we protect, because of so many things that this body does, but also because we are a compassionate nation, because we look at problems and we do not always worry about how they started. We worry about what to do to end them.

That is why this nation is so great.

At this, Senator Jesse Helms took the floor to conduct a rambling, vicious attack on the "homosexual lobby" for exaggerating the crisis and minimizing the role of gay sex as a contributing factor to it. He denounced the proposed Hatch-Kennedy bill as needlessly expensive—for robbing funds from treatment for other diseases, and for representing "another legislative flagship for the homosexual segment of the AIDS lobby and its apologists in and out of Congress, and in and out of the major news media." He proclaimed, "Being whipped up today is a hysteria bordering on terror by the repeated proclamation, and we have heard it this afternoon, that AIDS is everywhere and that we are on the verge of another bubonic plague. I think one of the saddest things is that the taxpayers' money is being proposed to be used to proselytize a dangerous lifestyle." Helms condemned the invocation of Ryan White's name by advocates of the bill as a cynical political ploy.

Helms's attitudes may seem prehistoric by today's standards, but at the time he was a conservative giant in the Congress, commanding the attention of many followers and allies on a wide range of issues, as well as the power of a high-tech direct-mail fund-raising juggernaut. Despite ninety-five senators wanting to bring the bill to a vote, Helms managed to raise enough objections and the implicit threat of a filibuster to delay the vote from May 15 to early August. Hatch and Kennedy agreed to several amendments to the final bill, including a provision that "punted" to state authorities the controversial issue of partner notification of a positive HIV test result, and another that excluded needle-exchange programs from the legislation.

Thanks to the work of Ryan White, countless determined and courageous gay and nongay AIDS activists, Orrin Hatch, Ted Kennedy, and most of the US Senate, the Ryan White CARE Act was passed with overwhelming support in Congress on August 4 by a vote of 95 to 4 in the Senate and 408 to 14 in the House of Representatives, where a version of the bill had first been introduced by Representative Henry Waxman, a Democrat from California. The legislation was a model of bipartisanship. President George H. W. Bush signed the bill into law on August 18, 1990, without a signing ceremony, just three weeks after he signed the Americans with Disabilities Act. The Bush administration had been curiously ambivalent and even hostile to the bill, arguing in a hollow official statement that its "narrow, disease-specific approach sets a dangerous precedent, inviting treatment of other diseases through similar ad hoc arrangements."[279]

The legislation initially allocated over $4 billion to address the AIDS crisis on a national level and became the biggest program providing services to those living with HIV/AIDS. It remains so today. Included in the original bill were emergency aid to cities and rural areas most affected by AIDS and grants to states and local governments and private and nonprofit health-care and social service providers. Other provisions of the bill focused on testing and early intervention, home care, continuity of insurance coverage, and special support for infants and children, expectant mothers, prisoners, low-income patients, hemophiliacs, Native Americans, and the homeless.

In 1995, Hatch and Kennedy again teamed up to assemble wide bipartisan support to successfully reauthorize funding for the Ryan White CARE Act. On July 26, Hatch again took the Senate floor as the chief conservative and Republican champion of the life-and-death measure, and his remarks included appeals to both intellect and emotion:

> People are dying.
>
> People are dying and we have the chance today or tomorrow to enact legislation that will really make a difference—really make a difference in their lives, and the lives of their families and friends who love them.
>
> We have the chance to enact legislation that will help alleviate some of the pain and suffering of individuals who are infected with HIV....

I think back to the early days of AIDS, and how the growing numbers of infected individuals and the resultant death toll caused this country so much alarm and panic.

Unfortunately, as with any unsuspected crisis, the immediate response from many—including members of both houses of Congress—could be characterized as denial, anger, and blame. Fortunately, over time, our compassion has grown for those infected with this insidious virus, as our understanding about the causes of and treatments for this devastating disease increased.

As I look back, I think of the swift reaction of our health care community, yet how painfully clear it was that both our research and service delivery infrastructures lacked the capacity to address the growing number of cases of HIV infection.

As I look back, I recall how the service delivery programs evolved—the AIDS service demonstration projects, the home and community-based health services grant programs, and the AIDS drug reimbursement program—yet we still could not keep pace with the need for services in our communities. They came out of our Labor Committee, and we were proud to authorize those programs, which have really served to help people. But they were not enough.

Out of this great need for community-based, compassionate care was born the Ryan White Comprehensive AIDS Resources Emergency [CARE] Act of 1990, a bill I was pleased to author with my colleague from Massachusetts, Senator Kennedy.

We named the bill after Ryan White, a courageous, intelligent and caring young man from Indiana, who worked tirelessly to educate others about HIV and AIDS. Ryan helped replace fear and indifference with hope and compassion. One of the great lessons of his life—that we should not discriminate against those with the HIV virus or other illness—remains true today. His tireless efforts, indeed, his legacy, is being carried on by his mother, Jeanne White. And I met with her a number of times. And I have to say she is doing a good job.

There are so many others who have spoken out with the same spirit and eloquence, including Mary Fisher, founder of the Family AIDS Network, who is a tireless crusader against AIDS, and our much-missed friend Elizabeth Glaser, who established the Pediatric AIDS Foundation, which has done so much to improve the lives of children infected with HIV.

I can remember when she first walked into my office. I did not know a lot about pediatric AIDS. I knew about adult AIDS. But I did not realize so many children were being infected at that time. When she walked in and explained it to me, I have to say we decided to help her. Our colleagues, Senator Metzenbaum and others, helped her raise her first million dollars for the Pediatric AIDS Foundation at a wonderful dinner here in Washington, DC; and she went on from there to raise several more million dollars in the fight against AIDS, and, of course, she is one of the most valued heroines in this country, as far as I am concerned. There have been so many unnamed others in countless communities across the Nation.

Today, we have before us reauthorization of the Ryan White CARE Act.

Let me discuss a few dramatic facts in order to highlight the tremendous impact of this disease and explain why this bill should be passed. The most revealing fact is that the No. 1 cause of death for males aged 29 to 44 is now AIDS.

In the last decade, the proportion of cases represented by women has almost tripled.

Even in my small home state of Utah, it is estimated by the Department of Health that there are 5,000 people infected with the HIV virus. To date, 1,110 have been diagnosed with full-blown AIDS, and 644 have died.

Indeed, our knowledge of AIDS has expanded dramatically since those early days.

We now know that AIDS is not a gay disease, or a Haitian disease.

We know that it cannot be transmitted by casual contact.

We know that it affects man, woman and child, whatever race, whatever nationality.

AIDS does not play favorites. It affects rich and poor, adults and children, men and women, rural communities and the inner city.

Since its enactment in 1990, the Ryan White AIDS Care Act has provided the necessary assistance to those persons and their families affected by the AIDS epidemic.

Often, the funding provides for models of HIV service delivery that are considered to be some of the most successful health care delivery models in history.

I am very proud of Utah's Ryan White program. Let me tell you of some of our accomplishments.

Ryan White funds were used to establish a home health services program which provides much needed homemaker, health aide, personal care, and routine diagnostic testing services.

A drug therapy program has been established that offers AZT and other drugs to individuals infected with HIV.

Ryan White funds have been used to provide health and support services through an HIV Care Consortium, which offers vital services such as dental, mental health counseling, transportation, benefits advocacy, eye exams and glasses, legal advocacy, information and education, nutrition counseling, and substance abuse counseling.

Many have noted that AIDS brings out the best and worst in people. Let us hope that this debate reflects the best of the great American traditions of reaching out to those in our community.

I plead with my colleagues today, and I will tomorrow, let us not backslide on this.

Once again, Senator Jesse Helms rose up to attack the heart of the measure, by proposing a prohibition that any funds would not be used to advance homosexuality. As journalist Susan Milligan wrote, "The amendment could have limited cities' ability to reach into the gay community to promote condom use and other ways to prevent the spread of the disease." But Orrin Hatch realized that this was an ingenious move by Helms, since many Democratic senators were thinking of running for president the following year and would not want to seem to endorse gay promiscuity and the spread of AIDS. "Kennedy thundered against Helms on the Senate floor, his decibel level rising," reported Milligan, "but he was getting nowhere. Then Hatch took on Helms."[280]

Hatch later explained, "I stood up and said 'Senator, I know you're sincere. But this is not a gay rights bill. This is a public health bill.'"[281] Once again, Hatch's actions gave both Republicans and Democrats the political cover to do the right thing and support the reauthorization of the Ryan White CARE Act.

"That was the end of the battle, and Helms knew it," Hatch noted.

In the thirty years since its enactment, the Ryan White CARE Act and its reauthorizations, all supported by Orrin Hatch, have continued to benefit millions of Americans by supporting comprehensive HIV care and providing services for those without health insurance. Today, programs funded by the act serve over five hundred thousand people living with HIV, or more than half of those diagnosed with HIV in the United States, the majority of whom are Black or Latinx and have incomes at or below the federal poverty level. The program funds research, primary health care, mental health support, home care, gynecological support, access to medication, dental services, family counseling, and a network of eight regional AIDS Education and Training Centers.

Ryan White programs are credited both with major improvements in viral suppression for HIV/AIDS patients and with sharply reducing the number of children born HIV-positive by reducing transmission rates between mother and child. In 2015, President Obama's top AIDS officials reported that "clinics funded by the Ryan White HIV/AIDS Program now are retaining more than

8 out of 10 patients in care—and very nearly as many have successfully achieved 'viral suppression,' significantly reducing their risk of transmitting HIV. This is extraordinary, especially compared to the much lower national rates of retention in care and viral suppression."[282]

In 2020, Dr. Judith Feinberg, the chair of the HIV Medicine Association, and Dr. Anna Person, the cochair of the Ryan White Medical Providers Coalition, wrote, "As clinicians and researchers committed to HIV medicine, we have witnessed remarkable advances in HIV care and treatment over the last three decades. Without the Ryan White Program too many of our patients who face significant barriers accessing healthcare would not benefit from those advances." The doctors added, "The average rate of viral suppression—the virus suppressed in patients to levels so low that it is undetectable, protecting their health and eliminating their risk of sexual transmission—among people receiving Ryan White services nationally is 87.1%, compared to a national viral suppression rate among people with HIV reported by the Centers of Disease Control and Prevention of 62.7%."[283]

Back in Utah, Dr. Kristen Ries, the state's longtime lone "AIDS doctor," witnessed the direct impact of the Ryan White CARE Act among her own patients soon after its enactment. At first, Dr. Ries explained, funding for HIV/AIDS treatment was almost nonexistent. "Everything was done on a shoestring, people would donate money, and we would help develop programs for people to get their medicines from the donations," she recalled. But after the 1990 passage of the Hatch-Kennedy-sponsored Ryan White CARE Act, she explained, "That's when the money really started coming in. Patients could get their medical appointments paid for. It helped get people mental health therapy. The lawyers came in. We were able to get dentists and specialty care in that program, and it evolved into what it is today."

In 2020, living in retirement with Maggie Snyder, her now wife and longtime partner in AIDS work, Dr. Ries said she has "always been amazed" by the behind-the-scenes, national impact that Orrin Hatch made in the fight against AIDS. Whenever she hears someone criticize Hatch, she tells them about his work on the Ryan White Act. "Nobody knows about that here in Utah," she reported.[284]

Dr. Kristen Ries never got a chance to meet Orrin Hatch and express her gratitude for his long history of supporting HIV/AIDS research and treatment, since, she explained, Hatch was a big player on the national stage, and "I was just a nobody." One day in 1995, though, Dr. Ries did make it to Washington, DC, to try to thank Hatch for giving his full support to the Ryan White CARE Act and to urge him to fight for its renewal and continued funding. She was welcomed graciously by Hatch's Senate staff, but Senator Hatch was unable to join them.

Orrin Hatch has called the Ryan White CARE Act one of his proudest achievements and "one of the finest pieces of legislation to come out of the Senate."[285]

In one astonishing burst of legislative leadership in the summer of 1990, Orrin Hatch helped defeat AIDS hysteria on the floor of the US Senate and saved the landmark Americans with Disabilities Act from probable death or indefinite delay, then went on to facilitate—just a few weeks later—the passage of the Ryan White CARE Act for HIV/AIDS. Both pieces of legislation backed by Hatch, as well as their direct-successor laws and amendments, continue to benefit multitudes of citizens to this day three decades later and form social pillars of the nation.

There was no one who was more responsible for these achievements than Orrin Hatch.

According to Michael Iskowitz, who served as Senator Kennedy's chief AIDS adviser at the time, much of the work on AIDS by Hatch and Kennedy was done with small groups of key senators and experts over dinners the two hosted at Kennedy's home. There, senators could privately ask questions and educate themselves on the science of this emotional, politically explosive issue. Hatch and

Kennedy directed their staffs to prepare a jointly sponsored one-thousand-page book of AIDS facts, statistics, and charts and had a copy delivered to each of the other ninety-eight members of the Senate. "There was no constituent-driven, Utah-driven reason for Hatch to be as involved in AIDS as he was," Iskowitz recalled. "He did it because he really believed strongly in access to health care, and the importance of public health, and because of his relationship with Senator Kennedy. There was also a lot of actual resistance in Utah to him being as out there as he was on these things. Yet it didn't deter him because he really believed strongly in it and wanted to make it happen."

In 2021, Iskowitz made a startling, sweeping assertion about Hatch's impact and effectiveness on the issue of AIDS: "The Ryan White Act would never have happened without him, there's no doubt about that. As someone who has worked on AIDS for over thirty years, there is no doubt in my mind that the US response to AIDS would have been significantly more delayed if it wouldn't have been for Hatch. Especially in the early days when the response to AIDS was so stuck in fear, that without Orrin Hatch, the US response to AIDS would have waited a lot longer had it not been for someone like him who was willing to put partisanship aside and do something big and important for the country."[286]

He concluded, "We will be forever indebted to him for that—forever."

The nearly simultaneous victories of the Americans with Disabilities Act and the Ryan White CARE Act during what could be called a "summer of glory" in 1990 literally reshaped and rebuilt the United States for the better.

*   *   *

In the ways in which he dealt with the separate but often related issues of HIV/AIDS and LGBTQI+ rights over his forty-two-year public career, Orrin Hatch proved himself to be among the most surprising of politicians—one who adhered to a strong ideological foundation but was also capable of admitting mistakes and showing surprising complexity, change, and growth in his views. In the process, he often allied himself with the "better angels" of the American spirit.

Orrin Hatch was capable of being contradictory and making mistakes on issues of concern to gay Americans, as many people have been. Hatch did not always support proposals put forward by mainstream gay rights groups, and sometimes he opposed them.

For many years, Orrin Hatch held firm to his fundamental, faith-based belief that, in the familiar phrase, "marriage is between a man and a woman," a belief that was widely held and long shared among many leading Democrats, including Bill Clinton and Barack Obama. In the 1990s, Hatch championed the Defense of Marriage Act (DOMA), which denied same-sex couples federal benefits and recognition. He was also the lead author of a 2013 brief signed by ten senators that unsuccessfully urged the Supreme Court to uphold DOMA.

When the Supreme Court struck down DOMA in 2013's *United States v. Windsor* decision, Hatch criticized the majority for basing its ruling on "its own personal opinion." That year, in a poor choice of phrases, Hatch said that if traditional male-female marriage is devalued, "I got to tell you they'll be every Tom, Dick and Harry in there with some crazy marital scheme demanding the same rights and the same privileges."[287] Hatch reiterated that he doesn't think people choose to be gay, but that he draws the line on "traditional marriage."

In 2009, Hatch voted against the Matthew Shepard and James Byrd Jr. Hate Crimes Prevention Act, which broadened federal hate crime laws to encompass crimes against people based on their sexual orientation and gender identity. Hatch did not think such legislation was necessary, and believed that "most all crimes" motivated by prejudice and bias were being punished at the state level.[288] In

2012, Hatch opposed the renewal of the Violence Against Women Act, which he had cosponsored with Senator Joe Biden in 1994. He disagreed with "divisive projects" in the law's updated provisions,[289] such as language barring discrimination against LGBTQI+ people in programs funded through the law.

However, through the 1980s and into the 2010s, Hatch often called for compassion for all Americans, including LGBTQI+ citizens and people with HIV/AIDS, both gay and nongay. Hatch spearheaded, as the lead Republican senator, legislation that provided billions of dollars of critical new federal funding for HIV/AIDS research, treatments, medications, and social support—laws that saved lives and shaped the lives of tens of millions of Amercans for the better. He spent countless hours on these issues, meeting with constituents and experts in Utah; arm-twisting and negotiating behind the scenes in hallways, cloakrooms, and conference rooms in the Capitol; horse-trading and partnering with Republicans and Democrats; and juggling a host of intractable opinions, competing interests, and deep emotions in shaping the legislation so that it could actually pass and become the law of the land.

In 2013, Hatch was one of only ten Republican senators to vote in favor of the Employment Non-Discrimination Act (ENDA), which would explicitly prohibit employment discrimination on the basis of sexual orientation and gender identity. The Senate passed the bill, but it did not receive a vote in the House of Representatives. The Senate vote was 64 to 33, with Hatch joining nine other Republicans and all voting Democrats. Hatch explained that he voted for the bill "because it prohibits discrimination that should not occur in the workplace, it protects the rights of religious entities, and minimizes legal burdens on employers."[290] Despite the House's inaction, a similar result was achieved in 2020 by the US Supreme Court's ruling in *Bostock v. Clayton County, Georgia*, that Title VII of the Civil Rights Act of 1964 barred discrimination against employees based on their gender identity and sexual orientation.

In 2013, Hatch suddenly changed his longtime opposition to marriage rights for LGBTQI+ Americans by expressing support for a civil unions law that would, in his words, "give gay people the same rights as married people," a position that had also been held by mainstream Democrats like Bill Clinton and Barack Obama. Hatch viewed civil unions as a means of protecting "traditional marriage" for heterosexual couples.

In 2014, Hatch acknowledged that nationwide marriage equality was inevitable. He told a radio audience, "Let's face it, anybody who does not believe that gay marriage is going to be the law of the land just hasn't been observing what's going on," and "The trend right now in the courts is to permit gay marriage, and anybody who doesn't admit that just isn't living in the real world."[291] His prediction was verified in the US Supreme Court's *Obergefell v. Hodges* decision in 2015, which declared that same-sex couples have a constitutional right to marry under the Fourteenth Amendment and are guaranteed equal protection under the law.

In 2015, with Hatch's strong support, leaders of The Church of Jesus Christ of Latter-day Saints worked with LGBTQI+ advocates and Utah legislators to pass a state law that safeguards LGBTQI+ citzens from discrimination in housing and employment, while providing exemptions for religious organizations. The agreement, known as "the Utah compromise," is a model of the pragmatic, moderate, and constructive role often played behind the scenes by Latter-day Saint leaders like Orrin Hatch.

And in July 2017, Senator Hatch spoke in favor of transgender Americans in response to President Donald Trump's announcement that he would reinstate a ban on transgender people serving in the military. "I don't think we should be discriminating against anyone," Hatch said in a statement.[292]

On one of his last days as senator before his retirement in 2019, then eighty-four-year-old Orrin Hatch honored Pride Month by sending what he called "a message of love" to "my LGBT brothers and sisters" on the Senate floor and issued a heartfelt plea for tolerance in the face of chronic antigay prejudice and tragic rates of suicide among gay youth. "These young men and women deserve to feel loved, cared for, and accepted for who they are," he declared. "I don't think they chose to be who they are. They're born the way they are. And we ought to understand that. They deserve to know that they belong and that our society is stronger because of them."

Hatch continued, "No one should ever feel less because of their gender identity or sexual orientation. LGBT youth deserve our unwavering love and support. They deserve our validation and the assurance that not only is there a place for them in this society, but that it is far better off because of them. These young people need us—and we desperately need them. We need their light to illuminate the richness and diversity of God's creations. We need the grace, beauty, and brilliance they bring to the world."[293]

It was as heartfelt a plea for compassion for LGBTQI+ Americans as had ever been made in the halls of Congress.

✳   ✳   ✳

On October 11–13, 1991, a firestorm erupted on live national television in which Orrin Hatch played a central role.

The drama was the events surrounding the Senate Judiciary Committee's confirmation hearings for conservative Republican attorney and federal judge Clarence Thomas to be appointed an associate justice of the US Supreme Court, and the last-minute appearance of his former employee at the Department of Education and the Equal Employment Opportunity Commission, Anita Hill, who accused him of making graphic, unsolicited sexual comments to her ten years earlier when she worked for him. Thomas vehemently denied the accusations. Both Hill and Thomas were African Americans.

Their diametrically opposing testimonies—and televised questioning by US senators on the Judiciary Committee—triggered a full-scale social and political earthquake and a media spectacle that opened up a fault line in American history on the subject of sexual harassment. Nothing like it had ever happened before, and Orrin Hatch played a key role in the drama as an uncompromising defender of Thomas and a skeptic of Hill's charges, which he attempted to discredit.

To explore the charges, rebuttals, alleged facts, events, and personalities of the Anita Hill–Clarence Thomas controversy is to fall into a rabbit hole connected to a hall of mirrors that reveal nothing but confusion. Without direct third-party witnesses to, or tape recordings of, the conversations in question between Thomas and Hill, it is impossible to tell which person was telling the truth. To this day, some Americans believe Hill, who taught at the University of Oklahoma law school at the time of the hearings, and others believe Thomas.

The political ferocity of the partisan debate over Thomas's confirmation had roots in President Reagan's 1987 nomination of conservative jurist Robert Bork to the Supreme Court, which Senator Hatch strongly supported on the Judiciary Committee. Hatch later wrote, "I was here when Democrats started the confirmation wars with their treatment of Robert Bork. Just one year earlier, Senator Ted Kennedy had attempted to filibuster Justice William Rehnquist's elevation to Chief Justice, but those efforts were thwarted by a bipartisan cloture vote and a subsequent 65–33 confirmation vote. But in 1987, Senate Democrats twisted Judge Bork's words, misrepresented his record, and did their best to turn a good and decent man into some sort of monster."[294]

After a bitter debate over Bork's views on civil rights and abortion and his role as a Justice Department official during the Watergate scandal, his nomination was defeated by fifty-eight senators voting against it. Senator Ted Kennedy, Hatch's colleague on the committee, made the provocative charge that "in Robert Bork's America, there is no room at the inn for blacks and no place in the Constitution for women; and, in our America, there should be no seat on the Supreme Court for Robert Bork."[295]

Hatch strongly supported Bork, who he said was "experiencing the kind of innuendo and intrigue that usually accompanies a campaign for the Senate."[296] Hatch was appalled by the episode, which he viewed as an unfair, politically motivated hit job by liberals and Democrats. What Kennedy did "was disgraceful," said Hatch. "I felt it was hitting below the belt."[297]

To Hatch, the Thomas nomination was a hit job, too, but now the explosive dimension of sex was added to the mix. Hill's charges became public when an FBI interview with her was leaked to the press just as Thomas's confirmation hearings were ending. Hatch knew and admired Thomas and thought him utterly incapable of saying the things Hill said he did. Hatch told Thomas he should "be himself," "tell the truth," and not "take any crap from anyone."

Hatch played the role of chief friend, supporter, and strategist for Thomas through the final drama, which riveted and sometimes appalled millions of TV viewers, creating a series of indelible images in the national memory. There was the spectacle of a panel of powerful white men, including Judiciary Committee chairman and future president Joseph Biden, asking deeply personal, embarrassing questions of a Black woman in public before millions of viewers. Hatch himself did not directly question Hill during the hearings.

There were startling images of Anita Hill calmly recounting her memories of Thomas discussing graphic sexual matters with her in his office, and of Orrin Hatch, in sympathetic dialogue with Thomas, reading a quote from William Peter Blatty's 1971 horror novel *The Exorcist* to suggest that the book, not Thomas, was the source of Hill's account of one such comment. Hill "would have us believe," Hatch asked Thomas incredulously, "that you were saying these things because you wanted to *date her*?" Hatch may have hoped the discovery of this quote would fully vindicate Thomas in the court of public opinion, but viewpoints remained largely polarized along party lines.

Finally, there was the dramatic scene of Clarence Thomas publicly and forcefully denying all the accusations to Hatch and denouncing the proceedings as a "national disgrace," and a "high-tech lynching for uppity blacks." After this, Hatch stepped out of the hearing room and encountered National Public Radio correspondent Nina Totenberg, who told him, "I don't know what to believe, I believe them both!" Hatch responded, "No, Nina, only one of them is telling the truth, and it's Judge Thomas."[298]

Witnesses came forward to testify to Thomas's good character and behavior, and there was speculation that at least one other person was prepared to come forward to lend credibility to Hill, but the hearings, which seemed to be veering out of control, were abruptly shut down by Chairman Biden. On October 15, 1991, the Senate narrowly voted to confirm Thomas by a vote of 52 to 48. Years later, Hatch recalled, "I said, 'There's something wrong here.' Did I like Anita Hill? Yes. Did I think she was a wonderful witness? Yes. Do I wish her well? You bet. But I believe Clarence Thomas." In 1993, Hatch admitted, "I don't know if anybody is ever going to have the actual full and final true story on that, but I believe Clarence Thomas."[299]

In 2002, Hatch wrote of the Clarence Thomas hearings, "Some claim I was too unwilling to overlook a serious allegation purely for partisan, political reasons. Obviously, I disagree, although I have found this accusation rather ironic given the thunderous silence from these very same critics when reports of President Clinton's assorted misuses and abuses of women came to light."[300] In 1998 and 1999, Clinton's presidency was consumed by impeachment proceedings in the House and Senate over charges of perjury and obstruction of justice stemming from a civil sexual harassment lawsuit, and Clinton also faced separate multiple allegations in the press of sexual assault and misconduct. Hatch argued that "at most, if you believe her (Hill), what he (Thomas) said in her presence was crude and insensitive but on the whole rather tame in comparison to more recent developments."[301]

The Thomas-Hill drama predated the "MeToo" era by a full twenty-five years. Hatch wrote, "We who were involved in the hearings will never be the same," and the same could be said of the nation. "If any good came out of the needlessly tortured and vicious confirmation," wrote Hatch in a fitting epitaph for the events, "it was that the nation was forced to confront the reality, too often ignored or discounted, of sexual harassment in the workplace."[302]

Hatch went on to play a key role in every Supreme Court appointment confirmation that followed, a process that became increasingly—and bitterly—partisan. According to Hatch, "When Bill Clinton became President, Senate Republicans did not retaliate" for the Rehnquist, Bork, and Thomas battles. He explained, "Instead, we gave Judges (Ruth Bader) Ginsburg and (Stephen) Breyer fair hearings and confirmed them overwhelmingly. Indeed, as ranking member on the Senate Judiciary Committee, I helped shepherd through both of President Clinton's nominees."[303] Judge Ginsburg, widely regarded to be on the liberal spectrum, wrote, "During my confirmation hearings, perhaps my biggest supporter was Orrin Hatch."[304]

In fact, Hatch directly suggested court of appeals judges Ruth Bader Ginsburg and Stephen Breyer to President Clinton, and they were confirmed with Hatch's support in 1993 and 1994. "I knew them both and believed that, while liberal, they were highly honest and capable jurists and their confirmation would not embarrass the president," Hatch recalled. "From my perspective, they were far better than the other likely candidates from a liberal Democrat administration."[305]

In Hatch's mind, everything changed in the 2000s, when Democrats blocked the nominations of several Republican-backed federal appellate court justice nominees. "For the first time in history, Senate Democrats successfully filibustered ten court of appeals nominees," Hatch wrote in 2017. "These were nominees who would have been confirmed had they gotten an up-or-down vote. What Senate Democrats did during George W. Bush's presidency changed the Senate—forever.

"What happened when Barack Obama became president?"

Hatch asked. "Once again, after Senate Democrats had escalated the confirmation wars, Senate Republicans chose not to reciprocate. To be sure, many Republicans voted against Judges Sotomayor and Kagan, but no Republican attempted to filibuster their nominations. And how did Democrats respond to our restraint? They eliminated the filibuster for lower-court nominees. The irony of this particular move is rich. It was the Democrats who, ten years earlier, for the first time in Senate history, began filibustering court of appeals judges in an effort to stop Bush's nominees. When Senate Republicans did not roll over for Obama's lower-court nominees, Democrats simply changed the rules back to what they were in practice ten years prior. Democrats, that is, raised the effectual confirmation threshold to 60 votes by instigating filibusters to block Republican nominees, and then lowered it back down to 50 votes to push through Democratic nominees."

Hatch concluded, "I have participated in this process for 40 years, during every combination of partisan control in both the Senate and White House. I have seen the confirmation process degrade from cooperation to, now, all-out partisan conflict. That is not a direction that is good for the country or for the institutions of the Senate and the judiciary."[306]

Hatch participated in the confirmation of more than eighteen hundred members of the federal judiciary, including all sitting members of the Supreme Court at the time of his retirement. "Arguably more than any other senator, Orrin Hatch has helped shape the Supreme Court for decades," wrote Jonathan Turley, a law professor at George Washington University, in 2018. "Hatch's success in the Senate is due in large part to his reputation for candid and honest advice. He has consistently voted for conservative causes, however he's one of the dwindling number of members who works well with the opposing party."[307]

Another intense partisan clash broke out in 2018 when President Trump nominated to the Supreme Court Brett Kavanaugh, a judge on the United States Court of Appeals for the District of

Columbia Circuit. Kavanaugh was engulfed in hotly disputed public allegations of sexual misconduct from when he was a young man, charges that Hatch found not credible and that Kavanaugh emotionally denied in his confirmation hearing. In strong echoes of the Hill-Thomas events, Kavanaugh was eventually confirmed with Hatch's help, as opinions hardened along partisan lines.

When political combat over judicial appointments first erupted in the Senate in the 1980s, Orrin Hatch's nemesis on the Judiciary Committee was often the liberal lion of the Senate, Ted Kennedy.

But at the same time, on the Senate Education and Labor Committee (called the Health, Education, Labor, and Pensions Committee from 1999), the two men were forging an increasingly momentous partnership together in Senate showdowns over AIDS legislation and the Americans with Disabilities Act.

They would come together again in the 1990s as brothers-in-arms in two historic endeavors—a fight to guarantee religious freedom to all citizens and a campaign to provide medical care for millions of poor American children.

CHAPTER 7

Brothers-in-Arms: Religious Freedom and Children's Health

ONE OF THE REASONS I ran for the Senate was to fight Ted Kennedy," Orrin Hatch once said of the senior Democratic senator from Massachusetts, "who embodied everything I felt was wrong with Washington."[308]

But through the 1980s and 1990s, the two men became the yin and yang, the oddest couple of American politics—the disheveled, überliberal, hard-partying, superrich libertine Ted Kennedy, and the abstemious, buttoned-up, conservative church-bishop-from-a-poor-family Orrin Hatch.

And sometimes, they shaped American history together.

"We did not agree on much, and more often than not, I was trying to derail whatever big government scheme he had just concocted," recalled Hatch in 2009. "And, in those years that Republicans held the majority in the Senate, when it came to getting some of our ideas passed into law, he was not just a stone in the road, he was a boulder. Disagreements over policy, however, were never personal with Ted. I recall a debate over increasing the minimum wage. Ted had launched into one of his patented histrionic speeches, the kind where he flailed his arms and got red in the face, spewing all sorts of red meat liberal rhetoric. When he finished, he stepped over to the minority side of the Senate chamber, put his arm around my shoulder, and said with a laugh and a grin, 'How was that, Orrin?' "[309]

After countless knock-down, drag-out battles on the Senate floor and in committee rooms, Hatch remembered, "We'd both reach out for each other and hug each other.[310]

"When I came to Washington, I hadn't the slightest idea that I would eventually have a strong working relationship with and love for the man that I came to fight," Hatch recalled in 2018. "And if you would have told me that he would become one of my closest friends in the world, I probably would have suggested that you need professional help."[311]

A turning point in their relationship occurred in 1981 when Hatch took over the chairmanship of the Labor and Human Resources Committee, which was dominated ideologically by a 9–7 majority of Democrats joined by two liberal Republicans. Hatch needed Kennedy's assistance to get anything done, because Kennedy largely controlled the committee's votes. "I went to Ted and said, 'I've got to have your help,'" Hatch later explained. "And to his credit, he did help. And we became friends." In 2020, Hatch recalled, "To have Kennedy pulling for me on occasion was very, very good."[312]

"When we got together," Hatch remembered of his work with Kennedy, "people would say, 'Oh, gosh, if those two can get together, anybody can,' and they'd get out of the way."[313] According to Kennedy aides Nick Littlefield and David Nexon, "The beauty of an early bipartisan alliance is that it provides at least some measure of instant credibility on both sides of the aisle. When Hatch and Kennedy signed on to a compromise, it gained instant credibility. They were so far apart on the conservative-liberal spectrum that when they agreed on a bill, it immediately had the potential for broad support. Hatch would sometimes joke that the only way they got together was that one of them must not have read the legislation. Hatch was a particularly desirable cosponsor because once he agreed to join with Kennedy on a piece of legislation, he was a tenacious advocate."[314]

In 2009, Hatch remembered Kennedy as a powerful force of opposition, but also of possible cooperation on certain shared causes: "Well, he was the leading liberal in the United States Senate for all the years I've been in the Senate. I've been there thirty-three years. And bar none, he was the leader. And he had more control over the Democrat Party base than anybody else. He's the only one who could bring them along on issues that were down the middle and really bipartisan, but he could bring them along. They would have to listen to him."[315]

"Ted was a lion among liberals, but he was also a constructive and shrewd lawmaker," Hatch once recounted. "He never lost sight of the big picture and was willing to compromise on certain provisions in order to move forward on issues he believed important. And, perhaps most importantly, he always kept his word. When our carefully balanced compromise legislation came to the Senate floor, Ted often had to lead the opposition to amendments offered by Democratic colleagues that he would rather have supported. But, he took the integrity of our agreement seriously and protected the negotiated package."[316]

Hatch's willingness to work with Kennedy sometimes earned him sharp criticism from fellow conservatives, both in public and in private. The *National Review*, a conservative journal, described him as a "latter-day liberal,"[317] and in closed-door Senate meetings, fellow Republican senator Phil Gramm often teased Hatch by calling him a "flake"[318] with liberal, left-wing ideas. Hatch was undeterred, once explaining, "Whenever I can move him (Kennedy) to the center on something that really makes a difference in people's lives, why shouldn't I?"

Kennedy was the flesh-and-blood definition of a larger-than-life character. The son of megawealthy financier and ambassador to the United Kingdom Joseph P. Kennedy and a scion of a legendary political family, Kennedy was so handsome in 1961 that journalist Clare Boothe Luce said he "looked like a Greek God."[319] Elected to the Senate in 1962, he went on to become one of the institution's hardest working and most respected and formidable legislators.

By 1991, Kennedy—after thirty years of hard living punctuated by the scandals of his causing the death in a car accident of Mary Jo Kopechne in 1969, and a 1991 incident in Palm Beach, Florida, when his nephew William Smith was charged with sexually assaulting a woman after a night of drinking with his uncle Teddy—*Time* magazine described him in much less flattering terms: "Kennedy's face sometimes looks flushed and mottled, with the classic alcoholic signs of burst capillaries, puffiness and gin-roses of the drunk. Sometimes he simply looks like hell—fat, dissolute, aging, fuddled. But his powers of recuperation are amazing. He has, when he needs it, an organizing inner discipline that allows him, by an act of sheer will, to pull himself together, to focus and resume a senatorial, Kennedy star quality."[320]

In 2009, John Broder of the *New York Times* wrote of Kennedy, "He was a Rabelaisian figure in the Senate and in life, instantly recognizable by his shock of white hair, his florid, oversize face, his booming Boston brogue, his powerful but pained stride. He was a celebrity, sometimes a self-parody, a hearty friend, an implacable foe, a man of large faith and large flaws, a melancholy character who persevered, drank deeply and sang loudly. He was a Kennedy."[321] He was, in other words, the extreme polar opposite of Orrin Hatch.

Kennedy once explained his relationship with Hatch as one of pragmatism and shared goals: "We are beyond the point where we let our differences get in the way of opportunities for progress. We have just learned it is a lot easier to work together than it is to fight each other. We have differences in terms of perhaps how we achieve the objectives, but I don't really feel that I have a differ- ence with Orrin in terms of what the objectives ought to be. If you build upon that kind of understanding and respect, you get a lot of things done."[322]

For many years, the two senators sat next to each other in the Senate's Education and Labor Committee room, where smoking was allowed until the early 1990s. "You could always tell when Teddy and I were in an argument or were fighting, by the amount of cigar smoke that he blew my way, as a nonsmoking Mormon," Hatch remembered. "If there was a particularly strong disagree- ment, he would just sit back in his chair, puffing smoke my way, giving me an actual headache to go along with the political head- aches he gave to all of us on the Republican side."

Sometimes, Hatch recalled, "Teddy would lay into me with the harshest, red meat, liberal rhetoric you could imagine. But just minutes later, he would come over and put his arm around me and ask, 'How did I do, Orrin?' "[323]

At one point in the 1980s, Hatch was so alarmed at Kennedy's self-destructive habits of partying, womanizing, and drinking that he confronted his friend. "Ted, it's time for you to grow up and quit acting like a teenager," said Hatch. "You know what you've got to do, don't you? You've got to quit drinking." Kennedy seemed "very stunned" by the intervention, according to Hatch, and gently replied, "I know."[324] On another occasion, Hatch said, "I'm going to have to send the Mormon missionaries after you." Kennedy looked away and concurred, "I'm ready for them."[325]

Their friendship intensified over the years, to the point that the two resembled battling brothers who cherished a deep love for each other. Kennedy went to the funeral of Hatch's mother, and when Hatch attended the service for Kennedy's mother he tried to slip into the back of the church, but Kennedy beckoned Hatch to join him in the front row.

David Kessler, a medical doctor who served as a health policy adviser to Hatch in the 1980s, observed what he saw as "an extreme personal fondness and an extreme degree of caring" between Kennedy and Hatch. "Perhaps they knew the kind of life they led, what it was like to be in public view all the time, the kind of pounding, the kind of beating up that they take, the kind of pressure that they take. If you've experienced it and you're there and you have those kind of pounding pressures—always being criticized by someone, battling sometimes your friends even more than people from the other side—it almost took somebody who was a senior senator to be able to understand another senator." Kessler recalled seeing Hatch speak of Kennedy "with a fondness that transcended anything that I had seen."[326]

Sometimes it seemed that for much of their time together in the Senate, which spanned from 1977 to Kennedy's death in 2009, Kennedy and Hatch were fighting each other like gladiators on issues such as spending bills, foreign policy, and judicial appointments. But other times, they were fighting together shoulder to shoulder to move America forward on great issues like disability rights and AIDS funding, and on two of their proudest achievements—religious freedom and health insurance for poor children.

*   *   *

One day in 1984, a drug and alcohol abuse counselor named Alfred Leo Smith attended a Native American religious ceremony in Oregon.

What happened there caused him to be fired from his job, denied unemployment compensation, and forced into a seven-year legal struggle that culminated in a stunning decision by the US Supreme Court.

It also inspired conservative senator Orrin Hatch to forge the proudest bipartisan achievement of his career in 1993, in partnership with a man he came to love like a brother—the liberal leader of the US Senate, Ted Kennedy of Massachusetts.

Al Smith was a Klamath Nation tribal member who endured years of homelessness and alcoholism and had been sober since

1957 with the help of Alcoholics Anonymous. Part of his job at a nonprofit drug and alcohol treatment center was to learn about Native cultural and spiritual practices that could aid his work, such as sweat lodges and spiritual ceremonies. When his coworker Galen Black was invited to a Native American religious ceremony and then summarily fired by the center for ingesting a small amount of ritual peyote, a mescaline-containing hallucinogen derived from cactus that was considered a sacred medicine to Native American practitioners, Smith was indignant.

Native Americans had used peyote in such ceremonies for fifty-five hundred years, and some believed that the ritual could help in recovery from addiction. Smith resolved to attend an upcoming ceremony himself, but his bosses told Smith that if he ingested peyote, he would lose his job too. Smith's immediate response was, "You can't tell me that I can't go to church!" He wondered, "How could they tell me I was attending a drug party when the ceremony was one of the most sacred Native American ceremonies that has survived for thousands of years?" Smith went to the ceremony, ingested a small quantity of peyote, told his employer about it, and was fired. He and Black applied for unemployment benefits, but the state denied the claims on the basis that ceremonial use of peyote, then technically criminal in Oregon, was "misconduct." An Oregon state court ruled that their conduct was safeguarded by the First Amendment and ordered the state to pay them their benefits. The state refused, appealed to the US Supreme Court, and demanded that the two men confess to engaging in misconduct and repay the court-mandated unemployment they'd already received.[327]

Some people advised Smith to seek an out-of-court settlement with the state. He woke up one morning and told himself, "Your kids are going to grow up and the case is going to come up one of these days and someone will say, 'Your dad is Al Smith? Oh, he's the guy that sold out.'" He decided, "I'm not going to lay that on my kids. I'm not going to have my kids feel ashamed. Even if we lose the case, they are going to say, 'Yeah, my dad stood up for what he thought was right.' "

In taking his stand, Smith was exercising the most fundamental of all American freedoms, the one chosen by the founders of the United States to be expressed in the very First Amendment to the Constitution, which guaranteed the freedom of religious worship by specifying that "Congress shall make no law respecting an establishment of religion, or prohibiting the free exercise thereof." The Supreme Court had ruled that the clause applied to both federal and state governments.

It was a principle that dated back to the first European settlers on the continent, including citizens in the Dutch outpost of New Amsterdam, which was later called New York. In 1657, they protested against religious discrimination in a declaration called the "Flushing Remonstrance," which is considered to be a precursor to the Bill of Rights, which declared that "the law of love, peace and liberty" extends to "Jews, Turks and Egyptians" as well as "Presbyterian, Independent, Baptist or Quaker."

Freedom of worship was also a principle that was very dear to the heart of Orrin Hatch, an intensely religious man who began each day by reading Scriptures. He once explained, "Daily prayer and scripture study remind me of the principles in which I believe, the reason why I am here, and what I should be fighting for. This puts things in the right perspective and allows me to focus my efforts on what really matters."[328] Hatch even saw the possibility of a divine hand guiding his career. "I actually believe I was destined to do this," he once explained. "I'm not saying it was divinely sanctioned, but it could very well have been."[329]

Jace Johnson, Hatch's onetime Senate chief of staff, recalled that if a weighty decision presented itself, Hatch would say, "Why don't we just kneel down and pray right here? And let's get our answer." Johnson recalled being "really shocked" by Hatch's faith, his belief, and his ability to call on spiritual guidance when needed. "It blew me away,"[330] Johnson remembered. In a 2017 tribute to her father, Hatch's daughter Marcia spoke about his compassion to others, even those who disagreed with him. "I know he believes that all children are children of our Heavenly Father and he treats them that way," she said. "He does this, I believe, because he is striving to be like our Savior Jesus Christ. I know he has great love for Him and for His gospel and for all mankind."[331]

Hatch once explained how he saw the relationship between religion and politics. "Every issue in government to me involves morality," he said in 1980. "Every issue involves folkways and mores; every issue involves religious belief and non-religious belief. There is no such thing as a purely political issue that doesn't involve alternative beliefs of various people." He ended on a note of humility: "I'm willing to admit that I may be wrong in some of my approaches, but I don't believe so or I wouldn't fight as hard as I do for them. But if I can be shown that I am wrong, I will admit that I am wrong in public and go on from there. I think good representatives should do that. We can't be right in everything."[332]

Hatch's own faith, The Church of Jesus Christ of Latter-day Saints, had been subjected to prejudice, discrimination, and periodic mob violence. In 1906, a US Senate committee recommended that a Republican US senator from Utah, Reed Smoot, a Latter-day Saint who was elected to office in 1903, be declared ineligible to serve amid false allegations that members of the church took a secret loyalty oath to the church over the nation and that they still practiced polygamy in secret, despite its renunciation by the church in 1890. On February 20, 1907, Reed Smoot's ordeal, which he endured with dignity, finally ended when a vote by the full Senate to expel him failed. He served until 1933, a full thirty years in office. It was, in effect, a trial of his church, and in the words of the Senate historian's office, "The U.S. Senate took a stand in support of religious freedom for all Americans."[333]

Hatch also enjoyed an intense bond with the Jewish faith, which translated into his becoming one of Israel's biggest supporters in Congress and serving on the governing board of the US Holocaust

Memorial Museum. Behind the scenes, he worked hard to assist Jews who were endangered in the old Soviet Union and those who wanted to immigrate to Israel. "Anything I can do for the Jewish people, I will do," Hatch once said.[334] "I feel sorry I'm not Jewish sometimes."[335] He wore a golden mezuzah prayer scroll necklace every day, adorned the doorways of his homes in Washington and Utah with mezuzahs, kept a replica of a Torah in his Senate office, and once wrote a hip-hop Hanukkah song.[336] In 2018, the Jewish *Forward* publication thanked Hatch "for four exemplary decades as a friend of Israel, a symbol of bipartisanship, and a true American *Mensch* (person of integrity and honor)."[337]

In a 2020 interview, Israeli prime minister Benjamin Netanyahu reported, "I have always admired Senator Hatch's love of the Jewish people and the depth of his commitment to Israel's security and well-being. In March 2015, I spoke before a joint meeting of Congress about the threat posed by a nuclear Iran to Israel, to the Middle East, and to the entire world. Senator Hatch was then the president pro tempore of the Senate and sat with Speaker Boehner on the rostrum. How symbolic it was that as I brought Israel's message not only to the Congress but also to the American people, one of Israel's greatest friends would be sitting right behind me. As was true throughout his career, Senator Hatch had Israel's back. And Israel will be eternally grateful for a lifetime of his unwavering support."[338]

Through his career, Hatch would prove steadily consistent on the subject of freedom to worship. In 2010, when a private organization announced plans to build an Islamic center and mosque on private property near Ground Zero in downtown Manhattan, drawing protests from many Republican leaders and others, Hatch defended the group's right to do so. "The only question is are they being insensitive to those who suffered the loss of loved ones?" Hatch asked. "We know there are Muslims killed on 9-11 and we know it's a great religion." Hatch said that even if public opinion was against building the Mosque, "that should not make a difference if they decided to build it and I'd be the first to stand up for their rights."[339]

Religious freedom as expressed in the First Amendment was a concept strongly endorsed by virtually every American president and politician since the nation's founding, and it was repeatedly upheld by the nation's courts. When Alfred Leo Smith's case was finally ruled on by the US Supreme Court, he had every reason to expect that the Oregon courts' rulings in his favor would be upheld. In its 1963 *Sherbert v. Verner* decision, the US Supreme Court had established a legal test for courts to follow when considering unemployment compensation claim denials that might be affected by the First Amendment's religious Free Exercise Clause: the government must prove it is acting to further a "compelling state interest" in the manner least restrictive, or least burdensome, to religion. This did not appear to apply in the Smith case.

But in a surprise decision on April 17, 1990, the Supreme Court stunned legal observers and managed to shock and alarm Orrin Hatch as well as liberals, conservatives, the religious community, and civil liberties advocates. In the case of *Employment Division, Department of Human Resources of Oregon v. Smith*, a majority of the justices held in favor of the state of Oregon's denial of unemployment claims for Smith and his colleague.

By declaring that the free exercise of religion did not protect minority religions from "neutral, generally applicable laws," the court effectively abandoned the *Sherbert* test and rewrote the prevailing interpretation of the First Amendment. "They contend that their religious motivation for using peyote places them beyond the reach of a criminal law that is not specifically directed at their religious practice," wrote Justice Antonin Scalia, but the "free exercise of religion" did not shield minority religions from "neutral, generally applicable laws"—even if those laws were developed by an indifferent or ignorant majority. In other words, the court held that the Free Exercise Clause protects religious beliefs but does not exempt religious actions from laws unless the laws specifically target a religion for unfavorable treatment. The "compelling state interest" test no longer applied.[340]

Al Smith was especially dismayed by the ruling, saying, "I think it was a horrendous decision, like they drove a spike through the Bill of Rights. If the First Amendment doesn't protect me, how in the hell is it going to protect you?"

Both religious leaders and civil liberties advocates alike realized that the *Smith* decision could be applied widely to threaten all religious-freedom claims. A powerful, unlikely cross-ideological coalition quickly mobilized to seek a solution in the US Congress. The coalition included politicians, scholars, religious organizations, civil rights groups, the American Civil Liberties Union, the conservative Traditional Values Coalition, and organizations like the Christian Legal Society, the Baptist Joint Committee for Religious Liberty, the American Jewish Congress, and the National Association of Evangelicals. Their fears were well-founded: in the two years after *Smith*, a Congressional Research Service analysis reported federal and state court decisions were being made that limited all kinds of religious exercise claims. Within months of the Supreme Court's *Smith* decision, congressional Democrats introduced legislation to counteract it.

In the Senate, both Orrin Hatch and Ted Kennedy decided that the *Smith* ruling posed a danger to religious liberty. "The compelling interest test has been the legal standard protecting the free exercise of religion for nearly 30 years," Kennedy later said. "Yet, in one fell swoop the Supreme Court overruled that test and declared that no special constitutional protection is available for religious liberty as long as the Federal, State, or local law in question is neutral on its face as to religion and is a law of general application."[341]

Hatch and Kennedy worked together to develop legislation that would effectively negate the *Smith* decision, restore the *Sherbert* test, and strengthen protection for the free exercise of religion. The Hatch-Kennedy bill matched a bill introduced in the House of

Representatives by then Democratic representative from New York Charles "Chuck" Schumer. It was a brief 797-word law called the Religious Freedom Restoration Act of 1993 (commonly referred to as RFRA, or "rifra") that declared, "Laws 'neutral' toward religion may burden religious exercise as surely as laws intended to interfere with religious exercise," and "Governments should not substantially burden religious exercise without compelling justification," and the "compelling interest" test should be restored.

The legislation quickly attracted support from a wide range of groups on the political left and political right. "When the American Civil Liberties Union and the (conservative) coalitions for America see eye-to-eye on a major piece of legislation," noted Hatch, "I think it is certainly safe to say that someone has seen the light."[342] Hatch fought hard for the bill alongside Kennedy and defended it against protests from antiabortion activists who feared that it would allow women to claim a religious right to abortion and state authorities who worried that prison inmates would demand luxury treatment because some invented religion required it. But Hatch insisted that if exemptions were allowed, the bill would fall apart. In 2013, he recalled that "Republicans and Democrats were united on one fundamental principle, that the right of all Americans to the free exercise of their religion should be equally protected by the same rigorous legal standard. We refused to give an advantage to some religious claims or to prevent others from being considered."[343]

On the Senate floor, Hatch argued for swift passage of the bill in its unadulterated form: "This bill involves the rights of every American citizen. The *Smith* case was wrongly decided and the only way to change it is with this legislation. Mr. President, I hope this legislation is not amended in any way, because religious freedom ought to be encouraged in this country. It is the first freedom mentioned in the Bill of Rights. And, frankly, that is what Senator Kennedy and I are arguing for here today with a wide, vast coalition across the country that believes in restoring religious freedom to the point where it was before the Supreme Court decision in *Smith*."

As was the case in many such bipartisan bills, Hatch's support gave nervous or wavering Republicans the political "cover" to back it. The bill was approved by a unanimous voice vote in the House and a 97 to 3 vote in the Senate, and President Clinton signed it into law in a White House Rose Garden ceremony on November 16, 1993, with Hatch and other members of Congress standing behind him. Clinton said, "What [RFRA] basically says is that the Government should be held to a very high level of proof before it interferes with someone's free exercise of religion."[344]

In 1997, the Supreme Court ruled that RFRA applied only to federal—not state or local—laws, and Hatch responded by spearheading congressional passage of the Religious Land Use and Institutionalized Persons Act (RLUIPA). The law protected all religions' right to build church facilities on private property, and it was signed into law by President Bill Clinton in September 2000. Additionally, twenty-two states have passed RFRA-like laws of their own, and state courts in an additional ten states have strengthened religious liberty protections.

Over the past thirty years, the RFRA and RLUIPA laws championed by Orrin Hatch have proved to be durable, vital instruments for protecting the free exercise of religion in the United States and have been successfully invoked by religious minorities including Orthodox Jews, Muslims, Sikhs, and Native Americans. Through the laws, a Sikh accountant was permitted to pass through security at a federal building while possessing a religious kirpan, a small dull dagger that is a symbol to Sikhs like the cross is to Christians. A group of Native Americans obtained an exemption from federal law to possess eagle feathers in spiritual ceremonies. Observant Sikhs were enabled to serve in the US military with their religious beards and turbans. A group of Buddhists overcame a zoning challenge to residential gatherings for silent meditation, and a Presbyterian church in Washington, DC, overcame a zoning challenge to its program of feeding thousands of homeless citizens, enabling it to continue.[345]

As a student at Brigham Young University, circa 1958. The values Hatch learned from his faith in The Church of Jesus Christ of Latter-day Saints greatly informed his political career. *(Courtesy of the Office of Orrin G. Hatch)*

Hatch was anointed as a superstar in the making by the conservative Sun King himself, Ronald Reagan, who backed Hatch's stunning come-from-nowhere triumph to capture a US Senate seat in 1976. Hatch described Reagan as "an older brother who was always there for me." *(Mark Philbrick, Brigham Young University)*

Erma Byrd, her husband, Senator Robert Byrd, Democrat of West Virginia, and Hatch in 1987, nine years after the two men clashed in an epic showdown on the Senate floor over labor law reform, an issue that Hatch believed could kill the Republican Party. *(Courtesy of the Office of Orrin G. Hatch)*

President Ronald Reagan signs bipartisan compromise Voting Rights Act renewal legislation with Senator Bob Dole, Representative Bob Michel, Howard Baker, Vice President George Bush, and Senators Charles Mathias and Joseph Biden in the White House East Room, June 29, 1982. *(Ronald Reagan Presidential Library)*

Hatch and President Reagan at the Rose Garden signing ceremony on September 24, 1984, for the Drug Price Competition and Patent Term Restoration Act of 1984. Hatch's co-champion of the bill, which came to be known as the Hatch-Waxman Act, was Democratic representative from California Henry Waxman, second from right. The bill created the modern generic drug industry and continues to save consumers many billions of dollars to this day. *(Ronald Reagan Presidential Library)*

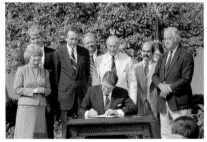

The Hatch family in 1985. Back row: Mia Hatch, John Catron, Kim Hatch Catron, Senator Orrin G. Hatch, Jess Hatch, Randy Whetton, Scott Hatch, Wendy Hatch. Front row: Stephanie Hatch, Brent Hatch, Tierney Hatch, Elaine Hatch (Senator Hatch's wife), Christopher Whetton, Marcia Hatch Whetton, Alysa Hatch. *(Courtesy of the Hatch Family.)*

Greeting Queen Elizabeth II on May 17, 1991, the day she became the first British monarch to address a joint session of the US Congress. In her speech, she noted, "Our societies rest on mutual agreement, on contract, and on consensus," a fitting description of Hatch's legislative philosophy. *(Courtesy of the Office of Orrin G. Hatch)*

To reshape the world: Senator Hatch and Democratic US representative Steny Hoyer, left, with jubilant disability advocates in the Capitol building on July 13, 1990, moments after Congress passed the Americans with Disabilities Act, the greatest civil rights legislation since the 1960s and a great turning point in the lives of the disabled. The man in the hat is Justin Dart Jr., sometimes referred to as the Martin Luther King Jr. of the disability civil rights movement. Hatch worked passionately to repeatedly rescue and eventually pass the ADA on behalf of 43,000,000 disabled Americans. "If it wasn't for Senator Hatch," said disability rights leader Pat Wright in 2020, "we would still be fighting the ADA and there probably wouldn't be final passage of the ADA." The act inspired similar measures by 157 nations. *(John Duricka, AP)*

Ryan White, the young activist who inspired Hatch and Kennedy to name their landmark HIV/AIDS legislation after him. In 2021, former Kennedy aide Michael Iskowitz said of Hatch, "The Ryan White Act would never have happened without him. There's no doubt about that. As someone who has worked on AIDS for over thirty years, there is no doubt in my mind that the US response to AIDS would have been significantly more delayed if it wouldn't have been for Hatch. Especially in the early days when the response to AIDS was so stuck in fear that without Orrin Hatch, the US response to AIDS would have waited a lot longer had it not been for someone like him who was willing to put partisanship aside and do something big and important for the country." He concluded, "We will be forever indebted to him for that—forever." *(Bettmann/Getty)*

Hatch with Elder M. Russell Ballard, Quorum of the Twelve Apostles of The Church of Jesus Christ of Latter-day Saints, at the White House on November 1993 for President Bill Clinton's signing of the Religious Freedom Restoration Act into law. *(Courtesy of the Office of Orrin G. Hatch)*

Israeli prime minister Benjamin Netanyahu said in a 2020 interview for this book, "I have always admired Senator Hatch's love of the Jewish people and the depth of his commitment to Israel's security and well-being. In March 2015, I spoke before a joint meeting of Congress about the threat posed by a nuclear Iran to Israel, to the Middle East, and to the entire word. Senator Hatch was then the president pro tempore of the Senate and sat with Speaker Boehner on the rostrum. How symbolic it was that as I brought Israel's message not only to the Congress but also to the American people, one of Israel's greatest friends would be sitting right behind me. As was true throughout his career, Senator Hatch had Israel's back. And Israel will be eternally grateful for a lifetime of his unwavering support." *(Caleb Smith, Office of Speaker John Boehner)*

President Barack Obama meets with Hatch in the Oval Office, May 5, 2010. Hatch opposed Obamacare and Obama's nomination of Merrick Garland to the Supreme Court, but he also helped forge major achievements with the young president. "I had what was arguably my most productive Congress during President Obama's final two years in office," Hatch recalled. "While things may have appeared acrimonious on cable news, Democrats and Republicans worked late nights and weekends to secure a number of substantive bipartisan victories, from historic trade legislation to a comprehensive legislative package to address our nation's opioid crisis. We also found common ground on issues as diverse and varied as intellectual property, transportation infrastructure, rare diseases, and even education reform. True, tensions ran high. But from tension was born some of the most meaningful bipartisan work of the past decade." *(White House photo)*

Face of the apocalypse: on January 20, 2017, a military officer like this one appeared at Orrin Hatch's side, equipped with a "nuclear football" satchel (in his right hand) that would give Hatch the power to bring much of the world to an end. *(Leon Neal/Getty Images)*

Celebrating twenty years of the State Children's Health Insurance Program at the Utah State Capitol Building, 2017. *(Courtesy of the Office of Orrin G. Hatch)*

Hatch with Chief of Staff Matt Sandgren before a Senate Judiciary Committee meeting in 2018, his last full year in office, when the two worked to pass a striking burst of bipartisan legislation. *(Courtesy of the Office of Orrin G. Hatch)*

Meeting with his successor, Senator-elect Mitt Romney in his Utah office, 2018. *(Courtesy of the Office of Orrin G. Hatch)*

"I am honored to commend you on forty-two years of public service," President Donald Trump said when he awarded Hatch the Presidential Medal of Freedom at the White House in 2018. Trump added, "During your time in the Senate, you have been a tremendous advocate for the people of Utah, having led on countless important issues, from confirming judges who apply the law as written to passing historic tax cut legislation. You are a true American statesman, and I was pleased to award you with the Presidential Medal of Freedom. I hope you are filled with tremendous pride as you reflect on all that you have accomplished. I am truly grateful for your friendship." Hatch backed President Trump and many of his policies and congratulated his successor, Joe Biden, when he became president. *(Courtesy of the Office of Orrin G. Hatch)*

US Supreme Court associate justices Brett Kavanaugh, Neil Gorsuch, Samuel
Alito, and Ruth Bader Ginsburg congratulate Hatch at the Medal of Freedom
ceremony at the White House on November 16, 2018. Hatch championed the
nomination of Clarence Thomas to the court in 1991, a tumultuous drama that
predated the "MeToo" era by a full twenty-five years. Hatch wrote, "We who
were involved in the hearings will never be the same," and the same could be
said of the nation. "If any good came out of the needlessly tortured and vicious
confirmation," wrote Hatch in a fitting epitaph for the events, "it was that the
nation was forced to confront the reality, too often ignored or discounted, of
sexual harassment in the workplace." Hatch went on to play a key role in every
Supreme Court appointment confirmation that followed, a process that became
increasingly, and bitterly, partisan. Hatch championed the appointment of conservative justices to federal posts, but he also shepherded President Clinton's
nominations of Stephen Breyer and Ruth Bader Ginsburg to the Supreme Court.
"During my confirmation hearings," wrote Ginsburg, "perhaps my biggest supporter was Orrin Hatch." *(Courtesy of the Office of Orrin G. Hatch)*

Hatch with then Vice President Joe Biden, his longtime colleague in the US Senate. After the 2020 election, Hatch congratulated Biden and Vice President Kamala Harris, saying, "Having had the opportunity to serve with both of them in the Senate, I saw up close the love they have for our country and the American people." He added, "I am confident that the president will serve our nation now just as he has served it over more many decades in elected office—with drive, dedication, and a heart full of optimism. His success will be America's success, which is why I wish him the very best." *(Courtesy of the Office of Orrin G. Hatch)*

The strangest of bedfellows: when they weren't battling with each other (which was very often), Hatch and Massachusetts Democratic senator Edward M. "Ted" Kennedy forged one of the most consequential bipartisan partnerships in US Senate history. Their work helped create four monumental achievements for the American people: the Americans with Disabilities Act, the Ryan White CARE Act for HIV/AIDS relief, the State Children's Health Insurance Program, which provided coverage for millions of lower-income children, and the Religious Freedom Restoration Act. This 2008 Capitol Hill photo captures their farewell meeting before Kennedy's death from brain cancer, when the two lions of the Senate talked at length about their memories of decades of working with each other as battling brothers in arms. *(Courtesy of the Office of Orrin G. Hatch)*

With author William Doyle in Salt Lake City, Utah, February 2020. *(Author's collection)*

In recent years, the philosophy advanced by RFRA has come into conflict with the views of LGBTQI+ advocates, who object to protections that enable, for example, religiously affiliated organizations or companies to deny medical coverage for birth control or abortion or deny service to gay customers. Recent Supreme Court decisions in the *Burwell v. Hobby Lobby Stores* (2014) and *Masterpiece Cakeshop, Ltd. v. Colorado Civil Rights Commission* (2017) cases have sharpened this tension and led Democrats to propose legislative exceptions to the RFRA framework. Hatch strongly opposed any revisions to the original law he authored with Senator Kennedy in 1993, asserting, "The day we begin carving out exceptions to RFRA is the day RFRA dies."[346]

In 2018, Hatch said if he had to pick "one bill that I love more than anything else," it would be the Religious Freedom Restoration Act. "We could not pass that today," he said. "That has protected religious freedom like never before. It's something you would think you wouldn't have to protect, but believe me, you have to protect it."[347]

✳   ✳   ✳

In 1997, Hatch met with two families from Provo, Utah, and experienced what he once called one of the defining moments of his career as a senator.

"The parents in these families were humble and hardworking, they were prudent, they were frugal," Hatch explained. "And they were able to provide food and shelter for their children, but the one necessity they couldn't afford was health insurance."[348] Hatch was troubled that these children and over thirty thousand other children of the working poor in Utah could not access the nation's healthcare system. Their families earned too much to qualify for public assistance and too little to afford health insurance. There were more than seven million children like them across the United States.

Hatch had long been interested in issues affecting children, having stood up for the Head Start Program in Utah and cosponsored the Act for Better Child Care Services of 1989 with liberal senator

Christopher Dodd from Connecticut, which was passed by the Senate but then indefinitely postponed. In that effort Hatch was opposed by nearly the entire Republican Party, which led him to lament on the Senate floor, "I have been personally likened to Karl Marx, Benedict Arnold, and even Brutus."[349]

Hatch realized that the only way to help the children of the working poor without health insurance was with a bipartisan solution. His own Republican Party controlled both the House and the Senate, but he figured many Republicans would never support a major new federal entitlement program. Democrats had no interest in supporting a Republican plan anyway, he thought, because it would deny them a political victory.

To Hatch's amazement, Senator Kennedy was focusing on the same issue, three years after the collapse of "Hillarycare," the Clinton administration's proposed overhaul of the American healthcare system. "He had introduced legislation in the past to address the issue, but it was so expensive and unwieldy that it fell under its own weight. Ted came to me and asked whether I was interested in working with him,"[350] Hatch said.

The two men then, in Hatch's words, "negotiated, fought, and screamed at each other, and our staffs had numerous battles as we tried to fashion an approach we could both live with."[351] At one tough point in the negotiations, Kennedy dispatched his chief of staff, Nick Littlefield, to serenade Hatch with "Freedom's Light,"[352] a patriotic song written by Hatch.

The result was an ingenious piece of legislative engineering the two men introduced in March 1997 that came to be known as the State Children's Health Insurance Program (SCHIP). The final version of the bill hiked the federal excise tax on cigarettes by 43 cents a pack, to raise $10 billion over five years to reduce the federal deficit and over $20 billion for children's health insurance to be distributed not through a new federal bureaucracy, but through block grants to the states. Hatch and Kennedy shaped it so it could not be considered an entitlement, which reduced potential Republican opposition, and they cleverly attached the proposal to an emerging agreement between Republicans, Democrats, and the Clinton White House to reduce the deficit.

The two senators unveiled their plan at a press conference at the Children's Defense Fund in Washington, DC. It was the biggest expansion of the nation's social safety net since the launch of Medicaid in 1965. Hatch explained that he proposed the bill to demonstrate that the Republican Party "does not hate children," and he added that "as a nation, as a society, we have a moral responsibility" to provide coverage for vulnerable children. "Children are being terribly hurt and perhaps scarred for the rest of their lives" when they don't have health insurance, he noted.[353]

For the next 144 days, Hatch and Kennedy fought together to bring the bill to a vote. At first, Hatch remembered, "Our bill upset everyone."[354] It faced opposition from conservative critics, tobacco companies, and their congressional allies—and especially from Republicans. Republican Senate majority leader Trent Lott of Mississippi immediately condemned the bill, saying, "A Kennedy big-government program is not going to be enacted,"[355] without mentioning Hatch. According to Hatch, when he told Lott the bill would pass, Lott replied, "No, it isn't." Hatch's fellow Republican senator from Utah, Robert F. Bennett, first promised his support, then publicly backed off. At this, Hatch declared, "I am disappointed, but I accept whatever my colleague wants to do. As for me, I am going to fight my guts out for these kids."[356]

"There may not be two more relentless legislative advocates than the Utah Mormon and the Massachusetts Democrat," wrote the *Wall Street Journal*'s Al Hunt. The bill, Hunt reported, "is driving Mr. Lott and Oklahoma Sen. Don Nickles, the Senate GOP whip, crazy. They demagogue it as big government and tax-and-spend, misrepresenting what it would do. And they are strongarming every Republican in sight to oppose it."[357]

Children's health advocates rejoiced at news of congressional approval of the Hatch-Kennedy State Children's Health Insurance

Program (SCHIP), which was incorporated into the Balanced Budget Act of 1997 and signed into law by President Bill Clinton on August 5, 1997. Marian Wright Edelman, the civil rights giant and founder of the Children's Defense Fund, wrote to Hatch, "Yet again you have proven that deep commitment and hard work will prevail at the end of the day! Without you, there would be no children's health initiative of 1997." She marveled, "At every turning point you were there to keep the issue alive. Against all odds, you succeeded."[358] Days after the bill's passage, a *New York Times* headline announced, "Through Senate Alchemy, Tobacco Is Turned into Gold for Children's Health."[359]

According to an account in Hatch's hometown publication the *Deseret News*, "Delegates to the 1998 Utah GOP Convention actually passed a resolution condemning Hatch's children's health insurance program. In a show of defiance, Hatch took the stage and lectured the 5,000 hard-core GOP delegates on the responsibility of man helping fellow man."[360]

The SCHIP program created by Hatch and Kennedy went on to serve many millions of American families and earn near-universal praise from politicians in both parties and from state governors across the country. In 2018, as one of Orrin Hatch's final acts in Congress, he helped secure full funding to continue the program for another ten years.

In 2008, Ted Kennedy was diagnosed with brain cancer. One day, Hatch's chief of staff, Jace Johnson, got a call from his counterpart on Kennedy's staff, who said, "Listen, Ted's getting to the point where he's probably not going to be able to be in the Senate much longer. We have him in a really convenient office over in the Capitol off of the Senate floor. Could the Senator come by and meet with him?"

Johnson related what happened next: "And so, Senator Hatch and I went over there, and I sat down as the two of them, and Ted Kennedy's two dogs that were with him, sat down with him and sat by the fireplace and [they] just talked about this long career that they had shared in the Senate. And it was incredible how much they remembered about all the things that they had worked on together. Children's health insurance, labor laws, they could just go through the list of all these areas where they had partnered, religious freedom, they knew all the bills and all the laws that they had done together and how they had kind of fought these wars in their mind and did it for the good of the country. I love that moment. And at the end, they stood up and I took a picture of the two of them that I still have today, and, tearfully, tearfully, you know, [we] walked out. They were joking about some of the songs that Senator Hatch had written for Vicky and Ted, and it was just a great moment. It was well over an hour in there and the two of them just talking. They really cared about each other."[361]

Hatch offered a tribute to Kennedy at his memorial service at the John F. Kennedy Presidential Library and Museum on August 29, 2009. He called Kennedy "one of my closest friends in the world," and added, "Like all good leaders, when he struck out on a mission, he was able to inspire many to follow him until the job was done, no matter how long it took or how hard the task was." It was a skill that could also be ascribed to Orrin Hatch.

Hatch concluded by telling Kennedy's widow and his assembled family and friends, "I miss fighting in public, and joking with him in the back room. I miss all the things I knew we could do together."

CHAPTER 8

The Once and Future Golden Age of Bipartisanship

O RRIN HATCH'S SUCCESS in the 1980s and 1990s in spearheading the passage of historic legislation on generic drugs, orphan drugs, AIDS funding, disability rights, religious freedom, children's health insurance, and a range of other vital issues can be seen as high-water marks in a Golden Age of Bipartisanship that appeared at certain times when the stars aligned in the political firmament.

Then, the conventional narrative reports, at some point in the 1990s and 2000s, the Senate and the culture underwent a radical change, and bipartisanship died, never to be reborn. Politics became a game of scorched-earth, total war. Political opponents became demonic enemies. In the 2010s, Hatch himself often lamented the breakdown of civility in American politics and in the Senate, which he said had never been so bad in his experience.

"The Senate is more dysfunctional today than at any other

point during my nearly four decades as a Member of this body," Hatch declared on the Senate floor on July 22, 2014. "It would be hard to find a current Member of this body who, in moments of honest reflection, did not feel as if the Senate is in many respects broken. Most importantly, the American public has lost faith in this body and largely views the Senate as an institution characterized by dysfunction. To say that today Congress is held in low esteem is an understatement. Our approval rating ranges from the teens to the single digits. One survey found that the public has a higher opinion of brussel sprouts, root canals, and used car salesmen than of Congress. In many respects, this popular assessment is justified. Throughout my thirty-eight years of service in this body, I have never seen it this bad. To my colleagues who as a matter of firsthand experience don't know anything different, let me say this: The Senate has not always been as dysfunctional as it is today. Quite the opposite. Until recently, this Chamber often lived up to its reputation as the world's greatest deliberative body. We regularly worked together in an orderly and constructive fashion to advance the common good, and we routinely defended our institutional prerogatives against executive encroachment. Unfortunately, none of that is true of the Senate today."

Perhaps, or so goes the narrative, the death of bipartisanship was triggered by the arrival of a record number of new senators from the more combative House of Representatives in the 1990s, or by the fierce maneuvering by both parties over filibusters that erupted in the 2000s. Or it could have been the appearance of tidal waves of dark money and social media that perverted and polarized political opinions to the extremes, inflamed emotions, and fanned conspiracy theories.

Perhaps, some think, the death of bipartisanship resulted from the passing from the scene of a giant like Ted Kennedy, who had the power to push the Democratic and liberal centers of gravity toward the center on bipartisan initiatives. Orrin Hatch has speculated that if Kennedy had been alive, he could have helped hammer out a bipartisan alternative to the 2010 Affordable Care Act, or "Obamacare," which Hatch wound up bitterly opposing as putting the nation "on a fast-track to socialism."

Maybe the breakdown in bipartisanship occurred with the arrival of cheap air travel, which enabled senators to return to their home states more often on weekends and holidays, thus losing opportunities to bond socially with their peers from the other party, which rarely happens anymore. Perhaps, some think, it resulted from leadership failures of Bill Clinton, or George W. Bush, or Barack Obama, or Donald Trump, or Joe Biden. Or perhaps it was the fault of hardfighting party leaders like House Speaker Newt Gingrich, Senate Democratic leader Harry Reid, or Senate Republican leader Mitch McConnell, and the erosion of the Senate's traditional "regular order" process of amendments and committee hearings by multiple senators, and its replacement by bills written by diktat in the leaders' offices. Maybe it was the sudden collapse of America's political culture into hatred, division, and demagoguery inflamed by cable news networks—a culture that could never sustain a new player with a character, personality, and pragmatism like that of Orrin Hatch.

Some or all of this may be true. But the conventional narrative misses a central point of American politics: beyond the headlines, the cable news clips, and the online shouting matches—and often underreported by the media—the work of government continues in the corridors of the nation's Capitol, and it often happens with quiet compromise, consultation, and accommodation between Republicans and Democrats.

Orrin Hatch's final years in the Senate are a case in point. He continued to be a passionate conservative crusader on many fronts, especially when it came to Supreme Court and federal judiciary appointments. But for him, bipartisanship never died—it was a vital part of his daily work routine.

In 2003, as a senior member of the Senate Finance Committee, Hatch helped negotiate the Medicare Prescription Drug, Improvement, and Modernization Act, the biggest revision of Medicare since its inception. As Judiciary Committee chairman, he authored the PROTECT Act, which simplified prosecution against pedophiles and child pornographers. The following year, Hatch played a key role in passing the Justice for All Act of 2004, which provided much-needed funding and assistance to realize the full potential of DNA technology in solving crimes and protecting the innocent and was a critical step toward eliminating the nationwide backlog of rape cases.

In 2005, Hatch helped to create a comprehensive energy bill and a National Cord Blood Stem Cell Bank Network to prepare, store, and distribute human umbilical cord blood stem cells for the treatment of patients and to support peer-reviewed research using such cells. In 2006, Hatch's sex offender registry bill was signed into law as the Adam Walsh Child Protection and Safety Act, which increased penalties for sex crimes against children and required convicted offenders to register their location or face additional jail time. In 2008, Hatch again teamed up with Ted Kennedy to reauthorize the Traumatic Brain Injury Act and pass the Serve America Act, which expanded national and community-based service opportunities for all Americans.

In the 2010s, Hatch helped pass the Biologics Price Competition and Innovation Act, the America Invents Act patent reform bill, the State Child Welfare Innovation Act provisions that were incorporated into the Child and Family Services Improvement and Innovation Act, the American Taxpayer Relief Act of 2012, the Middle Class Tax Relief and Job Creation Act of 2012, the Medical Device Access and Innovation Protection Act, and the Defend Trade Secrets Act. Working with Democratic senator Amy Klobuchar, Hatch strongly backed the STOP School Violence Act of 2018, which authorized grant award programs to strengthen school safety and was passed into law as part of the Consolidated Appropriations Act of 2018. In a striking display of support, the act was praised by both Sandy Hook Promise and the National Rifle Association.

In his final years on Capitol Hill, Hatch also championed legislation to provide funding to support health clinics and veterans' services, update music licensing laws for the digital age, improve the Food and Drug Administration's approval process for new drugs and medical devices, and strengthen the Trade Promotion Authority, providing major support for America's global competitiveness and economic performance. By the end of the 114th Congress, Hatch had passed more than thirty legislative proposals into law—the most of any of his colleagues and more than twice as many as the average senator. A great many of these were bipartisan achievements.

In 2018, Hatch announced that he would retire at the end of his seventh six-year term in office, and he endorsed Mitt Romney in his successful bid to succeed him as senator from Utah. As Hatch prepared to finally leave the Senate in January 2019, he was praised by luminaries from across the political spectrum. President Jimmy Carter, the first of seven presidents under whom Hatch served, told the senator, "Your legacy reflects your passion for your constituents, your humble respect for the institution, and a true love of our great country," adding, "America is stronger because of your life's work."[362]

Two days before George H. W. Bush died on November 30, 2018, the former president wrote to Hatch, "You have been a wonderful friend and supporter over the years. More importantly, you've been an exemplary public servant and patriot. The entire country is grateful for your service. As chair and member of the Judiciary Committee, you were instrumental in shepherding hundreds of judges through the Senate. Your commitment to the Constitution and the rule of law is a legacy that will help govern our democracy for decades to come."[363] The following month, former president Bill Clinton wrote to Hatch, "I will always appreciate the opportunity to have worked with you while I was president, especially on the creation of the Children's Health Insurance Program."[364]

On December 12, 2018, a long line of senators assembled in the

Senate chamber to pay tribute to Hatch. Democratic senator Ron Wyden of Oregon, Hatch's colleague on the Senate Finance Committee, said, "If you had told this body or this country in the winter of 2017 that you would pass in this Congress a bipartisan ten-year reauthorization of the Children's Health Insurance Plan, you would be charged with hallucinating. People would say no way, it couldn't possibly happen. If you had said in the winter of 2017 that you were going to pass a major set of reforms on foster care, reforms that Marian Wright Edelman of the Children's Defense Fund has been dreaming about for decades, they would simply have said impossible, it couldn't possibly happen, you're hallucinating. If you had said, and colleagues listen to this, if you had said in the winter of 2017 that you were going to start a transformation of Medicare, with over fifty million seniors, a transformation from a program that traditionally used to be about acute illness and now is largely about chronic illness, cancer, diabetes, heart disease, and strokes; if you told people in 2017 that you were going to transform Medicare to update the Medicare guarantee to help seniors, once again they would have said impossible. Colleagues, that's happened in this Congress, because Chairman Hatch was willing to reach across the aisle."

In his floor tribute, Senate majority leader Mitch McConnell explained of Hatch, "He's led the charge often and hasn't flinched from the big battles. But at the very same time, there was Orrin, constantly working quietly behind the scenes and across the aisle to tick off victories for vulnerable Americans who could easily have been left behind. One perfect illustration of this was Orrin's friendship with the late Ted Kennedy. For many of the years they spent here in the Senate, it seemed like they managed to rank among each other's closer friends, top collaborators, and most persistent sparring partners all at the same time." McConnell added, "You can't help but respect Orrin. Because his own respect—for this institution, and for the dignity of every individual he meets—is so evident. Orrin has been so generous to his colleagues, to this institution, to the state and the nation he's served. He has given us so much."

In 2021, Barbara Mikulski, a Democrat from Maryland who served in the House of Representatives from 1977 to 1987 and the Senate from 1987 to 2017, recalled, "Senator Hatch and I have a couple of things in common. He is the longest serving Republican senator and the awardee of the Medal of Freedom. I am the longest-serving woman in congressional history and I also am a Medal of Freedom awardee. We served on the Health, Education and Labor committee. He was a man of principle. He was a very principled person in terms of his political philosophy, and in his personal philosophy, a man of Utah and a man of the Mormon faith. He was very clear about those. But he was also a very congenial person, and a very civil person, and he always treated people with the utmost respect, which led to mutual trust and dignity."

Mikulski remembered after-work encounters together with Hatch and Senator Ted Kennedy that were so convivial they seemed from a different era than today's Washington, DC, when senators from opposing parties rarely socialize. Kennedy held periodic dinners at his house, when groups of senators would assemble without their staff members for good food, some wine, and good conversation about issues pending before Congress. As the evenings wore on, if the conversations got too intense, Kennedy would exclaim, "Hey, Orrin, let's have a song!" which was the signal for senators to gather around the piano.

"I get kind of choked up about it," remembered Mikulski, "because I think about an era when we actually did things like this. We would gather around the piano, Senator Hatch would play, and Teddy Kennedy would always want to sing an Irish ballad. We would politely humor him that thank God it was never a career choice on his part. Senator Hatch would always have a new cowboy ditty that he had written. We would have a couple of songs, and a lot of good laughs and teasing each other. When Orrin finished playing, the dinner was over. On the way out, we would talk about things we could do together and have our staffs follow up on. It was an atmosphere of conviviality that led to collegiality, that led to actually strategically working through things and getting things done."[365]

Michael Iskowitz, former HIV-AIDS policy adviser to Senator Kennedy, saw the partnership between Hatch and Kennedy in similarly historic terms. "The relationship between them was a beautiful thing to see," he marveled. "The reason they are one and two on the [most effective senators] list is they both had a solid commitment to doing things for the greater good, and they both understood that relationships are a part of how you get there, in particular in the Senate. They had deep, deep, deep affection for each other. They were in many ways like brothers. They fought a lot and they loved on each other a lot. They had this dance where sometimes there was just no way to find agreement and they would be pretty much at each other's throats. My favorite time was about forty-eight hours after they'd had a huge blowup, which would be the most fertile ground for something good that they could come together on. I always looked for those moments, because they both had a deep desire to find their way back to working together and being together and being on the same side. They were always both quite anxious to find a way back there. They both realized that if they could find those areas of common ground and use that as a basis to build trust, that upon that trust they could go out of their comfort zone and reach for some big things together." And in terms of impact, on issues like HIV-AIDS, disability rights, and children's health, the Kennedy-Hatch partnership had few parallels in modern congressional history.[366]

Gordon Smith, an Oregon Republican senator from 1997 to 2009, saw his shared faith in The Church of Jesus Christ of Latter-day Saints as a key to understanding Hatch. "I think he had a genuinely Christian heart," Smith said. "He loved God and he loved his neighbors. And that enabled him to see others who had differences of opinion with him in very noble terms. I think that's at the center of who Orrin Hatch was. That breaks down a lot of political walls that otherwise separate Americans. He saw his opponents as equal to himself, believing that we are all the offspring of heavenly parentage. When you see others as a brother or a sister, regardless of race or ethnicity or national origin or sexual orientation, that enables you then to treat them with respect and give them the dignity that should be accorded to all of divine heritage."[367]

According to Scott Anderson, a Utah business leader and long-time friend to Hatch, "His secret was that he was conservative but he was not blinded by ideology to new ideas. He always stayed true to his conservative anchors, but he knew how to move forward almost in spite of them, and how to compromise without surrendering. I think that's really what made him great. He has been a champion for doing what's right. He listens to his opponents and reaches out to them. Above all, he's an American. He loves the country and he loves the people. When you look at his legislation as a total portfolio, I've come to realize that he was trying to make life better for all Americans. He was guided by two principles that really were his bedrock. One was that all Americans should have a truly equal opportunity to prosper. The second principle is that economic inclusion is essential to creating these opportunities. So you have his push for education, for health care, for religious freedom, for tax cuts, for drug competition. He saw us as being united in our differences instead of being pulled apart by them, where we could disagree and still be friends. And he could reach across the aisle and compromise without feeling that he had surrendered. He believed in the idea of pluralism, where you can come together and be united and benefit from your differences, and celebrate your differences while addressing issues that are important. He was passionate about this, and determined to make a difference. He brought America together."[368]

In the words of Susan Collins, the Republican senator from Maine since 1997, "Orrin was an outstanding legislator because he always would try to get a result. He was not interested in scoring partisan political points and instead he often worked across the aisle, such as his famous friendship with Ted Kennedy. He wanted to get things done. He wanted accomplishments. He was always very kind and nice to everybody whether it was an elevator operator or a Senate colleague. He was brilliant in the range of his knowledge about issues. Many senators know a great deal about one particular issue or topic. But Orrin was encyclopedic in his knowledge of so many different areas, whether it was health care, education, criminal justice, defense, scientific research, or tax reform. He influenced public policy on an extraordinarily broad range of issues where he could add to the debate or lead the legislative effort. I think history will judge Orrin very kindly. His collaboration with Ted Kennedy, which produced the Children's Health Insurance Program, was one of his greatest accomplishments. Orrin really set the example for those of us who believe that bipartisanship produces better legislation and it is the way to get things done. I think the Senate is a lesser place without Orrin in it because he was someone who could reach across the aisle while staying very true to his principles. He recognized that collegiality and collaboration produced compromises that in turn lead to good laws."[369]

To Martin Gold, a former Senate staffer and historian of Senate parliamentary procedure, Hatch was not an ideologue, but both a conservative and a centrist. "He was a conservative in the sense that he began from conservative positions. But he was also a centrist in the sense that he understood how to write legislation, and how to make deals. He understood that if you just stood on your own principles and insisted that everybody come to you, you weren't going to get much done. Hatch was much more of a Ronald Reagan type. Reagan would say if you go into a negotiation and you get 70 or 80 percent of what you want, consider it a victory. You're never going to get 100 percent of what you want. You can't just impose it on people. So you have to figure out where the compromise is. And a skilled legislator will have a sense of how to do that, and be trusted enough so that the other side is willing to make deals with him. That's why he was so good at it. He had a sense of the possible, he knew where he could make deals, and people trusted him personally, so that when he gave his word on something they knew they could rely on it."[370]

Frank Madsen, Hatch's former neighbor, campaign volunteer, and Senate aide, saw Hatch as a giant in his home state's history. In a 2009 oral history, Madsen recalled, "What the state of Utah doesn't realize is that he has been the most significant and powerful Senator this state has ever had by far. No one has ever achieved the presence he has achieved, no one has achieved the stature, nobody has ever come close to where he is. He is one of the most powerful men in the Senate—from little Utah, it's just amazing." Madsen described Hatch as "the most powerful and most caring Senator Utah has ever had, and the one who did more for the state of Utah than any other politician has come close to doing."[371]

Like most of us, Senator Orrin Hatch was far from perfect, and he was no stranger to mistakes and failures. He had a temper, and in the stress of political life he sometimes made snap comments that he regretted and often apologized for. In 1983, he made what he called "one of the worst decisions I have made as a senator,"[372] by voting against the creation of the Martin Luther King Jr. Day federal holiday. For decades, Hatch unsuccessfully tried to pass a balanced budget amendment to the US Constitution, which was one of his most bitter disappointments. Depending on your political persuasion, you may find much to praise or much to disagree with in Hatch's actions and positions over the decades.

But through his skill, his creativity, his faith, and his courage in forging great legislative achievements, Orrin Hatch has left us a road map for how to achieve a new Golden Age of Bipartisanship in America in the not-too-distant future. "I am not ashamed to work in a bipartisan manner on key issues," Hatch said nearly forty years ago. "Moreover, I believe working across the aisle and knitting together political coalitions to get things done is an element of leadership."[373]

It is not impossible to envision how a new and even more powerful form of the periodic Hatch-Kennedy bipartisan alliance could take shape. In a narrowly divided Senate, a small force of six to nine centrist senators from both parties could unite behind key initiatives and insist to their party leaders that bipartisanship prevail. As former Democratic senator Byron Dorgan pointed out in 2020, "It requires people to join the US Senate who say, 'You know what? Party is second. The most important thing is what do we do to put the country back on track. Political party is second place.' These days it's very hard. I think ultimately the American people will find a way to reward good behavior and punish bad behavior in the Senate, and if they figure out how to do that, I think the Senate will change."[374]

Orrin Hatch of Utah has left us a living example for how we can again some day create moments in time when Democrats and Republicans step back from the brink of political Armageddon, break out of the poisonous fog of social media, acknowledge the faults in ourselves and the nobility of our opponents, and come together as sisters and brothers to build a better world.

The United States deserves nothing less—and its survival as a nation may well depend on it.

ORRIN HATCH: FAREWELL SPEECH TO THE US SENATE

December 2, 2018

Mr. President, for more than four decades, I have had the distinct privilege of serving in the United States Senate, what some have called the world's greatest deliberative body. Speaking on the Senate floor; debating legislation in committee; corralling the support of my colleagues on compromise legislation—these are the moments I will miss. These are the memories I will cherish forever.

To address this body is to experience a singular feeling—a sense that you are a part of something bigger than yourself, a minor character in the grand narrative that is America.

No matter how often I come to speak at this lectern, I experience that feeling—again and again. But today, if I'm being honest, I also feel sadness. Indeed, my heart is heavy. It aches for the times when we actually lived up to our reputation as the world's greatest deliberative body. It longs for the days in which Democrats and Republicans would meet on middle ground rather than retreat to partisan trenches.

Now some may say I'm waxing nostalgic, yearning—as old men often do—for some golden age that never existed. They would be wrong.

The Senate I've described is not some fairy tale but the reality we once knew. Having served as a senator for nearly forty-two years, I can tell you this: things weren't always as they are now.

I was here when this body was at its best. I was here when regular order was the norm, when legislation was debated in committee, and when members worked constructively with one another for the good of the country. I was here when we could say, without any hint of irony, that we were members of the world's greatest deliberative body. Times have certainly changed.

Over the last several years, I have witnessed the subversion of Senate rules, the abandonment of regular order, and the full-scale deterioration of the judicial confirmation process. Polarization has ossified. Gridlock is the new norm. And like the humidity here, partisanship permeates everything we do.

On both the Left and the Right, the bar of decency has been set so low that jumping over it is no longer the objective. Limbo is the new name of the game. How low can you go? The answer, it seems, is always lower.

All the evidence points to an unsettling truth: The Senate, as an institution, is in crisis. The committee process lies in shambles. Regular order is a relic of the past. And compromise—once the guiding credo of this great institution—is now synonymous with surrender.

Since I first came to the Senate in 1978, the culture of this place has shifted fundamentally—and not for the better. Here, there used to be a level of congeniality and kinship among colleagues that was hard to find anywhere else. In those days, I counted Democrats among my very best friends. One moment, we would be locking horns on the Senate floor; the next, we would be breaking bread together over family dinner.

My unlikely friendship with the late senator Ted Kennedy embodied the spirit of goodwill and collegiality that used to thrive here. Teddy and I were a case study in contradictions. He was a dyed-in-the-wool Democrat; I was a resolute Republican. But by choosing friendship over party loyalty, we were able to pass some of the most significant bipartisan achievements of modern times—from the Americans with Disabilities Act and the Religious Freedom Restoration Act to the Ryan White bill and the State Children's Health Insurance Program.

Nine years after Teddy's passing, it's worth asking: Could a relationship like this even exist in today's Senate? Could two people with polar-opposite beliefs and from vastly different walks of life come together as often as Teddy and I did for the good of the country? Or are we too busy attacking each other to even consider friendship with the other side?

Mr. President, many factors contribute to the current dysfunction. But if I were to identify the root of our crisis, it would be this: the loss of comity and genuine good feeling among Senate colleagues.

Comity is the cartilage of the Senate—the soft connective tissue that cushions impact between opposing joints. But in recent years, that cartilage has been ground to a nub. All movement has become bone on bone. Our ideas grate against each other with increasing frequency—and with nothing to absorb the friction. We hobble to get any bipartisan legislation to the Senate floor, much less to the president's desk.

The pain is excruciating, and it is felt by the entire nation.

We must remember that our dysfunction is not confined to the Capitol.

It ripples far beyond these walls—to every state, to every town, and to every street corner in America.

The Senate sets the tone of American civic life. We don't mirror the political culture as much as we make it. It's incumbent on us, then, to move the culture in a positive direction, keeping in mind that everything we do here has a trickle-down effect. If we are divided, then the nation is divided. If we abandon civility, then our constituents will follow.

And so, to mend the nation, we must first mend the Senate. We must restore the culture of comity, compromise, and mutual respect that used to exist here. Both in our personal and public conduct, we must be the very change we want to see in the country. We must not be enemies but friends. Though passion may have strained, it must not break our bonds of affection. The mystic chords of memory...will yet swell...when again touched...by the better angels of our nature.

These are not my words but the words of President Abraham Lincoln.

They come from a heartfelt plea he made to the American people long ago on the eve of the Civil War. Lincoln's admonition is just as timely today as it was then. If ever there were a time in our history to heed the better angels of our nature, it is now.

How can we answer Lincoln's call to our better angels? In the last year, I have devoted significant time and energy to answering that question. Today, I wish to put flesh on the bones of Lincoln's appeal.

Our challenge is to rise above the din and divisiveness of today's politics. It is to tune out the noise and tune in to reason. It is to choose patience over impulse, and fact over feeling. It is to reacquaint ourselves with wisdom by returning to core principles.

Today, allow me to offer a prescription for what ails us politically.

Allow me to share just a few ideas that—when put into practice—can help us not only fix the Senate but put our nation back on the right path.

Heeding our better angels begins with civility. While our politics have always been contentious, an underlying commitment to civility has held together the tenuous marriage of right and left. But the steady disintegration of public discourse has weakened that marriage, calling into question the very viability of the American experiment. As the partisan divide deepens, one thing becomes increasingly clear—we cannot continue on the current course. Unless we take meaningful steps to restore civility, the culture wars will push us ever closer toward national divorce.

We would do well to remember that without civility, there is no civilization. Civility is the indispensable political norm—the protective wall between order and chaos. But more than once, that wall has been breached.

Consider recent events: the pipe bomb plot in the midterm election, the terrorist attack in Charlottesville last year, and the shooting at the congressional baseball practice before that. These are stark reminders that hateful rhetoric, if left to ferment, becomes violence.

Restoring civility requires that each of us speak responsibly. That means the president. That means Congress. And that means everyone listening today.

We live in a media environment that favors outrage over reason, and hyperbole over truth. The loudest voices—not the wisest ones—now dictate the terms of public debate. For evidence, simply turn on the TV. But be sure to turn down the volume.

The media deserves some culpability in creating this environment by adopting outrage as a business model. But we are complicit when we use words to provoke rather than to persuade, to divide rather than to unite. We only make the problem worse when the object of our discourse becomes to belittle the other side—to own the libs, for example, or to disparage the deplorables. If you're looking to convert someone to your side, humiliating them is probably not the best place to start.

Who among us would make friends with the same person who would make him a fool?

Put simply, pettiness is not a political strategy. It is the opposite of persuasion, which should be the ultimate aim of our dialogue. Our better angels call on us to persuade through gentle reason. They call on us to inspire and unite rather than to provoke and incite. In short, they call on us to embrace civility.

In addition to embracing civility, we must rediscover a forgotten virtue, one that lies at the heart of our nation's founding: pluralism. Pluralism is the adhesive that holds together the great American mosaic. It is the idea that we can actually be united by our differences, not in spite of them.

In a pluralist society, we can be polar opposites in every respect yet still associate freely with one another. I can be white, conservative, and Christian, and my friend can be Black, progressive, and Muslim. We can be different but united precisely because we are united by our right to be different. That, in a nutshell, is pluralism.

Pluralism is the alchemy that makes out of many, one possible. It is the means by which we have been able to weave together the disparate threads of a diverse society more successfully than any nation on earth. At the heart of pluralism is the understanding that our country was built not on a collection of common characteristics but on a common purpose. When we approach political problems from a pluralist perspective, we recognize that the majority of our disagreements are not matters of good vs. evil but good vs. good. Pluralism acknowledges that there is more than one way to achieve the good life. Accordingly, it seeks to accommodate different conceptions of the good rather than pit them against each other.

The adversary of pluralism is zero-sum politics, which we embrace at our own peril. Zero-sum politics tempts us to view life through an absolutist prism—one that filters all nuance and recasts everything as an either-or fallacy. This distorted way of thinking renders every policy squabble as a Manichaean struggle for the soul of the country.

If the Republican tax bill passes, it will be Armageddon. If a Democrat takes the White House, it will be the end of America as we know it. Funny how these prophecies never come to fruition.

Answering the call to our better angels requires us to reject zero-sum politics in favor of pluralism. It requires us to make room for nuance and to see our differences not as competing but as complementary.

Nowhere is the pluralist approach more needed than in the fraught relationship between religious liberty and LGBTQI+ rights.

As my colleagues know, I've made religious liberty a priority of my public service. Of all the hundreds of pieces of legislation I've passed during my forty-two years in the Senate, the one that I'm most pleased with, and the one that I hope will most define my legacy, is the Religious Freedom Restoration Act. Religious liberty is a fundamental freedom.

It deserves the very highest protection our country can provide.

At the same time, it's also important to take account of other interests, especially those of our LGBTQI+ brothers and sisters. We are in the process now of working out the relationship between religious liberty and the rights of LGBTQI+ individuals here in America. There are some who would treat this issue as a zero-sum game, who would make the religious community and LGBTQI+ advocates into adversaries. This is a mistake.

Pluralism shows us a better way. It shows us that protecting religious liberty and preserving the rights of LGBTQI+ individuals are not mutually exclusive. I believe we can find substantial common ground on these issues that will enable us to both safeguard the ability of religious individuals to live their faith and protect LGBTQI+ individuals from invidious discrimination. We must honor the rights both of believers and LGBTQI+ individuals. We must, in short, find a path forward that promotes fairness for all.

In my home state, we were able to strike such a balance with the historic Utah Compromise, a bipartisan antidiscrimination law that both strengthened religious freedoms and offered special protections to the LGBTQI+ community. No doubt we can replicate that same success on a federal level. That's why, as one of my final acts as a US senator, I challenge my colleagues to find a compromise on this crucially important issue—a compromise that is true to our founding principles and that is fair to all Americans.

Our better angels invite us to walk the path of civility and to embrace the principles of pluralism. But above all, they call on us to strive for unity. Today our house is as divided as at any time since the Civil War.

Each year, red and blue America drift further apart. As progressives move to the coasts and conservatives retreat to the interior, we increasingly sort ourselves by geography. We also sort ourselves by ideology, with media diets catered to quiet our cognitive dissonance and confirm our preconceived notions. It's a sad consequence of the information age that Americans can now live in the same city but inhabit completely different worlds.

Something has to give; the status quo cannot hold. These are, or should be, the United States of America. While that name has always been more aspirational than descriptive, it at least gives us an ideal to strive for.

To achieve the unity that is our namesake we must reject the politics of division, starting with identity politics. Identity politics is nothing more than dressed-up tribalism. It is the deliberate and often unnatural segregation of people into categories for political gain. This practice conditions us to define ourselves and each other by the groups to which we belong—in other words, the things that divide us rather than unite us.

When institutionalized, identity politics causes us to lose sight of our shared values. In time, we come to see each other not as fellow Americans united by common purpose but as opposing members of increasingly narrow social subgroups. And thus begins the long descent into intersectional hell.

Our better angels call on us to resist identity politics by recommitting ourselves to the American idea, the idea that our immutable characteristics do not define us. It's the idea that all of us—regardless of color, class, or creed—are equal, and that we can work together to build a more perfect union. When we heed this call, we can achieve unity. And ideas—not identity—can resume their rightful place in our public discourse.

Mr. President, this is the last request I will ever make from this lectern—that as a Senate and as a nation, we listen to our better angels; that we recommit ourselves to comity; that we restore civility to the public discourse; that we embrace wholeheartedly the principles of pluralism; and that we strive for unity by rejecting the rhetoric of division.

When we heed our better angels—when we hearken to the voices of virtue native to our very nature—we can transcend our tribal instincts and preserve our democracy for future generations. That we may do so is my humble prayer....

Last, and perhaps most importantly, I wish to thank my Father in heaven, who has allowed me to serve for much longer than my detractors would have hoped. Each time I walk into this chamber, I am humbled by the significance of it all. And I am reminded of a passage of Scripture, one of my favorites: "For of him unto whom much is given, much is required." Truly, God has given me so much. In return, I've tried to give back as much as I could. I hope He will accept my best efforts.

ACKNOWLEDGMENTS

I am most grateful to Senator Orrin G. Hatch for his cooperation with this book, and to the staff of the Orrin G. Hatch Foundation, especially its Executive Director and the Senator's former Chief of Staff Matt Sandgren, Board Chair Scott Anderson, Board Member John K. Castle, Community Relations Director and the Senator's former State Director Melanie Bowen, and Administrative Director Sara Ebert.

I thank my editors, Alex Pappas and Kathryn Riggs of Center Street, and my longtime literary agent, Mel Berger of WME. Thanks also to production editor Jeff Holt and copy editor Deborah Wiseman.

For their interviews and insights on Orrin Hatch and on the inner workings of Congress, I thank current and former US Senators Joseph Lieberman, Chuck Grassley, Susan Collins, Trent Lott, Jake Garn, Dennis DeConcini, Byron Dorgan, David Durenberger, Jon Kyl, Gordon Smith, Saxby Chambliss, Barbara Mikulski, Scott Brown, Ben Nighthorse Campbell, James DeMint, Richard Bryan, Phil Gramm; and former US Representative Henry Waxman.

In a sense, and without knowing it at the time, I began work on this book in the mid-1970s when I served as a college intern in the Capitol Hill office of US Senator James Buckley of New York, who

ACKNOWLEDGMENTS

won office in the 1970 election as the Conservative Party candidate in an unusual three-way contest against a liberal Democrat and a liberal Republican opponent. I did the work that lowly interns do, answering the phones, handling constituent relations cases for New York residents needing help with the federal bureaucracy, running the autopen automatic ink signature contraption that signed form letters from the senator, and hand-delivering time-sensitive messages from Buckley to other senators on Capitol Hill, which briefly brought me face-to-face with many of the legendary senators of that era. In recent years Buckley and I have renewed our friendship, and I am most grateful for his enthusiasm, encouragement, and relentless good humor.

The excellent staff of the US Senate Historical Office has been a huge help to me, especially archivist Dan Holt and director Betty Koed, and its former director Don Ritchie. The office shared over twelve thousand pages of research from their files on various senators and Senate history with me, a collection that forms a research pillar of this book.

A wide range of people who worked for, worked with, or otherwise came into the orbit of Orrin Hatch and his times were generous in sharing their memories and insights with me and otherwise helping with this project, including Benjamin Netanyahu, Ted Wilson, Kevin McGuiness, Nancy Taylor, Bobby Silverstein, Mark Disler, Celeste Gold, Pat Wright, Caleb McCarry, Randall Rader, Loren Israelen, Peter Carey, David Sundwall, Garland Dennett, Paul Matulic, Brent Hatch, Ray Marshall, Kristen Ries, Michael Iskowitz, Tom Bossert, and George Will.

I am grateful to leaders of The Church of Jesus Christ of Latter-day Saints for sharing insights on their faith and their friend Orrin Hatch with me, especially Dallin H. Oaks, First Counselor in the First Presidency and President of the Quorum of the Twelve Apostles; M. Russell Ballard, Acting President of the Quorum of the Twelve Apostles; Dieter F. Uchtdorf, member of the Quorum of the Twelve Apostles; and Elder Jack N. Gerard.

I also thank Craig Volden of the Center for Effective Lawmaking; Martin Gold, expert on US Senate parliamentary history; Phil Rokus, Office of the US Senate Curator; Sara Stefani, archivist for the Richard G. Lugar Senatorial Papers at Indiana University Libraries in Bloomington; Meredith Evans, director of the Jimmy Carter Presidential Library; Tony Clark of the Carter Library; Kris Bronstad, Modern Political Archivist, Political Science and Sociology Librarian, and Assistant Professor, University Libraries, Baker Center, University of Tennessee; Joseph E. Slater, Eugene N. Balk, Professor of Law and Values, Distinguished University Professor, University of Toledo College of Law; Catherine Fisk, Barbara Nachtrieb Armstrong, Professor of Law, University of California, Berkeley Law; Taylor E. Dark III, Professor and Chair, Department of Political Science, California State University, Los Angeles; Joseph A. McCartin, Professor of History, Director, Kalmanovitz Initiative for Labor and the Working Poor, Georgetown University; Ray Smock, Interim Director, Robert C. Byrd Center for Congressional History and Education at Shepherd University; and the archivists at the National Archives and the Ronald Reagan, George H. W. Bush, Bill Clinton, George W. Bush, and Barack Obama Presidential Libraries.

For details of the designated survivor process, I thank former presidential cabinet secretaries James Nicholson, John Block, Jeh Johnson, Donald Evans, Anthony Foxx, and Alberto Gonzales, each of which, I should stress, was careful not to reveal classified information. For historical and technical details of the process, I am grateful to the late Bruce Blair, a Princeton University nuclear historian and former Minuteman missile launch officer. For constitutional perspectives on the process, I thank John Fortier, the Director of Governmental Studies at the Bipartisan Policy Center.

Senator Orrin Grant Hatch was sworn in as the junior US senator from Utah on January 3, 1977, having had no prior experience in politics or elected office.

When Hatch retired after forty-two years of service on January 3, 2019, including four years as the president pro tempore, or senior officer and elder statesman of the United States Senate, he had served as a Republican senator for longer than anyone else in history, was the ninth-longest-serving US senator in American history, and the longest-serving officeholder in Utah history. The Center for Effective Lawmaking, a group of scholars at the University of Virginia and Vanderbilt University, has ranked him the number one most effective senator of any party of the post-Vietnam era.

Hatch served during the administrations of seven presidents—four Republicans and three Democrats. He was one of only a few senators in history to serve as chairman of three major Senate committees: the Senate Education and Labor Committee (now called the Health, Education, Labor and Pensions Committee); the Senate Judiciary Committee; and the Senate Finance Committee. In total, Hatch spent thirty-two of his forty-two years in Congress as either chairman or ranking member of a major committee.

Senator Hatch considered himself a protector of the nation's free market economy, individual liberty, and America's system of limited government under the Constitution, as well as a defender of the Senate's traditions, rules, precedents, and institutional prerogatives, and a champion for economic growth, tax reform, and fiscal responsibility. On the Health, Education, Labor and Pensions Committee, Hatch was a vital force in passing laws on cancer and HIV/AIDS research and treatment, pharmaceuticals, dietary supplements, mental health, and children's health welfare. As chairman of the Finance Committee, which included oversight of Medicare, Medicaid, and the Children's Health Insurance Program (CHIP), his priorities included pro-growth tax reform, opening foreign markets to American exports, and entitlement reform to ensure the long-term sustainability of Social Security and Medicare. On the Judiciary Committee, Senator Hatch opposed judicial activism and worked for civil justice reform, tough anticrime laws, property rights protections, technological innovation, and intellectual property and copyright protection. He tried for many years to pass constitutional amendments against abortion and for a balanced federal budget.

Hatch received awards and honors including fourteen honorary degrees from institutions such as the University of Pittsburgh, the University of Maryland, Pepperdine University, the University of Utah, and Utah State University.

He also received the National Intelligence Distinguished Public Service Medal from the director of National Intelligence; Gold and Platinum awards from the Recording Industry Association of America; the Presidential Medal of Freedom from President Donald Trump; and the Becket Fund's Canterbury Medal for religious freedom. He and his wife, Elaine, were married for more than sixty years and together had six children, twenty-three grandchildren, and dozens of great-grandchildren.

Leadership Positions

Chair of the Senate Labor and Human Resources Committee
1981–1987
Ranking Member of the Senate Judiciary Committee
1993–1995
Chair of the Senate Judiciary Committee
1995–2001
Ranking Member of the Senate Judiciary Committee
2001–2003
Chair of the Senate Judiciary Committee
2003–2005
Ranking Member of the Senate Finance Committee
2011–2015
Chair of the Senate Finance Committee
2015–2019
Chair of the Joint Taxation Committee
2016–2019
Chair of the Joint Pensions Committee
2018–2019
President Pro Tempore, US Senate
2015–2019

Chronology

1977

Hatch and fellow Utah senator Jake Garn worked to preserve funds for the water-reclamation Central Utah Project—funds that had been cut in President Jimmy Carter's budget. This project was completed and continues to provide water resources for Utah families, farms, and businesses to this day. Hatch consistently fought against what he considered to be Washington's encroachment on western lands.

Hatch introduced a joint resolution (S.J. Res. 84) proposing an amendment to the Constitution of the United States to protect the right to life of unborn children.

1978

Hatch spearheaded an epic filibuster battle that defeated the proposed Labor Law Reform Act backed by President Carter and many congressional Democrats, an act that Hatch believed would unreasonably increase union power.

1979

Hatch joined the "Sagebrush Rebellion"—which fought federal infringement on state land—when he introduced the Western Lands Distribution and Regional Equalization Act (S. 1680) to provide for the transfer of federally controlled western lands to states "west of the 100th meridian."

Hatch also introduced the Balanced Budget Amendment for the first time, beginning his decades-long fight to amend the Constitution to require a balanced federal budget.

Hatch opposed and defeated President Jimmy Carter's plan for basing MX strategic nuclear missiles on racetracks in Utah.

1981

After campaigning for Ronald Reagan in the 1980 presidential race, Hatch was catapulted to chairmanship of the Labor and Human Resources Committee when the Senate changed to Republican control. Hatch served as chairman for six years.

1982

Through his support of the Missing Children Act, Hatch helped establish the National Center for Missing and Exploited Children and partnered with John Walsh, host of *America's Most Wanted*, whose son Adam had been murdered the year before.

As the chairman of the Judiciary Subcommittee on the Constitution, Hatch authored the report *The Right to Keep and Bear Arms*, which argued that the Second Amendment was intended as an individual right to gun ownership, more than two decades before the Supreme Court affirmed that position.

Supported by President Ronald Reagan, Orrin Hatch won first reelection bid by 58 percent. His winning margins in 1988, 1994, 2000, 2006, and 2012 reelections were all over 60 percent, with each opponent never exceeding 32 percent.

1983

As Labor Committee chairman, Hatch opposed the Equal Rights Amendment (ERA), which he believed, among other provisions, threatened to render veterans' preference programs unconstitutional and outlaw single-sex schools and universities. "I believe in equal rights for women," Hatch argued, but "we have over twenty laws that guarantee them. I would prefer to work with those twenty laws than write a fifty-three-word definition into the Constitution that could be easily misconstrued." As of this writing in 2022, the ERA has not been adopted.

Hatch's Orphan Drug Act created incentives for private researchers to develop treatments and cures for rare disorders and resulted in a major increase in the marketing authorization of orphan drugs.

1984

Congress passed one of the most significant pro-consumer bills ever enacted, the Hatch-Waxman Drug Price Competition and Patent Term Restoration Act. Hatch-Waxman increased the availability of money-saving generic drugs, which today account for over 90 percent of all prescriptions issued in the United States. To this day, the law helps foster competition and patent strength, provides incentives to the development of generic versions of off-patent drugs, and permits patent owners to recover time lost during FDA approval. This law has saved consumers trillions of dollars since 1984.

Hatch's National Organ Transplant Act established a task force and a registry for organ procurement and transplantation, simplifying the bureaucratic process that patients must go through to obtain lifesaving transplants.

Hatch helped pass the Victims of Crimes Act, which grants victims the right to seek compensation for injury or losses from the offending criminals. He also helped pass the Bail Reform Act, which allows courts to detain offenders deemed too dangerous for release. (Both acts were included in P.L. 98-473.)

Hatch was the Senate leader on the Comprehensive Smoking Education Act (P.L. 98-474), with Representative Henry Waxman introducing the House version of the bill. This law required four specific health warnings on all cigarette packages and advertisements.

Hatch sponsored the first congressional AIDS bill, the Preventive Health Amendments of 1984.

1985

President Ronald Reagan sent Hatch on a diplomatic mission to Pakistan and Afghanistan, where he met with Pakistani officials and Afghan mujahideen. Hatch facilitated the delivery of Stinger missiles to the anti-Soviet Afghan fighters, which helped turn the tide of that war with a Soviet withdrawal in 1989.

1986

Hatch strongly supported an aid package to Contra rebels fighting the Soviet-backed Sandinista government in Nicaragua. The same year, Hatch became the first US senator to travel to the war zone of Angola in southern Africa, where he met with anti-Soviet fighters.

Hatch helped pass the Law Enforcement Officers Protection Act (P.L. 99-408), which banned "cop-killer" bullets.

1987

President Ronald Reagan traveled to Utah to campaign for Hatch's reelection, saying on June 17: "The United States has been strong enough to deter aggression and maintain the peace, in no small degree due to the efforts of Orrin Hatch. He's been a champion of those who fight for freedom in Afghanistan, Nicaragua, Angola, and other Third World countries. He's been a strong voice for America and for preparedness. He's been a representative the people of Utah can be proud of. He's a dear friend and a talented public servant who's there when you need him. If I could ask the people of Utah, my fellow westerners, one last favor, to stand with me one last time, it would be in support of Orrin Hatch's reelection to the United States Senate."

1988

Hatch successfully filibustered a bill (S. 837) to increase the federal minimum wage, because the measure did not include a youth-opportunity subminimum training wage to encourage companies to hire first-time workers, which unions adamantly opposed.

Hatch and Democratic senator Ted Kennedy of Massachusetts worked together to ban private employers from using lie detectors to screen workers and job applicants.

Hatch and Kennedy successfully fought for passage of the first comprehensive federal AIDS education, research, and treatment legislation, the Acquired Immunodeficiency Syndrome (AIDS) Research and Information Act, and the Health Omnibus Programs Extension Act of 1988.

1989

Hatch played a leading role in the US Civil Rights Commission Reauthorization (P.L. 101-810), which extended a 1957 law to monitor civil rights enforcement and undertake studies on civil rights.

1990

Hatch won approval for a provision in the Radiation Exposure Compensation Act (RECA) (P.L. 101-426), requiring that the federal government acknowledge its responsibility—and provide claims for compensation payments—to Utah "downwinders," miners, and others for injuries caused by fallout from aboveground atomic testing. In its first sixteen years, RECA delivered more than $1 billion to people hurt by the testing.

Hatch championed passage of the landmark Americans with Disabilities Act (P.L. 101-336), which expanded opportunities for citizens with disabilities by improving public access and barring discrimination in jobs, housing, and other key services. The act inspired similar measures in nations around the world.

Hatch and Democratic senator Chris Dodd of Connecticut authored the landmark Child Care and Development Block Grant Act, included in P.L. 101-508. The act makes grants to states and tribes to assist low-income families with child care.

1991

After President George H. W. Bush nominated Clarence Thomas to fill a vacancy on the Supreme Court, Hatch, as a senior member of the Senate Judiciary Committee, defended Thomas in televised hearings against accusations by former employee Anita Hill that Thomas made sexual comments to her years earlier. Thomas was confirmed by the Senate and today serves as a justice of the Supreme Court.

1992

Hatch and the Utah congressional delegation secured final authorization for the Central Utah Project Completion Act (P.L. 102-575), which helped to preserve and protect Utah's water sources, wildlife, and environment.

Hatch successfully led the defeat of the Opposed Workplace

Fairness Act (S. 53), or the striker replacement bill, which would have prohibited employers from hiring permanent replacements for workers engaged in strikes over economic issues.

With the Sanctions for Violation of Software Copyright Act (P.L. 102-561), Hatch protected the intellectual property rights of software authors.

1993

Hatch led the passage of the Religious Freedom Restoration Act, with the near unanimous support of congressional Democrats and Republicans. The bill was signed into law by President Clinton.

1994

Passage of the Dietary Supplement Health and Education Act (DSHEA) (P.L. 103-417), backed by Hatch and Democratic senator Tom Harkin of Iowa, facilitated Americans' access to dietary supplements like vitamins, minerals, and herbal products, while providing a framework for the FDA to remove harmful substances from the market. Opponents of the bill criticized it as being too favorable to the supplements industry, which is a major business in Utah. Supporters of the bill argued that existing laws and regulations, supplemented by DSHEA, gave consumers strong protection.

Hatch and then senator Joe Biden, Democrat of Delaware, created the Violence against Women Act (VAWA, P.L. 103-322), which allotted grants to fight violent crimes against women by strengthening law enforcement and prosecution strategies and improved services for women who had been subject to violent acts. From 1993 to 2001, the rate of intimate partner violence against females dropped by 49 percent and against males by 42 percent. Hatch opposed its renewal in 2007 due to what he saw as the addition of excessive and extraneous amendments.

1996

Following the Oklahoma City bombing, Hatch cosponsored the first comprehensive effort to protect against threats of domestic terrorism with the Antiterrorism and Effective Death Penalty Act (P.L. 104-132). The law limits all appeals to a writ of habeas corpus in capital cases and reduces the length of the appeal process by sharply limiting the role of the federal courts.

Hatch sponsored the Comprehensive Methamphetamine Control Act (P.L. 104-237), aimed at preventing the illegal manufacturing and use of methamphetamine.

Hatch led an effort to pass legislation to improve and simplify the tax code for small businesses, particularly S corporations. Many provisions enacted in the Small Business Job Protection Act were Hatch-led initiatives.

Hatch played a key role in enacting the welfare reform bill, known as the Personal Responsibility and Work Opportunity Reconciliation Act of 1996. He was especially involved in provisions on state training prerogatives and child care.

1997

Hatch worked to create the State Children's Health Insurance Program (SCHIP) to provide access to health-care insurance coverage for children from low-income families (P.L. 105-33). Hatch partnered with Democratic senator Ted Kennedy from Massachusetts to build bipartisan support for this legislation and eventually pass it into law. Since then, tens of millions of children have been enrolled in SCHIP.

1998

Under the Clinton administration, the Base Realignment and Closure (BRAC) Commission recommended the closing of Hill Air Force Base in Utah. Hatch spearheaded the successful effort to keep the base in operation.

Hatch cosponsored the Religious Liberty and Charitable Donation Protection Act (P.L. 105-183), which protects the tax status of charitable donations to religious institutions.

1999

Hatch provided continued funding for the National Center for Missing and Exploited Children and reauthorized the Runaway and Homeless Youth Act (P.L. 106-71).

Hatch joined with Democratic senators Max Baucus of Montana and Republican senator Charles Robb of Virginia, as well as high-tech industry leaders to announce the introduction of the Research and Development (R&D) Tax Credit.

Orinn Hatch voted to impeach President Bill Clinton, saying, "This great nation can tolerate a president who makes mistakes. But it cannot tolerate one who makes a mistake and then breaks the law to cover it up. Any other citizen would be prosecuted for these crimes."

2000

Hatch launched a bid for the Republican nomination for president of the United States but came in last in the Iowa caucuses and joined what he called the fraternity of senators who "had their delusions brutally eviscerated by reality." He later threw his full support behind then governor George W. Bush.

Hatch championed the Religious Land Use and Institutionalized Persons Act (P.L. 106-274), which helps religious institutions avoid state interference in their property through zoning laws. The law also expands religious freedoms to prisoners.

2001

Hatch became the leading pro-life Republican advocate of stem cell research, which holds promise for treating and curing many illnesses facing millions of Americans, including diabetes, Parkinson's, Alzheimer's, and cancer. Among the conservatives who supported Hatch on the issue was former First Lady Nancy Reagan, whose husband, President Ronald Reagan, suffered from Alzheimer's.

Following the September 11 terror attacks, Judiciary Committee chairman Hatch helped craft the USA PATRIOT Act (P.L. 107-56), which enhanced law enforcement tools against terrorism. In drafting the law, Hatch successfully argued for provisions to protect civil liberties.

2002

Hatch helped provide the necessary federal support for the 2002 Salt Lake City Winter Olympic Games, especially for security. Utah's Games have been called the most successful Winter Olympics ever.

Hatch's Technology, Education and Copyright Harmonization (TECH) Act (P.L. 107-273) revised federal copyright law to assist instructional broadcasting and distance education. Many rural residents of Utah and other states rely on distance learning to expand their educational opportunities.

Hatch wrote—and Congress passed—the Drug Abuse Education, Prevention, and Treatment Act, which emphasized prosecution for repeat violent offenders and drug traffickers; improved treatment for nonviolent and first-time offenders; and encouraged education to discourage drug use. Since 2003, the United States has invested heavily in compassionate, innovative programs flowing from this law, offering those addicted to drugs an opportunity to become productive members of society.

2003

Hatch reassumed the chairmanship of the Senate Judiciary Committee, a position he held until 2005.

As a senior member of the Senate Finance Committee, Hatch was on the negotiating team that developed the final version of the

Prescription Drug, Improvement, and Modernization Act (P.L. 108-173), the biggest revision of Medicare since its inception. The Act included a number of Hatch-written provisions, such as boosting physician reimbursement rates in rural areas, reducing the paperwork and regulatory burdens on physicians and other Medicare providers, and initiating a health-care quality study by the Institute of Medicine.

As Judiciary Committee chairman, Hatch authored the PRO-TECT ACT (P.L. 108-21), which simplified prosecution against pedophiles and child pornographers.

This same year, Hatch also helped establish a ban on partial-birth abortion.

2004

Hatch played a key role in passing the Justice for All Act of 2004 (P.L. 108-405), which provided much-needed funding and assistance to realize the full potential of DNA technology in solving crimes and protecting the innocent. It was also a critical step toward eliminating the nationwide backlog of rape cases and providing justice for the victims of crime, as well as those who are wrongfully accused and convicted.

Hatch cosponsored the Unborn Victims of Violence Act, also known as "Laci [Peterson] and Connor's Law" (P.L. 108-212). The law created a separate criminal offense for killing or harming an unborn child during a federal crime of violence against a pregnant woman.

Hatch supported the Law Enforcement Officers Safety Act (P.L. 108-277), which permitted qualified law enforcement officers, both current and retired, to carry concealed firearms in any state, notwithstanding any state or local law. The law also helped address the problem of revenge attacks against officers by criminals whom they helped send to prison.

2005

Congress passed a long-debated comprehensive energy bill (P.L. 109-58), which included several key initiatives sponsored by Hatch: increasing domestic oil supply through unconventional resources, such as oil shale and tar sands; enhancing refining capacity; and promoting geothermal and other alternative sources of energy.

A Hatch-sponsored law (P.L. 109-129) established a National Cord Blood Stem Cell Bank Network to prepare, store, and distribute human umbilical cord blood (HUCB) stem cells for the treatment of patients and to support peer-reviewed research using such cells. This research helps patients suffering from diseases such as leukemia, Hodgkin's disease, and sickle-cell anemia. The law significantly increases a patient's chance of finding a suitable genetic match when faced with a grave disease.

Hatch played a major role in bringing an immigration court to Utah to help the state cope with the burdens of unauthorized immigration.

2006

Hatch convinced the Department of the Interior (DOI) to reopen a public comment period on the proposed plan by Private Fuel Storage (PFS) to store spent nuclear fuel at the Skull Valley Goshute Indian Reservation in Tooele, Utah. Based on the comments by Utah citizens, the DOI denied PFS permission to either store or transport the nuclear material—killing the decadelong struggle to store waste dangerously close to the Utah Test and Training Range (UTTR), where live ordnance is used directly under the low-level flight path of seven thousand F-16s every year.

Hatch's sex-offender registry bill was signed into law as the Adam Walsh Child Protection and Safety Act (P.L. 109-248). The law increased penalties for sex crimes against children and requires convicted offenders to register their location in person every month or face additional jail time.

Hatch's proposed constitutional amendment (S.J. Res. 12), intended to empower Congress to ban desecration of the American flag, received 66 votes in the Senate—one vote short of the two-thirds required to pass, the closest Hatch's amendment has come to passing.

2007

Hatch became Utah's longest-serving senator.

Partnering with actor Michael J. Fox and former First Lady Nancy Reagan, Hatch led efforts to pass the Stem Cell Research Enhancement Act (S. 5), which would expand scientists' access to embryonic stem cell lines—opening the door to potential lifesaving cures for millions of Americans. Hatch argued, "It's the possible remedying of some of the worst diseases in our society....Stem cell research promotes life. It's the most pro-life position you could take." The legislation passed the Senate on April 11, 2007, by a vote of 63–34, then passed the House on June 7, 2007, by a vote of 247–176. President George W. Bush vetoed the bill on June 19, 2007.

2008

Hatch championed the reauthorization of the Special Immigrant Nonminister Religious Worker Program Act (P.L. 110-391), a program that awards up to five thousand foreign nationals annually the opportunity to come to the United States to serve in religious organizations and denominations.

Originally signed into law in 1996 (P.L. 104-66), the Traumatic Brain Injury (TBI) Act's authority expired in 2005. Recognizing the importance of reauthorizing TBI to meet the needs of military personnel and civilians with brain injuries, Hatch teamed with his Democratic colleague Senator Ted Kennedy of Massachusetts to enact the bill and send it to the president's desk for his signature (P.L. 110-206).

2009

Hatch was appointed chairman of the Senate Republican High-Tech Task Force, a position he would hold for a decade, promoting pro-growth, pro-innovation policies for the tech sector.

Hatch honored his longtime friend Senator Ted Kennedy by passing the Serve America Act, which expanded national and community-based service opportunities for all Americans. The legislation encouraged individuals of all ages to serve their communities, and supported social entrepreneurs with innovative solutions to tackle urgent national problems. Kennedy died on August 25 of that year, and Hatch spoke at his memorial service.

Hatch praised President Barack Obama for lifting the federal ban on stem cell research.

2010

After years of debate and negotiations, the Biologics Price Competition and Innovation Act was signed into law (P.L. 111-148). Hatch authored and led negotiations for this law, which ensured a balance of innovation and generic competition for the biotechnology industry, providing twelve years of market exclusivity.

In a joint *Salt Lake Tribune* op-ed with then Microsoft CEO Steve Ballmer, Hatch called for extending and strengthening the Research and Development (R&D) Tax Credit.

2011

Hatch was named ranking minority member of the Senate Finance Committee.

Hatch and Facebook founder Mark Zuckerberg held a technology and policy fireside chat before thousands of students at Brigham Young University.

The America Invents Act, a patent reform bill, was signed into law (P.L. 112-29). The law was the culmination of an effort that began in 2006 when Hatch introduced the first version of the legislation.

With Senate Finance Committee chairman Max Baucus, Democratic senator from Montana, Hatch introduced the State Child Welfare Innovation Act to make improvements to various child welfare programs and provide for limited state demonstration projects to improve outcomes for children and families. Major provisions of this bill passed as part of the Child and Family Services Improvement and Innovation Act (P.L. 112-34).

2012

Hatch was reelected to a historic seventh and final term in the US Senate.

Hatch helped lead the effort to make permanent the 2001 and 2003 tax cuts in the American Taxpayer Relief Act (P.L. 112-240).

Hatch introduced the WIN (Welfare Integrity Now) for Children and Families Act, which required states to demonstrate how they were prohibiting Electronic Benefit Transfer (EBT) cards from being used in casinos, liquor stores, and strip clubs. The bill passed as part of the Middle Class Tax Relief and Job Creation Act of 2012 (P.L. 112-96).

2013

Hatch led a bipartisan group of senators, including Amy Klobuchar (D-Minn.); Marco Rubio (R-Fla.); and Chris Coons (D-Del.), in introducing the Immigration Innovation ("I-Squared") Act, which, among other things, would greatly increase the number of H-1B visas for highly skilled immigrants working in science and technology fields.

Working with Senator Marco Rubio (R-Fla.), Senator Dianne Feinstein (D-Calif.), and Senator Michael Bennet (D-Colo.), Hatch also developed an immigrant guest worker program important for the agricultural sector. Both the technology and the agricultural reforms, along with many other Hatch amendments, were included in the Border Security, Economic Opportunity, and Immigration Modernization Act (S. 744), which Hatch supported and the Senate passed by a vote of 68–32.

Hatch hosted his twenty-seventh Utah Women's Conference, featuring former US secretary of state Condoleezza Rice. Over the years, Senator and Elaine Hatch hosted such prominent speakers as Laura Bush, Sandra Day O'Connor, Mary Tyler Moore, Henry Kissinger, Marie Osmond, and Eunice Kennedy Shriver.

Hatch and Senator Amy Klobuchar (D-Minn.) included in the Senate-passed Fiscal Year 2014 Budget Resolution an amendment to repeal the 2.3 percent excise tax on medical device products ranging from surgical tools to bedpans. Hatch would later introduce the bipartisan Medical Device Access and Innovation Protection Act in the 114th Congress. Hatch's work on the issue proved successful, as the medical device tax was suspended twice under his watch: The Consolidated Appropriations Act of 2016 (P.L. 114-113), signed into law on December 18, 2015, included a two-year moratorium on the medical device excise tax. And H.R. 195 (P.L. 115-120), signed into law on January 22, 2018, extended an additional two years the moratorium on the medical device excise tax.

2014

After a scandal over massive wait times in the Department of Veterans Affairs health-care system and widespread misconduct, Hatch fought for immediate reform. He joined his colleagues in enacting the Veterans' Access to Care through Choice, Accountability, and Transparency Act (P.L. 113-146), which provided funding to hire more health-care providers, build new health clinics, and support veterans and their families with more educational and mental health benefits.

With the aggressive spread of superbugs—or bacteria that are substantially resistant or unresponsive to any existing and available antibiotic—Hatch and Senator Michael Bennet (D-Colo.) first introduced the Promise for Antibiotics and Therapeutics for Health (PATH) Act, which would establish a new limited-population antibacterial drug approval pathway for antibiotics that treat serious or life-threatening infections for which there are few or no other options. The PATH Act was included in the 21st Century Cures Act (P.L. 114-255), a collection of nineteen bills that would make changes to how the Food and Drug Administration approved new drugs and medical devices.

2015

As the most senior senator of the majority party, Hatch was sworn in as the ninetieth president pro tempore of the Senate, making him presiding officer of the Senate and third in the line of succession to the presidency of the United States, behind only the vice president and the Speaker of the House of Representatives. In this capacity, he met with foreign dignitaries, including presidents, prime ministers, chancellors, and ambassadors on official travel to the United Kingdom, Germany, the Azores, Portugal, France, and Croatia.

Assuming his third committee chairmanship, Hatch became Senate Finance Committee chairman.

Hatch helped pass the Medicare Access and CHIP Reauthorization Act (P.L. 114-10), a bipartisan bill that permanently repealed and replaced the Medicare physician reimbursement formula with an improved payment system that rewards quality, efficiency, and innovation so seniors and doctors alike will no longer have to worry about annual crises affecting Medicare. The bill is fully paid for with provisions described as a "down payment" on long-term entitlement reform.

In partnership with Democratic senator Ron Wyden (Oregon), Hatch led the battle to pass bipartisan Trade Promotion Authority (TPA) (P.L. 114-26). The legislation established concrete rules for international trade negotiations to help the United States deliver strong trade agreements to support American exports and create new economic opportunities and better jobs for American workers, manufacturers, farmers, ranchers, and entrepreneurs.

Hatch helped enact the bipartisan, bicameral Protecting Americans from Tax Hikes (PATH) Act (P.L. 114-113), which made a number of temporary tax provisions permanent, putting an end to the repeated tax extender exercise that had plagued Congress for decades and giving greater certainty to US taxpayers across the board. Among other things, the PATH Act made permanent the Research and Development (R&D) Tax Credit and Section 179 small businesses expensing, which allows small businesses—the main force of American job creation—to grow and invest with more immediate tax benefits. The bill also extended the term for bonus depreciation, giving more companies greater incentives to invest in assets that will help their businesses grow and expand.

2016

During one of the most divisive presidential elections in American history, Hatch continued to forge consensus on major bipartisan proposals, including the Defend Trade Secrets Act (P.L. 114-153), the most significant intellectual property reform of the last decade. The law created a private right of action for companies to protect their trade secrets in federal court, enabling them to fight trade secret theft and recover stolen intellectual property.

Hatch helped enact the Judicial Redress Act (P.L. 114-126), which paved the way for approval of the EU-US Data Privacy Shield, a key to securing cross-border data flows and improving coordination among law enforcement on both sides of the Atlantic.

In the Fiscal Year 2017 National Defense Authorization Act (P.L. 114-328), Hatch included a provision that enhanced the Utah Test and Training Range by more than 625,000 acres to allow the Air Force to safely test "next generation" weapons, such as the F-35 Lightning II fighter jet, the F-22, and long-range strike bombers.

By the end of the 114th Congress, Hatch had passed more than thirty legislative proposals into law—the most of any of his colleagues and more than twice as many as the average senator.

2017

As president pro tempore, Hatch was appointed by Donald Trump to serve as designated survivor during the swearing-in ceremony of the president of the United States.

Hatch helped pass the Trump-supported Tax Cuts and Jobs Act (P.L. 115-97).

Hatch also laid the foundation for bipartisan legislation that would pass the following year, including: the HEAL (Healthy Environment for All) Act (P.L. 115-271), which enacted key reforms to Medicare, Medicaid, and family services to address the nation's opioid crisis; the Amy, Vicky, and Andy Child Pornography Victim Assistance Act (P.L. 115-299), which provided meaningful restitution to the victims of child pornography by giving them access to ample compensation from the Crime Victims Fund; and the Rapid DNA Act (P.L. 115-50), which empowered state and local law enforcement to use rapid DNA technology to reduce evidence backlogs and more quickly catch criminals.

2018

Hatch championed the bipartisan STOP School Violence Act (P.L. 115-141), which sought to curb gun violence by funding school security improvements and encouraging investments in early intervention and prevention programs to stop school violence before it happens. This law was praised by leadership of both Sandy Hook Promise and the National Rifle Association.

Hatch helped secure passage of the Orrin G. Hatch-Bob Goodlatte Music Modernization Act (P.L. 115-264), which updated music licensing laws for the digital age to ensure that songwriters and other music creators receive fair payment for their work; and long-term extension of the Children's Health Insurance Program (CHIP), the same program that Hatch had developed with Senator Ted Kennedy (D-Mass.) more than twenty years earlier to increase access to child medical care for low-income families.

In a series of tweets in July, Hatch said, "Russia interfered in the 2016 election. Our nation's top intelligence agencies all agree on that point. From the President on down, we must do everything in our power to protect our democracy by securing future elections from foreign influence and interference, regardless of what

Vladimir Putin or any other Russian operative says"; "I trust the good work of our intelligence and law enforcement personnel who have sworn to protect the United States of America from enemies foreign and domestic."

Hatch worked closely with the US Department of State and personally intervened with Venezuelan president Nicolas Maduro to secure the release of Josh Holt, a Utah resident who had been detained in brutal conditions on false charges as a prisoner in Venezuela for a year.

Working with Democratic senator Chris Coons of Delaware, Hatch included the CLOUD Act in the fiscal year 2018 funding bill (P.L. 115-141), which put the United States and other countries on a path toward resolving the problems of cross-border data requests by law enforcement in the age of email and cloud computing.

Laws Passed

America's Most Effective Lawmaker in Action

During his forty-two years in office, Senator Orrin Hatch passed more legislation than any other senator, Republican or Democrat.

Here is a partial chronological list of the record 791 laws that Senator Hatch sponsored or cosponsored during his tenure. Many of these laws passed and were signed into law with strong bipartisan support, including the legislation that Hatch considered among his proudest achievements, the Drug Price Competition and Patent Term Restoration Act (also known as Hatch-Waxman), which created the modern generic drug industry (1982); the Americans with Disabilities Act, which prohibits discrimination against and requires accommodations for persons with disabilities (1990); and the Ryan White CARE Act of 1990.

This list does not include other measurements of Hatch's congressional effectiveness, such as blocking legislation; influence on judicial confirmations, appropriations, and reauthorizations;

and shaping and passing legislation that he did not sponsor or co-sponsor, or was combined with or absorbed into other legislation that became law, or that originated in the House of Representatives.

Examples of these cases include three pieces of legislation that Hatch also considered among his greatest achievements. The first is the bipartisan 1993 Religious Freedom Restoration Act, which holds the government accountable for ensuring the free exercise of religion. The version passed by Congress originated in the House of Representatives but matched the Senate version that was hammered out by Senators Hatch and Kennedy. A second example is the State Children's Health Insurance Program (SCHIP) championed by Hatch and Kennedy, which provides health care for uninsured children from low-income families who do not qualify for Medicaid, was incorporated into the Balanced Budget Act of 1997 and became law.

A third example is Public Law 115-97, popularly known as the Tax Cuts and Jobs Act of 2017, a measure that originated with House Republicans, was championed by Hatch as chairman of the Senate Finance Committee and by President Trump, passed the House and Senate and was signed into law by Trump on December 22, 2017. The bill, which enacted the first comprehensive tax reform in more than three decades, was credited by its supporters as providing immediate relief to small and large businesses and helping to jump-start the largest economic expansion since the Great Recession.

Justice System Improvement Act of 1979

Comprehensive Alcohol Abuse and Alcoholism Prevention, Treatment, and Rehabilitation Act Amendments of 1979

A joint resolution to authorize the Vietnam Veterans Memorial Fund, Inc. to erect a memorial

Small Business Innovation Development Act of 1982

Older Americans Act Amendments of 1981

Prompt Payment Act

Saccharin Study and Labeling Act Amendment of 1981

Indian Mineral Development Act of 1982

Job Training Partnership Act

Missing Children Act of 1982

Victim and Witness Protection Act of 1982

Student Financial Assistance Technical Amendments Act of 1982

Orphan Drug Act

Record Rental Amendment of 1984

Longshore and Harbor Workers' Compensation Act of 1984

Saccharin Study and Labeling Act Amendment of 1983

Alcohol and Drug Abuse Amendments of 1983

Controlled Substance Registrant Protection Act of 1984

Radio Broadcasting to Cuba Act

Water Resources Research Act of 1983

Health Promotion and Disease Prevention Amendments of 1984

Domestic Volunteer Service Act Amendments of 1984

Rehabilitation Amendments of 1984

Education of the Handicapped Act Amendments of 1983

National Cooperative Research Act of 1984

National Organ Transplant Act

Rural Health Clinics Act of 1983

Utah Wilderness Act of 1984

Preventive Health Amendments of 1984

Alcohol Abuse, Drug Abuse, and Mental Health Amendments of 1984

Small Business Secondary Market Improvements Act of 1984

Education Amendments of 1984

Human Services Reauthorization Act

Older Americans Act Amendments of 1984

Firearms Owners' Protection Act

Children's Justice and Assistance Act of 1986

Handicapped Children's Protection Act of 1986

Protection and Advocacy for Mentally Ill Individuals Act of 1986

Orphan Drug Amendments of 1985

Health Services Amendments Act of 1986

False Claims Amendments Act of 1986

Fair Labor Standards Amendments of 1985

Comprehensive Smokeless Tobacco Health Education Act of 1986

Health Services Amendments of 1985

Education of the Deaf Act of 1986

Special Foreign Assistance Act of 1986

Higher Education Amendments of 1986

Education of the Handicapped Amendments of 1986

Prompt Payment Act Amendments of 1988

Abandoned Infants Assistance Act of 1988

Public Health Service Amendments of 1987

Developmental Disabilities Assistance and Bill of Rights Act Amendments of 1987

National Deafness and Other Communications Disorders Act of 1988

Sentencing Act of 1987

Trademark Law Revision Act of 1988

Age Discrimination Claims Assistance Act of 1988

Protection and Advocacy for Mentally Ill Individuals Amendments Act of 1988

Technology-Related Assistance for Individuals with Disabilities Act of 1988

Generic Animal Drug and Patent Term Restoration Act

Health Omnibus Programs Extension Act of 1988

Salt Lake City Watershed Improvement Act of 1990

Food and Drug Administration Revitalization Act

Americans with Disabilities Act of 1990

Education of the Handicapped Act Amendments of 1990

Ryan White Comprehensive AIDS Resources Emergency Act of 1990

Foreign Direct Investment and International Financial Data Improvements Act of 1990

Developmental Disabilities Assistance and Bill of Rights Act of 1990

Transplant Amendments Act of 1990

Cable Television Consumer Protection and Competition Act of 1992

Nontraditional Employment for Women Act

National and Community Service Technical Amendments Act of 1991

Professional and Amateur Sports Protection Act

Animal Enterprise Protection Act of 1992

Copyright Amendments Act of 1992

Patent and Plant Variety Protection Remedy Clarification Act

Trademark Remedy Clarification Act

A bill to amend title 18, United States Code, to impose criminal sanctions for violation of software copyright

Semiconductor International Protection Extension Act of 1991

Individuals with Disabilities Education Act Amendments of 1991

Higher Education Amendments of 1992

Fishlake National Forest Enlargement Act

ADAMHA Reorganization Act

Abandoned Infants Assistance Act Amendments of 1991

Alzheimer's Disease Research, Training, and Education Amendments of 1992

Terry Beirn Community Based AIDS Research Initiative Act of 1991

Medical Device Amendments of 1992

Public Health Service Act

Technical Amendments Act

Prescription Drug Amendments of 1992

Cancer Registries Amendment Act

Religious Freedom Restoration Act

National Institutes of Health Revitalization Act of 1993

Government Performance and Results Act of 1993

Utah Schools and Lands Improvement Act of 1993

Dietary Supplement Health and Education Act of 1994

Developmental Disabilities Assistance and Bill of Rights Act
Amendments of 1994

General Aviation Revitalization Act of 1994

Judicial Amendments Act of 1994

Unfunded Mandates Reform Act of 1995

Digital Performance Right in Sound Recordings Act of 1995

Ryan White CARE Act Amendments of 1996

Antiterrorism and Effective Death Penalty Act of 1996

Anticounterfeiting Consumer Protection Act of 1996

Safe Drinking Water Act Amendments of 1996

Jerusalem Embassy Act of 1995

Federal Courts Improvement Act of 1996

Comprehensive Methamphetamine Control Act of 1996

Federal Law Enforcement Dependents Assistance Act of 1996

Curt Flood Act of 1998

A bill to throttle criminal use of guns

A bill to provide for the establishment of not less than 2,500
Boys and Girls Clubs of America facilities by the year 2000

Sonny Bono Copyright Term Extension Act

Visa Waiver Pilot Program Reauthorization Act of 1997

Religious Workers Act of 1997

Religious Liberty and Charitable Donation Protection Act of 1998

Nazi War Crimes Disclosure Act

Bulletproof Vest Partnership Grant Act of 1998

Crime Victims with Disabilities Awareness Act

Crime Identification Technology Act of 1998

Arches National Park Expansion Act of 1998

Trademark Law Treaty Implementation Act

Missing, Exploited, and Runaway Children Protection Act

Deceptive Mail Prevention and Enforcement Act

Alaska Native and American Indian Direct Reimbursement Act
of 2000

Indian Tribal Economic Development and Contract Encouragement Act of 2000

Indian Tribal Regulatory Reform and Business Development Act of 2000

Federal Prisoner Health Care Copayment Act of 2000

Patent Fee Integrity and Innovation Protection Act of 1999

Trademark Amendments Act of 1999

Radiation Exposure Compensation Act Amendments of 2000

Continued Reporting of Intercepted Wire, Oral, and Electronic Communications Act

Kids 2000 Act

Ryan White CARE Act Amendments of 2000

Bulletproof Vest Partnership Grant Act of 2000

Native American Business Development, Trade Promotion, and Tourism Act of 2000

A bill to amend the Immigration and Nationality Act to provide a waiver of the oath of renunciation and allegiance for naturalization of aliens having certain disabilities

Religious Land Use and Institutionalized Persons Act of 2000

Animal Disease Risk Assessment, Prevention, and Control Act of 2001

Persian Gulf War POW/MIA Accountability Act of 2002

PROTECT Act

Postal Civil Service Retirement System Funding Reform Act of 2003

Partial-Birth Abortion Ban Act of 2003

Minor Use and Minor Species Animal Health Act of 2003

Mentally Ill Offender Treatment and Crime Reduction Act of 2004

Video Voyeurism Prevention Act of 2004

Cooperative Research and Technology Enhancement (CREATE) Act of 2004

Anabolic Steroid Control Act of 2004

A bill to revise and extend the Boys and Girls Clubs of America

Prevention of Child Abduction Partnership Act

Class Action Fairness Act of 2005

Family Entertainment and Copyright Act of 2005

Broadcast Decency Enforcement Act of 2005

Bankruptcy Abuse Prevention and Consumer Protection Act of 2005

Protection of Lawful Commerce in Arms Act

PREEMIE Act

Combating Autism Act of 2006

Controlled Substances Export Reform Act of 2005

Upper Colorado and San Juan River Basin Endangered Fish Recovery Programs Reauthorization Act of 2005

Palestinian Anti-Terrorism Act of 2006

Dietary Supplement and Nonprescription Drug Consumer Protection Act

Pandemic and All-Hazards Preparedness Act

Animal Enterprise Terrorism Act

Religious Liberty and Charitable Donation Clarification Act of 2006

Traumatic Brain Injury Act of 2008

Safety of Seniors Act of 2007

ALS Registry Act

PROTECT Our Children Act of 2008

Newborn Screening Saves Lives Act of 2007

Poison Center Support, Enhancement, and Awareness Act of 2008

National Guard and Reservists Debt Relief Act of 2008

Criminal History Background Checks Pilot Extension Act of 2008

Prioritizing Resources and Organization for Intellectual Property Act of 2008

ADA Amendments Act of 2008

Special Immigrant Nonminister Religious Worker Program Act

Military Spouses Residency Relief Act

Pedestrian Safety Enhancement Act of 2010

Lord's Resistance Army Disarmament and Northern Uganda Recovery Act of 2009

Judicial Survivors Protection Act of 2009

Prevent All Cigarette Trafficking Act of 2009

Cell Phone Contraband Act of 2010

Fair Sentencing Act of 2010

Criminal History Background Checks Pilot Extension Act

Stem Cell Therapeutic and Research Reauthorization Act of 2010

Criminal History Background Checks Pilot Extension Act of 2010

United States-Israel Enhanced Security Cooperation Act

Patent Law Treaties Implementation Act of 2012

Unlocking Consumer Choice and Wireless Competition Act

Victims of Child Abuse Act Reauthorization Act of 2013

Emergency Medical Services for Children Reauthorization Act of 2014

Traumatic Brain Injury Reauthorization Act of 2014

United States-Israel Strategic Partnership Act of 2014

Bulletproof Vest Partnership Grant Program Reauthorization Act of 2015

Ensuring Access to Clinical Trials Act of 2015

Justice for Victims of Trafficking Act of 2015

Older Americans Act Reauthorization Act of 2016

Ensuring Patient Access and Effective Drug Enforcement Act of 2016

Comprehensive Addiction and Recovery Act of 2016

Defend Trade Secrets Act of 2016

Justice against Sponsors of Terrorism Act

Justice for All Reauthorization Act of 2016

Protecting Our Lives by Initiating COPS Expansion Act of 2016

Emmett Till Unsolved Civil Rights Crimes Reauthorization Act of 2016

Nuclear Energy Innovation Capabilities Act of 2017

FISA Amendments Reauthorization Act of 2017

Trickett Wendler, Frank Mongiello, Jordan McLinn, and Matthew Bellina Right to Try Act of 2017

Childhood Cancer Survivorship, Treatment, Access, and Research Act of 2018

State Veterans Home Adult Day Health Care Improvement Act of 2017

Public Safety Officers' Benefits Improvement Act of 2017

Justice for Uncompensated Survivors Today (JUST) Act of 2017

Nuclear Energy Innovation and Modernization Act

Protecting Young Victims from Sexual Abuse and Safe Sport Authorization Act of 2017

American Law Enforcement Heroes Act of 2017

PROTECT Our Children Act of 2017

Protecting Religiously Affiliated Institutions Act of 2018

Department of Veterans Affairs Accountability and Whistleblower Protection Act of 2017

Abolish Human Trafficking Act of 2017

Trafficking Victims Protection Act of 2017

SAFER Act of 2017

Amy, Vicky, and Andy Child Pornography Victim Assistance Act of 2018

VA (Veterans Administration) MISSION Act of 2018

Marrakesh Treaty Implementation Act

Anti-Terrorism Clarification Act of 2018

CyberTipline Modernization Act of 2018

Missing Children's Assistance Act of 2018

When not otherwise indicated, words spoken in the US Senate since 1976 were obtained from speeches and dialogue printed in the *Congressional Record* (https://www.congress.gov/congressional-record). Since those words are sometimes revised by senators prior to publication, I have when possible checked them against original video recordings of Senate proceedings, which began in 1986 and are available in the C-Span Video Library (https://www.c-span.org), and corrected them to more closely match the original words spoken. Both websites are searchable by date.

Author interviews

Orrin Hatch, Joseph Lieberman, Chuck Grassley, Susan Collins, Trent Lott, Jake Garn, Dennis DiConcini, Byron Dorgan, David Durenberger, Jon Kyl, Gordon Smith, Saxby Chambliss, Barbara Mikulski, Scott Brown, Ben Nighthorse Campbell, James Buckley, James DeMint, Richard Bryan, Phil Gramm, Henry Waxman, Don Ritchie, Dan Holt, Scott Anderson, John K. Castle, Matt Sandgren, Melanie Bowen, Sara Ebert, Benjamin Netanyahu, Ted Wilson, Kevin McGuiness, Nancy Taylor, Bobby Silverstein, Mark Disler, Martin Gold, Patrisha Wright, Caleb McCarry, Randall

Rader, Peter Carey, David Sundwall, Paul Matulic, Ray Marshall, Kristen Ries, Tom Bossert, George Will, Dallin Oaks, Russell Ballard, Dieter Uchtdorf, Jack Gerard, Craig Volden, Joseph Slater, Catherine Fisk, Taylor Dark, Joseph McCartin, Ray Smock, James Nicholson, John Block, Jeh Johnson, Donald Evans, Anthony Foxx, Alberto Gonzales, Bruce Blair, and John Fortier.

Key Books and Publications

Davis, Lennard J. *Enabling Acts: The Hidden Story of How the Americans with Disabilities Act Gave the Largest US Minority Its Rights*. Boston: Beacon Press, 2015.

Doyle, William. *Inside the Oval Office: The White House Tapes from FDR to Clinton*. New York: Kodansha, 1999.

Gold, Martin. *Senate Procedure and Practice*. Lanham, MD: Rowman & Littlefield, 2018.

Gould, Lewis L. *The Most Exclusive Club: A History of the Modern United States Senate*. New York: Basic Books, 2009.

Hatch, Orrin. *An American, a Mormon, and a Christian: What I Believe*. Springville, UT: Plain Sight, 2012.

———. *Higher Laws: Understanding the Doctrines of Christ*. Salt Lake City, UT: Shadow Mountain, 1995.

———. *Square Peg: Confessions of a Citizen Senator*. New York: Basic Books, 2002.

MacNeil, Neil, and Richard A. Baker. *The American Senate: An Insider's History*. New York: Oxford University Press, 2013.

Perlstein, Rick. *Reaganland: America's Right Turn, 1976–1980*. New York: Simon & Schuster, 2021.

Roderick, Lee. *Gentleman of the Senate: Orrin Hatch, a Portrait of Character*. Washington, DC: Probitas Press, 2000.

———. *Leading the Charge: Orrin Hatch and 20 Years of America*. Carson City, NV: Gold Leaf Press, 1994.

Shapiro, Ira. *The Last Great Senate: Courage and Statesmanship in Times of Crisis*. Lanham, MD: PublicAffairs, 2013.

Vetterli, Richard. *Orrin Hatch: Challenging the Washington Establishment.* Chicago, IL: Regnery Gateway, 1982.

Vetterli, Richard, and Brad E. Hainsworth. *In the Lion's Den: The Story of Senator Orrin Hatch.* Springville, UT: Cedar Fort, 1994.

Young, Jonathan M. *Equality of Opportunity: The Making of the Americans with Disabilities Act.* Washington, DC: National Council on Disability, 2010.

Archives and Websites

Orrin G. Hatch Foundation, Orrin G. Hatch Senate Papers; Oral Histories conducted by Heather Barney of former Hatch chiefs of staff Stan Parrish, Dee Benson, Robert Dibblee, Michael Kennedy, Jace Johnson.

Edward M. Kennedy Oral History collection, The Miller Center, University of Virginia: Oral Histories of Edward Kennedy, Melody Barnes, Stephen Breyer, Anthony Fauci, Michael Iskowitz, David Kessler, Trent Lott, John McCain, Melody Miller, Carolyn Osolinik, Robert Byrd, Thomas Rollins, Lowell Weicker.

https://millercenter.org/the-presidency/presidential-oral-histories/edward-kennedy

United States Senate Historical Office: US Senate history and architecture files; biographical files on Orrin Hatch, Jesse Helms, Edward Kennedy, Robert Dole, Robert Byrd, Richard Lugar, Tom Harkin, Howard Baker, Mike Mansfield, Joe Biden, Jake Garn, Ernest Hollings, James Buckley.

National Archives and Records Administration: Center for Legislative Archives, Orrin Hatch files

https://www.archives.gov/legislative

Congress.gov, Legislation Sponsored or Cosponsored by Orrin G. Hatch

https://www.congress.gov/member/orrin-hatch/H000338?q
=%7B%22bill-status%22%3A%22law%22%7D

Richard G. Lugar Senatorial Papers, Indiana University Bloomington

Howard H. Baker, Jr. Senatorial Papers, University of Tennessee

Robert J. Dole Senatorial Papers, University of Kansas

Robert C. Byrd Senatorial Papers, Shepherd University

United States Senate Historical Office website:

https://www.senate.gov

United States Senate Historical Office: The United States Senate: an Institutional Bibliography

https://www.senate.gov/artandhistory/history/resources/pdf
/InstitutionalBibliography.pdf

Presidential Libraries of Jimmy Carter, Ronald Reagan, George H. W. Bush, William J. Clinton, George W. Bush, Barack Obama.

https://www.archives.gov/presidential-libraries

C-Span, "The Senate: Conflict and Compromise" (2019)

https://www.c-span.org/video/?455793-1/senate-conflict
-compromise

New York Times, Washington Post, CNN.com, FoxNews.com, AP News, *The Hill, Politico, Deseret News, Salt Lake Tribune,* NBC News, CBS News, ABC News.

Epigraphs

1. Author interview with Orrin Hatch.
2. "Sen. Orrin Hatch: Tolerance Has Become Intolerant. But There Is a Cure," *Time*, September 11, 2018.
3. Orrin Hatch retirement announcement, CNN, January 2, 2018, https://edition.cnn.com/2018/01/02/politics/orrin-hatch-retires/index.html.
4. Orrin Hatch, "Identity Politics Threatens the American Experiment," *Wall Street Journal*, May 18, 2018.

Introduction

5. Hatch effectiveness rankings: Author interview with Professor Craig Volden, codirector of the Center for Effective Lawmaking (www .thelawmakers.org).

Chapter 1

6. Details on the events of Inauguration Day 2017 and the designated survivor process in this chapter are from author interviews with Orrin Hatch; confidential interviews with three then high-level government officials with direct knowledge of events of that day; author interviews with former cabinet-level designated survivors Jeh Johnson, Jim Nicholson, John Block, Donald Evans, Anthony Foxx, and Alberto Gonzales; author interview with Bruce Blair, research scholar at the Program on Science and Global Security at Princeton University's Woodrow Wilson School of Public and International Affairs and former Minuteman

missile launch officer; and author interview with John Fortier, director of Governmental Studies, Bipartisan Policy Center. Also: James Bamford, *A Pretext for War: 9/11, Iraq, and the Abuse of America's Intelligence Agencies* (New York: Knopf, 2005); and Garrett M. Graff, *Raven Rock: The Story of the U.S. Government's Secret Plan to Save Itself—While the Rest of Us Die* (New York: Simon & Schuster, 2017).

7. In this book I have chosen to refer to the faith that is often known as the Mormon Church instead by its preferred name and punctuation: The Church of Jesus Christ of Latter-day Saints. The church refers to its adherents as "Latter-day Saints."

8. John Block's designated survivor experience: Author interview with John Block.

9. Mark Knoller, "One Night Spent a Heartbeat Away," CBS News, January 30, 2007.

10. Nicholson's experience as designated survivor: Author interview with James Nicholson.

11. "Alberto R. Gonzales, *True Faith and Allegiance: A Story of Service and Sacrifice in War and Peace* (Nashville: Nelson Books, 2016), 1. Additional details from author interview with Alberto Gonzales.

12. Alex Ginsberg, "Cheney's Bunker Revealed," *New York Post*, June 7, 2004, https://nypost.com/2004/06/07/cheneys-bunker-revealed/.

13. Daniel Craig, "Here's the Gigantic, Not-So-Secret Pennsylvania Bunker 'Where Nuclear War in the U.S. Would Begin,'" *PhillyVoice*, August 24, 2017, https://www.phillyvoice.com/story-behind-gigantic-not-so-secret -pennsylvania-bunker-where-nuclear-war-us-would-begin/.

14. Bruce Blair quotes in this chapter: author interview with Bruce Blair.

15. Hugh Shelton, *Without Hesitation: The Odyssey of an American Warrior* (New York: St. Martin's Press, 2010), 392.

16. Valerie L. Adams, *Eisenhower's Fine Group of Fellows: Crafting a National Security Policy to Uphold the Great Equation* (Lanham, MD: Lexington Books, 2006), 185.

17. Author interview with government official who was with Hatch on Inauguration Day 2017.

18. Author interview with Orrin Hatch.

19. Author interview with Jeh Johnson.

20. Potential ambiguities during an Inauguration Day emergency: Such confusion is not an impossibly far-fetched scenario. For five days beginning on Inauguration Day in 1989, for example, a well-respected but little-known outside-the-Beltway federal official named Michael Armacost was number three in the presidential line of succession after the vice president, despite the fact that only a small number of people outside of the capital had the slightest idea who he was. At noon

on January 20, 1989, President Ronald Reagan's term ended and George H. W. Bush took the oath of office as the forty-first president. At that moment, Reagan's secretary of state, George Shultz, had resigned, as had the number two person in the State Department, John Whitehead. The Senate would not confirm Bush's new secretary of state, James Baker, until five days later. This meant that the number three person at the State Department, the under secretary for political affairs, Michael Armacost, became the acting secretary of state, and fourth in line to the presidency, since in the words of a 2009 report by the bipartisan Continuity of Government Commission, "According to the Presidential Succession Act, an acting secretary of a department is in the line of succession as long as he or she has been confirmed by the Senate for some position." Scholar John Fortier called this an example of "potentially disabling quirks in the US presidential succession system." If an Inauguration Day 1989 attack at the Capitol had killed the three men before him in the line of succession, the term of President Michael Armacost would have begun. "This weird gap of time until new cabinet officers are confirmed raises a real nightmare scenario," said Fortier in an interview with the author.

21. William White, *The Citadel* (New York: Harper & Brothers, 1957), ix.
22. "The Senate through the Ages," https://www.senate.gov/artandhistory /history/senate_thru_ages/since_1950.htm.

Chapter 2

23. Neil Lewis, "Washington at Work; Orrin Hatch's Journey: Strict Conservative to Compromise Seeker," *New York Times*, March 2, 1990, https://www.nytimes.com/1990/03/02/us/washington-work-orrin -hatch-s-journey-strict-conservative-compromise-seeker.html.
24. Kirk Victor, "Hatch's High-Wire Act," *National Journal*, April 4, 1998.
25. *Washingtonian* magazine, quoted in Doug Robinson, "The Two Lives of Orrin Hatch," *Deseret News*, July 6, 2003, https://www.deseret .com/2003/7/6/19781926/the-two-lives-of-orrin-hatch#utah-sen -orrin-hatch-said-hell-continue-to-run-for-office-as-long-as-i-think-im -doing-well-i-can-do-so-much-for-our-state-and-for-our-country.
26. Richard Vetterli, *Orrin Hatch: Challenging the Washington Establishment* (Chicago, IL: Regnery Gateway, 1982), 72.
27. Lee Roderick, *Leading the Charge: Orrin Hatch and 20 Years of America* (Carson City, NV: Gold Leaf Press, 1994), 62.
28. Gilbert King, "A Halloween Massacre at the White House," *Smithsonian*, October 25, 2012, https://www.smithsonianmag.com/history/a -halloween-massacre-at-the-white-house-92668509/.

29. "About the Vice President, Nelson Aldrich Rockefeller, 41st Vice President (1974–1977)," https://www.senate.gov/about/officers-staff/vice -president/rockefeller-nelson.htm.

30. Tony Horowitz, "The Vice Presidents That History Forgot," *Smithsonian*, July 2012, https://www.smithsonianmag.com/history/the-vice -presidents-that-history-forgot-137851151/.

31. "About the Vice President, Nelson Aldrich Rockefeller, 41st Vice President (1974–1977)," https://www.senate.gov/about/officers-staff/vice -president/rockefeller-nelson.htm.

32. Ibid.

33. Lindsay Whitehurst, "Orrin Hatch Ends 4-decade Senate Run as Unique GOP Voice," AP News, January 4, 2019, https://apnews.com/article/salt -lake-city-utah-tax-reform-courts-supreme-courts-00861a8caa3f4d 34b7768af271a2c0a0.

34. Robinson, "Two Lives of Orrin Hatch."

35. Ibid.

36. John Heilprin, "A Man on a Mission," *Salt Lake Tribune*, September 5, 1999.

37. Bob Bernick Jr., "Hatch Is Defined by His Contradictions," *Deseret News*, July 4, 1999, https://www.deseret.com/1999/7/4/19454095 /hatch-is-defined-by-his-contradictions-br-compassionate-counselor-or -moralistic-stiff.

38. Robinson, "Two Lives of Orrin Hatch."

39. Author interview with Matt Sandgren.

40. Naftali Bendavid, "The Two Sides of Orrin Hatch," *Legal Times,* March 5, 1995.

41. Author interview with Kevin McGuiness.

42. Interview with Melanie Bowen.

43. Theodore Roosevelt, *The Works of Theodore Roosevelt*, vol. 23 (New York: Scribner, 1926), 24.

44. William Neikirk, "Orrin Hatch," *Chicago Tribune*, December 21, 1999, https://www.chicagotribune.com/news/ct-xpm-1999-12-21-9912210239 -story.html.

45. Heilprin, "Man on a Mission."

46. Lee Benson, "The Final Walk: Orrin Hatch Was in It for the Long Run," *Deseret News*, November 11, 2018, https://www.deseret.com/2018 /11/11/20658625/the-final-walk-orrin-hatch-was-in-it-for-the-long -run#sen-orrin-hatch-r-utah-is-pictured-on-capitol-hill-in-washington -d-c-on-monday-oct-22-2018-hatch-the-longest-serving-republican-sena tor-in-the-united-states-will-retire-at-the-end-of-the-year.

47. Leslie Tillotson, "Person 2 Person: Senator Orrin Hatch," KUTV, December 15, 2014, https://kutv.com/news/local/person-2-person-senator -orrin-hatch.

48. Heilprin, "Man on a Mission."

49. Stephen Goode, "Orrin Hatch Wore Many Hats on Long Journey to Capitol Hill," *Insight* magazine, February 24, 1997.

50. Bendavid, "The Two Sides of Orrin Hatch."

51. Robinson, "Two Lives of Orrin Hatch."

52. Neikirk, "Orrin Hatch."

53. Robinson, "Two Lives of Orrin Hatch."

54. "Robert J. Dole, U.S. Senator from Kansas: Tributes," Senate Document 104-19, US Government Publishing Office, https://www.govinfo.gov/content/pkg/CDOC-104sdoc19/html/CDOC-104sdoc19.htm.

55. Robinson, "Two Lives of Orrin Hatch."

56. Heilprin, "Man on a Mission."

57. Orrin Hatch, "I Helped Pass the Americans with Disabilities Act. Its Future Is Uncertain," *USA Today*, July 26, 2020, https://eu.usatoday.com/story/opinion/2020/07/26/americans-disabilities-act-anniversary-protect-legacy-column/5501105002/.

58. "Interview with Utah Sen. Orrin Hatch," *Daily Universe* (Brigham Young University), August 20, 2002, https://universe.byu.edu/2002/08/20/interview-with-utah-sen-orrin-hatch/.

59. Robinson, "Two Lives of Orrin Hatch."

60. Ibid.

61. Orrin Hatch, *An American, a Mormon and a Christian: What I Believe* (Springville, UT: Plain Sight Publishing, 2012), 138.

62. McKay Coppins, "The Most American Religion," *Atlantic*, January/February 2021, https://www.theatlantic.com/magazine/archive/2021/01/the-most-american-religion/617263/.

63. Bendavid, "The Two Sides of Orrin Hatch."

64. Undated news clipping in Hatch file, Senate Historian's Office, article by E. Michael Myers, The Hill, c. 2000.

65. Roderick, *Leading the Charge*, 10.

66. Benson, "Final Walk."

67. Robinson, "Two Lives of Orrin Hatch."

68. Roderick, *Leading the Charge*, 16.

69. Roderick, *Leading the Charge*, 32.

70. Coppins, "The Most American Religion."

71. Robinson, "Two Lives of Orrin Hatch."

72. Ibid.

73. Ibid.

74. Bendavid, "The Two Sides of Orrin Hatch."

75. Law school entry dialogue: Tillotson, "Person 2 Person," interview with Orrin Hatch.

76. William Neikirk, "Humble Start Made Hatch Gutsy, Tough," *Deseret News*, January 9, 2000.

77. Undated news clipping, Hatch file, Senate Historian's Office, c. 2000.
78. Roderick, *Leading the Charge*, 32.
79. Heilprin, "Man on a Mission."
80. Bendavid, "The Two Sides of Orrin Hatch."
81. Robinson, "Two Lives of Orrin Hatch."
82. Bendavid, "The Two Sides of Orrin Hatch."
83. Ibid.
84. Orrin Hatch, *Square Peg: Confessions of a Citizen Senator* (New York: Basic Books, 2002), 7.
85. Ibid.
86. Ibid., 4.
87. Lee Roderick, *Gentleman of the Senate: Orrin Hatch, a Portrait of Character* (Washington, DC: Probitas Press, 2000), 39.
88. Ibid., 32.
89. Roderick, *Leading the Charge*, 41.
90. Robinson, "Two Lives of Orrin Hatch."
91. Frank Madsen Oral History, Orrin G. Hatch Foundation.
92. Author interview with Orrin Hatch.
93. Rick Perlstein, *Reaganland: America's Right Turn, 1976–1980* (New York: Simon & Schuster, 2021), 31.
94. John Dart, "Ezra Taft Benson, Leader of Mormons, Dies at 94," *Los Angeles Times*, May 31, 1994.
95. Orrin Hatch, "Tribute to W. Cleon Skousen," *Congressional Record*, vol. 152, no. 5 (Senate—January 25, 2006), https://www.congress.gov/congressional-record/2006/1/25/senate-section/article/s114-2?resultIndex=6.
96. Matt Canham, "The Political Birth of Orrin Hatch," *Salt Lake Tribune*, January 31, 2012, https://archive.sltrib.com/article.php?id=53359198&itype=cmsid.
97. Vetterli, *Orrin Hatch,* 13.
98. Perlstein, *Reaganland*, 31.
99. Frank Madsen Oral History, Orrin G. Hatch Foundation.
100. Roderick, *Leading the Charge*, 41.
101. Perlstein, *Reaganland*, 38, 39.
102. Ibid., 39.
103. Hatch, *Square Peg*, 14.
104. Ibid., 15.
105. Neikirk, "Humble Start."

Chapter 3

106. Orrin Hatch, *Square Peg: Confessions of a Citizen Senator* (New York: Basic Books, 2002), 19.

107. Author interview with Kevin McGuiness.
108. Senate desks: Author interview with Phil Rokus, Office of the US Senate Curator.
109. Richard Vetterli, *Orrin Hatch: Challenging the Washington Establishment* (Chicago, IL: Regnery Gateway, 1982), 66.
110. Lee Roderick, *Gentleman of the Senate: Orrin Hatch, a Portrait of Character* (Washington, DC: Probitas Press, 2000), 43.
111. George Packer, "The Empty Chamber," *New Yorker*, August 2, 2010. https://www.newyorker.com/magazine/2010/08/09/the-empty-chamber.
112. Mary McGrory, "The Senate's Windowless World," *Cedar Rapids Gazette*, January 15, 1966.
113. Joyce Barrett, "America's House of Lords," *M* (magazine), May 1992.
114. Senate perks: Ibid., and Robert Shrum, "The Imperial Congress," *New Times,* March 18, 1977; Michael Satchell, "In Focus: Being a Member of Congress," *Washington Star,* January 17, 1977; "Not a Bad Lot," *Time,* March 14, 1977.
115. Richard A. Arenberg and Robert B. Dove, *Defending the Filibuster: The Soul of the Senate* (Bloomington: Indiana University Press, 2012), 4.
116. Adlai E. Stevenson, *Something of Men I Have Known: With Some Papers of a General Nature* (Books in Demand, 2020), 49.
117. "Martin Gold: Counsel to the Senate Republican Leader" (interview by Donald Ritchie), https://www.senate.gov/artandhistory/history/common/generic/GoldMartin_IdeaoftheSenate.htm.
118. Martin Gold, *Senate Procedure and Practice* (Lanham, MD: Rowman & Littlefield, 2018), 3.
119. "Senate Created": https://www.senate.gov/artandhistory/history/minute/Senate_Created.htm.
120. Lewis L. Gould, *The Most Exclusive Club: A History of the Modern United States Senate* (New York: Basic Books, 2009), vii.
121. Russell Baker, "Troublemaker," *New York Review*, August 12, 2004, https://www.nybooks.com/articles/2004/08/12/troublemaker/.
122. *Senate, 1789–1989, V. 1: Addresses on the History of the United States Senate,* U.S. Government Printing Office, p. 424.
123. Gold, *Senate Procedure and Practice*, ix.
124. Packer, "Empty Chamber."
125. "Alexis de Tocqueville," *Democracy in America*, vol. 1 (New York: J. & H. G. Langley, 1841), 219.
126. "President Washington's Inauguration in New York City": https://www.mountvernon.org/george-washington/the-first-president/inauguration/new-york/.
127. Senate Historical Office, "Bitter Feelings in the Senate Chamber," https://www.senate.gov/artandhistory/history/minute/Bitter_Feelings_In_the_Senate_Chamber.htm.

128. Senate Historical Office, https://www.senate.gov/artandhistory /history/minute/The_Caning_of_Senator_Charles_Sumner.htm.

129. *Congressional Globe*, July 6, 1861, p. 16.

130. Senate Historical Office, "Senate Stories: Cooling Off in the Senate," August 2, 2021, https://www.senate.gov/artandhistory/senate-stories /cooling-off-the-senate.htm.

131. Senate Historical Office, Jefferson Davis's Farewell, https://www.senate .gov/artandhistory/history/minute/Jefferson_Davis_Farewell.htm.

132. Noah Brooks, *Mr. Lincoln's Washington: Selections from the Writings of Noah Brooks, Civil War Correspondent* (New York: T. Yoseloff, 1967), 88.

133. Andrew Glass, "3 Brothers Battle for Senate seat, Jan. 17, 1871," *Politico*, January 16, 2017.

134. Senate Historical Office, "The Censure Case of John L. McLaurin and Benjamin R. Tillman of South Carolina (1902)," https://www.senate.gov /artandhistory/history/common/censure_cases/090Tillman_Laurin .htm.

135. Quotes and details on Boies Penrose: John Lukacs, "Big Grizzly," *American Heritage*, October/November 1978, https://www .americanheritage.com/big-grizzly.

136. Gould, *Most Exclusive Club*, xii.

137. Author interview with Don Ritchie.

138. George Smathers Oral History, History Department, University of Florida, https://ufdc.ufl.edu/UF00005600/00001.

139. Merle Miller, *Lyndon: An Oral Biography* (New York: Ballantine Books, 1981), 212.

140. George Reedy, *Lyndon B. Johnson: A Memoir* (New York: Andrews and McMeel, 1982), 130.

141. Walter Isaacson and Evan Thomas, *The Wise Men: Six Friends and the World They Made* (New York: Simon & Schuster, 1997), 708.

142. Gould, *Most Exclusive Club*, 214.

143. Saul Pett (Associated Press), "Mansfield of Montana: Saint of the Senate," Bridgeport Sunday Post, June 7, 1970.

144. Biden's gym experience: Joe Biden, *Promises to Keep: On Life and Politics* (New York: Random House, 2007), 85–86.

145. C-Span, "The Senate: Conflict and Compromise" (2019), https:// www.c-span.org/video/?455793-1/senate-conflict-compromise.

146. United States Census Bureau, "Income and Poverty in the United States," https://www.census.gov/library/publications/2021/demo/p60-273.html.

147. See for example Daniel Koretz, *The Testing Charade: Pretending to Make Schools Better* (Chicago: University of Chicago Press, 2017), 6, 187, 190, 191.

148. Senate Intelligence Committee report: United States Senate Select Committee on Intelligence, "Report on the U.S. Intelligence Community's Prewar Intelligence Assessments on Iraq," July 7, 2004, https://web.mit.edu/simsong/www/iraqreport2-textunder.pdf.

149. America's intervention in Afghanistan ending in failure: A fitting summary was provided by the Orrin G. Hatch Foundation, which wrote in its September 15, 2021, email newsletter "Washington Update: Is This the End of American Empire?": "$2,2160,000,000,000 (no, that's not a typo) paid by US taxpayers to finance the War in Afghanistan. That's $300 million per day or $50,000 for each Afghan citizen. All of this debt has been financed and is accruing interest. By 2050, the price tag will have reached $6.5 trillion. 2,448 US military deaths and 3,846 US contractor deaths, not to mention 20,000+ wounded Americans. 19 years and 10 months—the total duration of the US military's engagement in Afghanistan—making it the longest war in America's history. The question no one wants to ask: After so much sacrifice, what do we have to show for our efforts there? The tragic truth: Hardly anything. From a pure ROI perspective, Afghanistan could be considered one of the poorest investments in history. Taking stock: Yes, Osama bin Laden is dead. But the specter of Islamic extremism remains and the Taliban has seized power once again. Expert's take: Here's how Dan Fried, a former senior US diplomat now at the Atlantic Council, sees the Afghanistan situation: 'Finger-pointing is an ugly Washington sport...in this case, fingers could be pointed in all directions and probably be right in each case. A failure like this is collective. Everybody screwed up.'"

Chapter 4

150. Hatch-Carter meeting and background: Lee Roderick, *Leading the Charge: Orrin Hatch and 20 Years of America* (Carson City, NV: Gold Leaf Press, 1994), 89; Daily Diary of President Jimmy Carter, May 15, 1978, Jimmy Carter Presidential Library, https://www.jimmycarterlibrary.gov/assets/documents/diary/1978/d051578t.pdf. Background and details on Labor Reform battle: Author interviews with Orrin Hatch, Ray Marshall, and Frank Moore; Orrin Hatch, *Square Peg: Confessions of a Citizen Senator* (New York: Basic Books, 2002), 22–41; Roderick, *Leading the Charge*, 88–101; WGBH, "The Advocates: Should Congress Provide More Protection for Union Organizing," April 27, 1978, https://openvault.wgbh.org/catalog/V_68E3FA3FF77E4E21B68EF14B381322D5#at_2500.31_s.

151. Kevin Boyle, ed., *Organized Labor and American Politics, 1894–1994: The Labor-Liberal Alliance* (Albany: State University of New York Press, 1998), 256.

152. Everett Carll Ladd Jr., "The Unmaking of the Republican Party," *Fortune*, September 1977, http://digitalcollections.library.cmu.edu/awweb /awarchive?type=file&item=690029.

153. Norman Miller, "Ailing GOP May Not Recover," *Wall Street Journal*, May 25, 1977.

154. Rick Perlstein, *Reaganland: America's Right Turn, 1976–1980* (New York: Simon & Schuster, 2021), 133.

155. Ibid.

156. Perlstein, *Reaganland,* 38.

157. Author interview with James Buckley.

158. Richard Vetterli, *Orrin Hatch: Challenging the Washington Establishment* (Chicago, IL: Regnery Gateway, 1982), 78.

159. Perlstein, Reaganland, 46.

160. Roderick, *Leading the Charge*, 80.

161. Ibid.

162. Ibid., 89.

163. Carter's presidential background, Oval Office details, micromanagement: William Doyle, *Inside the Oval Office: The White House Tapes from FDR to Clinton* (New York: Kodansha, 1999), 224–42, 387–91.

164. Zbigniew Brzezinski, *Power and Principle: Memoirs of the National Security Adviser, 1977–1981* (New York: Farrar, Straus and Giroux, 1983), 522.

165. Author interview with Orrrin Hatch.

166. Doyle, *Inside the Oval Office*, 232, 235, 236.

167. Adam Clymer, "Senate Votes to Give Up Panama Canal," *New York Times*, April 19, 1978.

168. A. A. Raskin, "Labor's Controversial Agenda," *New York Times*, March 1, 1977.

169. Author interview with Orrin Hatch.

170. "AEI Forums: Labor Law Reform?" March 21, 1978, https://www.aei .org/wp-content/uploads/2016/03/AEIForums18.pdf.

171. WGBH, "The Advocates," April 27, 1978.

172. Author interview with Frank Moore.

173. Matt Canham, "1977: Hatch takes office as a freshman fighter," *Salt Lake Tribune,* January 30, 2012, https://archive.sltrib.com /content404v4.php?ref=/sltrib/news/53392378-78/hatch-office-1977 -orrin.html.csp.

174. Robert Kaiser, "Man Behind the Talkathon," *Washington Post*, June 16, 1978, https://www.washingtonpost.com/archive/politics/1978/06

/16/sen-hatch-man-behind-the-talkathon/fae8047a-b60a-45a0
-bd59-275370404ec0/.

175. Mafia influence on American unions, 1930s to 1980s: James Jacobs,
Ellen Peters, "Labor Racketeering: The Mafia and the Unions," *Crime
and Justice, A Review of Research*, vol. 30, 2003, https://www.ojp.gov
/pdffiles1/Digitization/202743-202750NCJRS.pdf; President's Commission on Organized Crime: *The Edge: Organized Crime, Business,
and Labor Unions: Report to the President and the Attorney General*
(Washington, DC: The Commission), 1986, https://babel.hathitrust
.org/cgi/pt?id=mdp.39015049047825&view=1up&seq=14.

176. Perlstein, *Reaganland*, 316.

177. Ibid.

178. Jacobs and Peters, "Labor Racketeering," *Crime and Justice*, 249.

179. Robert Press, "Waterfront Labor Racketeering Belayed for Now,"
Christian Science Monitor, March 11, 1980.

180. Jacobs and Peters, "Labor Racketeering," *Crime and Justice*, 237.

181. Alfonso Narvaez, "Trustee Ordered for Union Run by Provenzanos," *New
York Times*, February 9, 1984, https://www.nytimes.com/1984/02/09
/nyregion/trustee-ordered-for-union-run-by-provenzaorgynos.html.

182. Jacobs and Peters, "Labor Racketeering," *Crime and Justice*.

183. Rachel Cohen, "How the Labor Movement Is Thinking ahead to a Post-
Trump World," *Intercept*, January 21, 2018, https://theintercept.com
/2018/01/21/labor-movement-us-unions/.

184. Hatch, *Square Peg*, 24.

185. Ibid., 32.

186. Hatch, *Square Peg*, 26.

187. Ibid., 27.

188. WGBH, "The Advocates," April 27, 1978.

189. "Nation: A Filibuster Ahead," *Time,* May 28, 1978.

190. Ibid.

191. Burton Ira Kaufman, *The Carter Years* (New York: Infobase, 2009),
474.

192. Hatch, *Square Peg*, 29.

193. David Corbin, *The Last Great Senator: Robert C. Byrd's Encounters
with Eleven U.S. Presidents* (Potomac Books, 2012), ebook.

194. Eric Pianin, "A Senator's Shame," *Washington Post*, June 19, 2005, https://
www.washingtonpost.com/archive/politics/2005/06/19/a-senators
-shame/95f623af-7bed-4389-9369-05a428ae4994/.

195. Robert Byrd, *Robert C. Byrd: Child of the Appalachian Coalfields*
(Morgantown: West Virginia University Press, 2005), 53.

196. George Douth, *Leaders in Profile: The United States Senate* (New
York: Speer & Douth, 1972), 441.

197. Reuters, "Fact check: Photograph Does Not Show Robert Byrd; Byrd Was Not the Grand Wizard of the Ku Klux Klan," June 17, 2020, https://www.reuters.com/article/uk-factcheck-robert-byrd-photo-grand-wiz-idUSKBN23O2K1.

198. Michael Newton, *White Robes and Burning Crosses: A History of the Ku Klux Klan from 1866* (Jefferson, NC: McFarland, 2016), 89.

199. Ibid., 90.

200. Eugene Robinson, "Byrd's Change and Redemption," *Real Clear Politics*, June 29, 2010, https://www.realclearpolitics.com/articles/2010/06/29/byrds_change_and_redemption_106129.html.

201. Thomas Ferraro, "Senate Gives Rare Honor to Legend Robert Byrd," Reuters, July 2, 2010, https://www.reuters.com/article/us-usa-congress-byrd-idUSTRE6605KY20100701.

202. Hatch, *Square Peg*, 28.

203. Roderick, *Leading the Charge*, 70.

204. Paul Delaney, "Filibuster's Leader: James Browning Allen," *New York Times,* December 3, 1973, https://www.nytimes.com/1973/12/03/archives/filibusters-leader-james-browning-allen.html.

205. George Will, *The Pursuit of Happiness, and Other Sobering Thoughts* (New York: Harper & Row, 1978), 214.

206. M. A. Farber, "Senator James B. Allen Dies," *New York Times*, June 2, 1978, https://www.nytimes.com/1978/06/02/archives/senator-james-b-allen-dies-alabamian-led-canal-pact-fight-wizard-of.html.

207. Ibid.

208. Ibid.

209. *Congress: New Rules, New Leaders, Old Problems; Articles* (Washington, DC: Government Research Corporation, 1977), 9.

210. *New York Times*, June 2, 1978.

211. Hatch, *Square Peg*, 21.

212. Interview with Orrin Hatch.

213. Ibid.

214. Roderick, *Gentleman of the Senate*, 47.

215. Hatch, *Square Peg*, 32.

216. Roderick, *Leading the Charge*, 94.

217. Hatch, *Square Peg*, 35.

218. Roderick, *Leading the Charge*, 95.

219. Hatch, *Square Peg*, 38.

220. Ibid., 37.

221. Dialogue on Senate floor: Hatch, *Square Peg*, 38; Roderick, *Leading the Charge*, 98. The full text of the Senate floor debate is available in the *Congressional Record* for June 22, 1978.

222. Hatch, *Square Peg*, 41.

223. Author interview with Taylor Dark.

224. Author interview with Joseph McCartin.

225. Philip Shabecoff, "Labor Law Revisions Put Aside in the Senate," *New York Times*, June 13, 1978, https://www.nytimes.com/1978/06/23/archives/new-jersey-pages-laborlaw-revisions-put-aside-in-senate-fate-now.html.

226. Hatch, *Square Peg*, 41.

227. Ibid., 42.

228. Author interview with Orrin Hatch.

229. Ibid.

Chapter 5

230. Key sources for this chapter include author interviews with Orrin Hatch, and with David Durenberger, Mark Disler, Nancy Taylor, Bobby Silverstein, Pat Wright, Michael Iskowitz, and David Sundwall. Scenes and dialogue involving Hatch during the ADA climax are from interviews with Hatch, Taylor, Wright, and Iskowitz. Other key sources for the chapter include: ADA Files, Robert Dole Papers, University of Kansas, https://dolearchivecollections.ku.edu/collections/ada/files/s-leg_749_003_all.pdf. Lennard J. Davis, *Enabling Acts: The Hidden Story of How the Americans with Disabilities Act Gave the Largest US Minority Its Rights* (Boston: Beacon Press, 2015); *Congressional Record*, vol. 136, pt. 12, July 10, 1990 to July 18, 1990, pages 17029–17059; C-Span recording of Senate deliberations of July 11, 1990. The ADA Archive, Special Collection: The Chapman Amendment, The ADA Project, http://www.adalawproject.org/chapman-amendment; "Celebrating the Americans with Disabilities Act," Office for Civil Rights, US Department of Health and Human Services, 2020, https://acl.gov/ada; Jonathan M. Young, *Equality of Opportunity: The Making of the Americans with Disabilities Act* (National Council on Disability, 2010), https://ncd.gov/publications/2010/equality_of_opportunity_the_making_of_the_americans_with_disabilities_act.
In 1989, before the ADA was enacted, The Church of Jesus Christ of Latter-day Saints leadership announced that it was "seeking more creative ways of providing religious training for those with physical, mental, and emotional impairments. But there is an even greater need to reduce the barriers imposed by a lack of understanding and acceptance of those who have disabilities," https://www.thechurchnews.com/archives/1989-04-29/people-with-disabilities-face-more-than-physical-barriers-151474.
The National Restaurant Association lobbied for a similar amendment

NOTES

NOTES

to the Chapman Amendment during the struggle for the Civil Rights Act of 1964. The amendment would have permitted businesses to refuse to hire Black Americans if it would have hurt their business—the same argument made regarding employing people with AIDS. The ADA was the product of many years of work by a very wide range of disability advocates and Washington insiders in addition to Orrin Hatch. Prominent among them were Justin Dart, Pat Wright, Edward Kennedy, Tom Harkin, Robert Silverstein, Robert Burgdorf, Tony Coelho, Fred Fay, Judith Heumann, Lowell Weicker, Steve Bartlett, Tony Coelho, John McCain, David Durenberger, George H. W. Bush, Richard Thornburgh, Nancy Taylor, Hamilton Fish Jr., Silvio Conte, Boyden Gray, Steny Hoyer, Arlene Mayerson, Major Owens, Bob Dole, Bill Roper, John Wodatch, Melissa Schulman, Bob Tate, Maureen West, Lex Frieden, Dana Jackson, Evan Kemp, Sandra Parrino, Paul Marchand, Paul Simon, James Jeffords, Hamilton Fish Jr., Bob Kafka, Sheila Burke, Bob Williams, Wade Blank, Elizabeth Boggs, Liz Savage, Marca Bristo, Bonnie Milstein, Tim Cook, Jim Weisman, Karen Peltz-Strauss, Ralph Neas, Becky Ogle, Michael Iskowitz, Mark Disler, Chai Feldblum, Marilyn Golden, Carolyn Osolinik, and David Capozzi. Many of the three thousand disability advocates who converged at the White House for the ADA signing ceremony should also be added to that list.

231. Young, *Equality of Opportunity*, 172.
232. Ibid.
233. Centers for Disease Control and Prevention (CDC) (September 9, 1983), "Current Trends Update: Acquired Immunodeficiency Syndrome (AIDS)—United States," MMWR Weekly 32(35):465–67, https://www.cdc.gov/mmwr/preview/mmwrhtml/00000137.htm.
234. Young, *Equality of Opportunity*, 172.
235. Author interview with Patrisha Wright.
236. Susan M. Schweik, *The Ugly Laws: Disability in Public* (New York: New York University Press, 2010), 293.
237. Associations of University Centers on Disabilities, Justin Dart's 1990 ADA Statement, https://www.aucd.org/template/news.cfm?news_id=1413&parent=&parent_title=News%20/%20Document%20Search%20Results&url=/template/news_mgt.cfm?start=9504&sort=date%20desc,title.
238. National Public Radio, *Fresh Air*, March 7, 2016, interview with Adam Cohen about his book *Imbeciles: The Supreme Court, American Eugenics, and the Sterilization of Carrie Buck*, https://www.npr.org/sections/health-shots/2016/03/07/469478098/the-supreme-court-ruling-that-led-to-70-000-forced-sterilizations?t=1636880397605.

239. Senator Tom Harkin quoting George H. W. Bush on Senate floor, September 7, 1989, https://www.c-span.org/video/?c4418286/user-clip -senate-session-ada.
240. Orrin Hatch, "I Helped Pass the Americans with Disabilities Act. Its Future Is Uncertain," *USA Today*, July 26, 2020.
241. Robert Burgdorf, "Why I Wrote the Americans with Disabilities Act," *Washington Post*, July 24, 2015, https://www.washingtonpost .com/posteverything/wp/2015/07/24/why-the-americans-with -disabilities-act-mattered/.
242. Hatch, "I Helped Pass the Americans with Disabilities Act." https:// www.salon.com/2015/07/11/ted_kennedy_had_one_thing_in _common_with_the_heavyweights_gathered_to_negotiate_the_ada _experience_with_disability.
243. Lennard Davis, "Ted Kennedy Had One Thing in Common with the Heavyweights Gathered to Negotiate the ADA: Experience with Disability," Salon.com, July 11, 2015.
244. Author interview with Orrin Hatch.
245. Neil Lewis, "Orrin Hatch's Journey: Strict Conservative to Compromise Seeker," *New York Times*, March 2, 1990, https://www.nytimes .com/1990/03/02/us/washington-work-orrin-hatch-s-journey-strict -conservative-compromise-seeker.html.
246. Ibid.
247. Ibid.
248. Author interview with Pat Wright.
249. Young, *Equality of Opportunity*.
250. Author interview with Patrisha Wright.
251. Young, *Equality of Opportunity*.
252. Author interview with Mark Disler. The issue of homosexuality was excluded from the ADA, since the American Psychological Association had already removed it from their list of psychological disorders.
253. Details and dialogue of showdown with John Sununu: author interviews with Bobby Silverstein and Mark Disler.
254. https://acl.gov/ada/the-senate-and-bush-administration.
255. "U.S. Capitol Crawl: Wheels of Justice Action," March 12, 1990, https://vimeo.com/328233990.
256. Robert Burgdorf, "A dozen things to know about the ADA," https:// adachronicles.org/stories-essays/a-dozen-things-to-know-about-the-ada/.
257. Michael Kennedy Oral History, Orrin G. Hatch Foundation.
258. US Department of State, Bureau of Educational and Cultural Affairs, The Americans with Disabilities Act, Signing Ceremony, July 26, 1990, https://www.youtube.com/watch?v=dFKicqqVME8.
259. Justin Dart 1990 Statement on ADA: https://www.aucd.org/template /news.cfm?news_id=1413parent=parent_title=.

260. Robert Burgdorf, "Why I Wrote the Americans with Disabilities Act," *Washington Post*, July 24, 2015.

261. Joseph Shapiro, "How a Law to Protect Disabled Americans Became Limited around the World," *All Things Considered*, National Public Radio, July 15, 2015, https://www.wnyc.org/story/how-a-law-to -protect-disabled-americans-became-imitated-around-the-world/.

262. Orrin Hatch, "Op-Ed: Disabilities Treaty Would Put U.N. in Control of U.S.," *Salt Lake Tribune*, August 29, 2014, https://archive.sltrib.com /article.php?id=58348861&itype=CMSID.

263. Steny H. Hoyer, Orrin Hatch, Tom Harkin, Bob Dole, Steve Bartlett, "ADA Needs More Work at 25," *USA Today*, July 26, 2015, https:// eu.usatoday.com/story/opinion/2015/07/26/americans-disabilities -act-minority-rights/30625707/.

264. Author interview with Pat Wright.

265. Author interview with Bobby Silverstein.

266. Ruth Colker, *The Disability Pendulum: The First Decade of the Americans with Disabilities Act* (New York: New York University Press, 2007), 66.

Chapter 6

267. Dr. Kristen Ries on Utah, AIDS, and Orrin Hatch in this chapter: author interview with Kristen Ries.

268. Gillian Friedman, "Utah's AIDS Crisis, Then and Now," *Deseret News*, January 29, 2018, https://www.deseret.com/2018/1/29/20639142 /utah-s-aids-crisis-then-and-now-from-one-doctor-in-the-1980s -to-the-u-s-new-free-clinic.

269. Edward M. Kennedy Institute for the United States Senate, Edward M. Kennedy Oral History, August 8, 2007, https://www.emkinstitute.org /resources/edward-m-kennedy-oral-history-882007.

270. Lee Davidson, "Hatch, Kennedy Made Political Theater as 'Odd Couple,'" *Deseret News*, August 27, 2009, https://www.deseret.com /2009/8/27/20336963/hatch-kennedy-made-political-theater-as-odd -couple#sen-edward-kennedy-d-mass-in-1970.

271. Author interview with David Sundwall.

272. Author interview with Orrin Hatch.

273. Matt Canham, "1977: Hatch Takes Office as a Freshman Fighter," *Salt Lake Tribune*, January 31, 2012, https://archive.sltrib.com/article .php?id=53392378&itype=cmsid; Lewis, "Orrin Hatch's Journey," *New York Times*, March 2, 1990.

274. Interview with Orrin Hatch.

275. Author interview with David Sundwall.

276. Edward M. Kennedy Institute for the United States Senate, Thomas M. Rollins Oral History, May 14, 2009, https://www.emkinstitute.org /resources/thomas-m-rollins-05-14-2009.

277. Author interview with Orrin Hatch.

278. "Bush Reluctantly Signs AIDS Measure," *CQ Almanac 1990* (Congressional Quarterly, 1991), https://library.cqpress.com/cqalmanac /document.php?id=cqal90-1113427.

279. Ibid.

280. Susan Milligan, "A Towering Record, Painstakingly Built," *Boston Globe*, February 20, 2009, http://archive.boston.com/news/nation /articles/2009/02/20/a_towering_record_painstakingly_built/.

281. Ibid.

282. Douglas Brooks, Laura Cheever, "The Ryan White Program at 25— 'A Beacon,'" White House Briefing, September 17, 2015, https:// obamawhitehouse.archives.gov/blog/2015/09/17/tbt-ryan-white -program-25---'-beacon'.

283. Judith Feinberg, Anna Person, "Three Decades of the Ryan White HIV/AIDS Program Have Set an Example, and a Path Forward," HIV Medicine Association, August 18, 2020, https://www.hivma.org/news _and_publications/hivma_news_releases/2020/three-decades-of-the -ryan-white-hivaids-program-have-set-an-example-and-a-path-for ward/.

284. Author interview with Kristen Ries.

285. Feinberg and Person, "Three Decades of the Ryan White HIV/AIDS Program."

286. Author interview with Michael Iskowitz.

287. Matt Canham, "Hatch Says Civil Unions Could Ward Off Gay Marriage," *Salt Lake Tribune*, April 5, 2013. https://archive.sltrib.com /article.php?id=56112240&itype=CMSID.

288. "The Matthew Shepard Hate Crimes Prevention Act of 2009: Hearing Before the Committee on the Judiciary," United States Senate, June 25, 2009, pp. 7, 8, https://www.govinfo.gov/content/pkg/CHRG -111shrg56684/pdf/CHRG-111shrg56684.pdf.

289. "Hatch, Lee Vote against Gay-Inclusive Violence Bill," *QSaltLake Magazine*, February 13, 2013, https://www.qsaltlake.com /news/2013/02/13/hatch-lee-vote-against-gay-inclusive-violence-bill/.

290. Alex Lundry, "Voters in Both Parties Back Workplace Equality for Gays," CNN, October 22, 2013, https://edition.cnn.com/2013/10/22 /opinion/lundry-nondiscrimination-gay-workers/index.html.

291. Associated Press, "Utah Senator Hatch: Gay Marriage Will Become Law of the Land," May 29, 2014, https://www.nbcnews.com/news/us-news /utah-senator-hatch-gay-marriage-will-become-law-land-n116986.

292. Jessica Estepa, "Sen. Orrin Hatch: 'Transgender people are people and deserve the best we can do for them,'" *USA Today*, July 26, 2017, https://eu.usatoday.com/story/news/politics/onpolitics/2017/07/26/sen -orrin-hatch-transgender-people-people-and-deserve-best-we-can-do -them/512333001/.

293. Brady McCombs, "Utah's Hatch Urges Support for LGBT Youth in Senate Speech," Associated Press, June 14, 2018, https:// apnews.com/article/health-religion-utah-united-states-congress -ada70b0f29f0483ea15351152dca3a26.

294. Orrin Hatch, "Sen. Orrin Hatch: Democrats Have Only Themselves to Blame for Rules Change," *Time*, April 6, 2017, https://time .com/4730017/hatch-filibuster-nuclear-option/.

295. "Excerpts from Opening Statements and Testimony at Senate Hearing on Bork," *Washington Post*, September 16, 1987, https://www.washingtonpost.com/archive/politics/1987/09/16 /excerpts-from-opening-statements-and-testimony-at-senate -hearing-on-bork/0b23596b-5731-469b-a593-3d45e7eb0c43/.

296. UPI, "Excerpts from Opening Statements," September 16, 1987, https://www.upi.com/Archives/1987/09/16/Excerpts-from-opening -statements/7174558763200/.

297. Rick Atkinson, "Why Ted Kennedy Can't Stand Still," *Washington Post*, April 29, 1990, https://www.washingtonpost.com/wpsrv /national/longterm/jfkjr/stories/emk092990a.htm.

298. Hatch, *Square Peg,* 156; and author email with Nina Totenberg.

299. *Charlie Rose* TV show, June 16, 1993, https://charlierose.com/videos /6364. Also in 1993, Hatch received complete vindication by a Senate Ethics Committee report, which he requested, that found no improper conduct in his contacts with the failed Bank of Credit and Commerce International (BCCI).

300. Hatch, *Square Peg*, 156.

301. Ibid., 161, 162.

302. Ibid., 156.

303. "Sen. Orrin Hatch," *Time*, April 6, 2017.

304. Aron Heller, "Justice Ginsburg Bemoans Partisan Divide in Congress," Associated Press, July 5, 2018, https://apnews.com/article /7f49e206d3e64f74a48755a0f6bebad9.

305. Hatch, *Square Peg*, 180.

306. "Sen. Orrin Hatch," *Time*, April 6, 2017.

307. Thomas Burr, "Sen. Orrin Hatch's Impact on the Supreme Court," *Salt Lake Tribune*, July 29, 2018, https://www.sltrib.com/news /politics/2018/07/29/sen-orrin-hatchs-impact/.

Chapter 7

308. Newsweek Staff, "Sen. Orrin Hatch Remembers Ted Kennedy," *Newsweek*, August 26, 2009, https://www.newsweek.com/sen-orrin-hatch-remembers-ted-kennedy-78653.

309. Orrin Hatch, "The Ted Kennedy I Knew," *Politico*, August 26, 2009, https://www.politico.com/story/2009/08/the-ted-kennedy-i-knew-026482.

310. "Hatch Reflects on Friendship, Battles with Kennedy," *PBS News Hour*, August 26, 2009, https://www.pbs.org/newshour/show/hatch-reflects-on-friendship-battles-with-kennedy.

311. Kevin Hechtkopf, "Hatch: Kennedy and I Were Like 'Fighting Brothers,'" CBS News, August 28, 2009, https://www.cbsnews.com/news/hatch-kennedy-and-i-were-like-fighting-brothers/.

312. Author interview with Orrin Hatch.

313. PBS NewsHour, August 26, 2009, https://www.pbs.org/newshour/show/hatch-reflects-on-friendship-battles-with-kennedy.

314. Nick Littlefield, David Nexon, *Lion of the Senate: When Ted Kennedy Rallied the Democrats in a GOP Congress* (New York: Simon & Schuster, 2015), 87.

315. PBS NewsHour, August 26, 2009, https://www.pbs.org/newshour/show/hatch-reflects-on-friendship-battles-with-kennedy.

316. *Politico*, August 26, 2009.

317. Michael Tomasky, "The Sad Trajectory of Orrin Hatch," January 3, 2018, https://www.nytimes.com/2018/01/03/opinion/orrin-hatch-republicans.html.

318. Author interview with Phil Gramm.

319. Hugh Sidey, "The Presidency: Memories of John F. Kennedy," *Time*, November 26, 1973, http://content.time.com/time/subscriber/article/0,33009,908157,00.html.

320. Lance Morrow, "The Trouble with Teddy," *Time,* April 29, 1991.

321. John Broder, "Edward M. Kennedy, Senate Stalwart, Is Dead at 77," *New York Times*, August 27, 2009, https://www.nytimes.com/2009/08/27/us/politics/27kennedy.html.

322. Quoted by Senator Ron Wyden in *Congressional Record*, December 12, 2018, https://www.govinfo.gov/content/pkg/CREC-2018-12-12/html/CREC-2018-12-12-pt1-PgS7458-4.htm.

323. Orrin Hatch, in Memorial Services for Edward Moore Kennedy, John F. Kennedy Library and Museum, August 28, 2009, https://www.govinfo.gov/content/pkg/CDOC-111sdoc6/html/CDOC-111sdoc6.htm.

324. "Ted Kennedy," *CBS 60 Minutes*, June 7, 1998, https://search.alexanderstreet.com/preview/work/bibliographic_entity%7Cvideo_work%7C2856095.

325. Paul Richter, "The Two Images of Kennedy," *Los Angeles Times*, June 7, 1991, https://www.latimes.com/archives/la-xpm-1991-06-07-mn-101-story.html.

326. Edward M. Kennedy Institute for the United States Senate, David Kessler Oral History, March 9, 2008, https://www.emkinstitute.org/resources/david-kessler-oral-history.

327. Quotes and background on Al Smith's experiences: "Al Smith—Speaks to Berkeley 1990," https://www.youtube.com/watch?v=v8gL5P9-rkI&t=1055s.

328. "Interview with Utah Sen. Orrin Hatch," *Daily Universe*.

329. Lee Benson, "The Final Walk: Orrin Hatch Was in It for the Long Run," *Deseret News*, November 11, 2018.

330. Jace Johnson Oral History, Orrin G. Hatch Foundation.

331. Sarah Harris, "Sen. Orrin Hatch Honored as 2017 Distinguished Utahn for Service to Others," *Deseret News*, June 2, 2017, https://www.thechurchnews.com/archives/2017-06-02/sen-orrin-hatch-honored-as-2017-distinguished-utahn-for-service-to-others-18586.

332. "Politics and Piety: An Interview with Senator Orrin Hatch," *Sunstone*, September–October 1980, http://docplayer.net/154231974-Politics-and-piety-an-interview-with-senator-orrin-hatch-with-the-rise-of-new-right-organizations-in-the.html.

333. "Expulsion Case of Reed Smoot of Utah (1907)," https://www.senate.gov/about/powers-procedures/expulsion/091ReedSmoot_expulsion.htm.

334. Mark Leibovich, "A Senator's Gift to the Jews, Nonreturnable," *New York Times*, December 8, 2009, https://www.nytimes.com/2009/12/09/us/politics/09hanukkah.html?_r=2&partner=rss&emc=rss.

335. Christina Wilkie, "Sen. Hatch Writes a Hannukah Song," *The Hill*, December 10, 2009, https://thehill.com/capital-living/in-the-know/71539-sen-orrin-hatch-writes-a-hannukah-song.

336. Author interview with Orrin Hatch.

337. Gil Troy, "Why U.S. Jews Owe Senator Orrin Hatch a Hearty Thank You," *Forward*, January 3, 2018, https://forward.com/scribe/391362/why-us-jews-owe-senator-orrin-hatch-a-hearty-thank-you/.

338. Author interview with Benjamin Netanyahu.

339. "Utah Senator: Public Opinion 'Shouldn't Make a Difference' in Mosque Construction," BJC online, August 30, 2010, https://bjconline.org/utah-senator-public-opinion-shouldnt-make-a-difference-in-mosque-construction/.

340. "Otis H. Stephens Jr., John M. Scheb II, Colin Glennon, *American Constitutional Law*, vol. 2 (Stamford, CT: Cengage, 2014), 252.

341. Committee on the Judiciary, "The Religious Freedom Restoration Act: Hearing before the Committee on the Judiciary, United States Senate, vol. 4," 1.

342. Committee on the Judiciary, "Religious Freedom Restoration Act," 8.

343. Orrin Hatch, "Why Religious Freedom (Still) Matters," *USA Today*, June 30, 2014, https://eu.usatoday.com/story/opinion/2014/06/30/freedom-religion-civitasterrena-hatch-column/11353449/.

344. "Notable & Quotable: Bill Clinton on Religious Freedom," *Wall Street Journal*, May 30, 2015, https://www.wsj.com/articles/notable-quotable-bill-clinton-on-religious-freedom-1427758386.

345. Use of RFRA and RLUIPA laws: See, for example, Becket Fund: https://www.becketlaw.org/research-central/rfra-info-central/.

346. Senator Hatch Office tweet, @senorrinhatch, May 23, 2018, https://twitter.com/senorrinhatch/status/999106516010586113.

347. Dennis Romboy, "Sen. Orrin Hatch Library, Public Policy Institute to Be Built on South Temple in Salt Lake City," *Deseret News*, May 2, 2018.

348. Hatch, *Square Peg,* 110.

349. Lee Davidson, "Conservative Hatch Defends Support of Liberal-Sponsored Bill," *Deseret News*, June 16, 1989, https://www.deseret.com/1989/6/16/18811564/conservative-hatch-defends-support-of-liberal-sponsored-bill.

350. Hatch, *Square Peg,* 111.

351. Roderick, *Gentleman of the Senate*, 84.

352. Littlefield and Nexon, *Lion of the Senate*, 421.

353. Robert Pear, "Hatch Joins Kennedy to Back a Health Program," *New York Times*, March 14, 1997, https://www.nytimes.com/1997/03/14/us/hatch-joins-kennedy-to-back-a-health-program.html.

354. Hatch, *Square Peg*, 113.

355. Littlefield and Nexon, *Lion of the Senate*, 426.

356. Adam Clymer, "G.O.P. Fights Bill to Offer a Health Plan for Children," *New York Times*, April 12, 1997.

357. Roderick, *Gentleman of the Senate*, 86.

358. Ibid., 90.

359. "Through Senate Alchemy, Tobacco Is Turned into Gold for Children's Health": *New York Times* article by Jerry Gray, August 11, 1997.

360. Bob Bernick Jr., "Hatch Is Defined by His Contradictions," *Deseret News*, July 4, 1999, https://www.deseret.com/1999/7/4/19454095/hatch-is-defined-by-his-contradictions-br-compassionate-counselor-or-moralistic-stiff.

361. Jace Johnson Oral History, Orrin G. Hatch Foundation.

Chapter 8
362. Jimmy Carter letter to Orrin Hatch, undated, circa December 2018, Hatch Papers, Orrin G. Hatch Foundation.

363. George H. W. Bush letter to Orrin Hatch, November 28, 2018, Hatch Papers, Orrin G. Hatch Foundation.
364. Bill Clinton letter to Orrin Hatch, December 24, 2018, Hatch Papers, Orrin G. Hatch Foundation.
365. Author interview with Barbara Mikulski.
366. Author interview with Michael Iskowitz.
367. Author interview with Gordon Smith.
368. Author interview with Scott Anderson.
369. Author interview with Susan Collins.
370. Author interview with Martin Gold.
371. Frank Madsen Oral History, Orrin G. Hatch Foundation.
372. Hatch, *Square Peg*, 166.
373. Adam Clymer, "G.O.P. Fights Bill to Offer a Health Plan for Children," *New York Times,* April 12, 1997, https://www.nytimes.com/1997/04/12/us/gop-fights-bill-to-offer-a-health-plan-for-children.html.
374. Author interview with Byron Dorgan.

Timeline of Milestones

375. The information cited here comes from congress.gov, the Orrin G. Hatch Foundation, and the author's research.

William Doyle is a *New York Times* bestselling author and TV producer. His books include *Inside the Oval Office: The White House Tapes from FDR to Clinton* (*New York Times* Notable Book, 1999); *An American Insurrection: James Meredith and the Battle of Oxford, Mississippi, 1962* (Winner of the American Bar Association Silver Gavel Award, American Library Association Alex Award, Robert F. Kennedy Book Award Finalist; Doubleday, 2002); *A Soldier's Dream: Captain Travis Patriquin and the Awakening of Iraq* (NAL Caliber, 2011); *A Mission from God* (coauthored memoir of civil rights hero James Meredith; Simon & Schuster, 2012); *American Gun: A History of the United States in 10 Firearms* (coauthored with former US Navy SEAL Chris Kyle, HarperCollins, 2013); *Navy SEALs: Their Untold Story* (coauthored with former US Navy SEAL Dick Couch; HarperCollins, 2014); *PT 109: An American Epic of War, Survival and the Destiny of John F. Kennedy* (HarperCollins, 2015); *Let the Children Play* (coauthored with Pasi Sahlberg, Oxford University Press, 2019); and *Beyond Valor* (HarperCollins Nelson Books, 2020), coauthored with Jon Erwin.

In 2014, Doyle coproduced the top-rated PBS prime-time documentary special *Navy SEALs: Their Untold Story*, the companion

TV program for his book. In 2017, he was executive producer of the History Channel prime-time TV documentary inauguration special *Transition of Power: The Presidency.* He is a frequent guest on NPR, CNN, and Fox News, and has written opinion pieces for the *Wall Street Journal* and CNN.com.

Doyle is winner of the Writers Guild Award for Best TV Documentary, and has conducted more than one thousand interviews with key players in American history and Oval Office insiders dating back to the FDR administration. The *Indianapolis Star* has called him "a master of crackling prose and a tireless hunter for vital facts and perspectives."

Doyle was a 2015–2016 Fulbright Scholar and a 2017 Rockefeller Foundation Bellagio Center Resident Fellow. His first job was as an intern in the US Senate office of Senator James Buckley (Conservative-Republican, New York).

Praise for
William Doyle's Books

"Doyle, who won a Writers Guild award for a documentary on the same subject, uses these recordings to present an impressive, illuminating account of how presidents from FDR to Clinton managed the day-to-day operations of 'the world's most dangerous office.' Combining interviews, meticulous historical research, and transcripts of the tapes themselves, Doyle peeks behind the wizard's curtain to show us the nation's chief executives at work....Reading this book is a little like peering through a keyhole at history."
—*Publishers Weekly* on *Inside the Oval Office*

"One of the best narratives to chronicle the epic contest between African Americans bent on freedom and their most fanatic opponents."   —*Washington Post* on *An American Insurrection*

"A compelling account of how the last battle of the Civil War came to be fought...precise and evocative."
—*San Jose Mercury News* on *An American Insurrection*

"A fascinating contribution to civil rights history."
—*Booklist* on *An American Insurrection*

"A truly inspirational story about an American soldier who epitomized our country's values."
—*Huffington Post* on *A Soldier's Dream*

"Compelling, carefully reported, and briskly written. A tale of how even in modern warfare, with all its cultural intricacies and geo-political considerations, two men can play a decisive role through dint of personality, adept maneuvering, and, yes, a fair amount of individual ambition."

—*Los Angeles Times* on *A Soldier's Dream*

"Captures the essence of Naval Special Warfare from our storied beginnings to the current fight and gives us a glimpse of what the future might bring for the twenty-first-century Navy SEALs."

—Admiral William McRaven (USN, ret.),
former commander of US Special Operations Command,
on *Navy SEALS: Their Untold Story*

"I am impressed. If you want to read one book about Navy SEALs, this is it."

—Master Chief Rick Kaiser (USN, ret.), executive director,
National Navy UDT-SEAL Museum, and former Naval Special
Warfare Development Group training chief, on
Navy SEALS: Their Untold Story

"Cinematic. Doyle expertly brings this remarkable saga back to life." —*Christian Science Monitor* on *PT 109*

"A revealing and breathtaking account about what happened to John F. Kennedy's Patrol Torpedo boat 109, and the famous war story's engrossing aftermath." —James Patterson on *PT 109*

"William Doyle's *PT 109* is a masterfully written book on John F. Kennedy's World War II service. Every page sparkles with keen insight and fresh research. Highly recommended!"

—Douglas Brinkley, historian, on *PT 109*